Brian Hart
with Mario Rinvolucri, Herbert Puchta & Jeff

English in Mind

Second edition

Teacher's Resource
Book 4

CAMBRIDGE
UNIVERSITY PRESS

CAMBRIDGE UNIVERSITY PRESS
Cambridge, New York, Melbourne, Madrid, Cape Town,
Singapore, São Paulo, Delhi, Mexico City

Cambridge University Press
The Edinburgh Building, Cambridge CB2 8RU, UK

www.cambridge.org
Information on this title: www.cambridge.org/9780521184502

First published 2004
Reprinted 2012

Printed in the United Kingdom by Short Run Press, Exeter

A catalogue record for this publication is available from the British Library

ISBN 978-0-521-18450-2 Teacher's Resource Book
ISBN 978-0-521-18446-5 Student's Book with DVD-ROM
ISBN 978-0-521-18447-2 Workbook
ISBN 978-0-521-18451-9 Audio CDs (3)
ISBN 978-0-521-18455-7 Testmaker Audio CD/CD-ROM
ISBN 978-0-521-18452-6 DVD (PAL)
ISBN 978-0-521-18453-3 DVD (NTSC)
ISBN 978-0-521-18454-0 Classware DVD-ROM

Contents

Map of Student's Book 4

Introduction 6

Teacher's notes and keys

Welcome section 10

1 Sport with a difference 16
2 People are people 23
Check your progress 29

3 Time travellers 31
4 In and out of fashion 39
Check your progress 44

5 Do something 46
6 Our world 53
Check your progress 57

7 Peacemakers 59
8 Kindness matters 67
Check your progress 72

9 Language 74
10 Using fame to help 82
Check your progress 88

11 Music is everywhere 90
12 Nature's best 98
Check your progress 104

13 Natural health 106
14 Movie magic 113
Check your progress 119

Pronunciation 121
Get it right! key 125
Projects 126
Workbook key 129
Entry Tests 145
Entry Test key 155
Teaching notes for communication activities and grammar practice 157
Communication and grammar 1–14 166
Acknowledgements 194

Welcome section	A **Grammar** Past tense review; *be used to* + gerund vs. *used to* + infinitive; **Vocabulary** Personality; *make* and *do* **Reading** The Real Rain Man	B **Grammar** *should / should have; wish* **Vocabulary** Problems; friends **Reading** Magazine reader's problems

Unit	Grammar	Vocabulary	Pronunciation
1 Sport with a difference	Relative clauses review Relative clauses with *which*	Sports	Intonation in questions
2 People are people	*What* clauses Verbs + gerund/infinitive review	Personality Vocabulary bank: Personality	Sentence stress and rhythm
CHECK YOUR PROGRESS			
3 Time travellers	Reported speech review Reporting verbs review	Expressions with *time* Vocabulary bank: Expressions with *time*	Schwa /ə/
4 In and out of fashion	*Would* and *used to* Adverbs and adverbial phrases	Common adverbial phrases Vocabulary bank: Adverbial phrases	/æ/ *accident* and /e/ *excitement*
CHECK YOUR PROGRESS			
5 Do something!	Conditionals review Mixed conditionals	Ways of getting involved Vocabulary bank: Ways of getting involved	Contractions in third conditionals
6 Our world	Future continuous Future perfect	Global issues	/ð/ *the* and /θ/ *thing*
CHECK YOUR PROGRESS			
7 Peacemakers	Past perfect passive Past perfect continuous	Conflicts and solutions Vocabulary bank: Conflicts and solutions	Linking sounds
8 Kindness matters	Dummy *it* Modal verbs review	Making an effort Vocabulary bank: Making an effort	Linking sounds: intrusive /w/ and /j/
CHECK YOUR PROGRESS			
9 Language	Phrasal verbs review	Meanings of phrasal verbs Understanding language Vocabulary bank: Language	Words ending in *-ough*
10 Using fame to help	Reduced relative clauses Question tags review	Fame Expressing opinions Vocabulary bank: Expressions with *opinion*	Intonation in question tags
CHECK YOUR PROGRESS			
11 Music is everywhere	Indirect questions Verbs + *wh-* clauses	Qualifying comparisons Listening to music Vocabulary bank: Music	*Record* (noun) and *record* (verb)
12 Nature's best	Participle clauses *Didn't need to / needn't have*	Geographical features Travel verbs Vocabulary bank: Travel	/ɪ/ *sit* and /iː/ *seat*
CHECK YOUR PROGRESS			
13 Natural health	Passive report structures	Health and medicine Feelings Vocabulary bank: Feelings	/n/ *thin* and /ŋ/ *thing*
14 Movie magic	Clauses of purpose: *to / in order to / so as to* Result clauses with *so / such (that)*	Reacting to films Vocabulary bank: Reactions	Word stress in multi-syllabic words
CHECK YOUR PROGRESS			

Pronunciation • Vocabulary bank • Get it Right! • Projects • Speaking B • Irregular verbs and phonetics

C **Grammar** Present perfect and future passives; Future predictions
Vocabulary Crimes; getting into trouble
Reading Interview about young people and gangs

D **Grammar** *Make / let / be/ allowed to*; modals of deduction (past)
Vocabulary Television; anger
Reading Dialogue between mother and daughter

Speaking & Functions	Listening	Reading	Writing
Talking about new sports Talking about sportsmen and sportswomen	An interview with two sportswomen	Article: chessboxing Culture in mind: Weird sports from around the world	A composition about a sport
Important qualities in a friend Talking about jokes	Practical jokes	Questionnaire on personality Photostory: You're both being a pain	A physical and personality description
Using expressions with *time* Talking about revision for exams Talking about time travel	An interview about a TV series	Article: *Dr Who* Magazine: advice column Literature in mind: *The Time Machine*	An email
Toy crazes Talking about flash mobs	Flash mobs Song: 'Accessory'	Popular gimmicks	A formal letter
Talking about raising money for charity Talking about voluntary work Talking about politicians and voting Coming of age	An interview about politicians and voting	Article: Run, Izzie, run! Culture in mind: Raising money for charity	A letter to raise money for charity
Talking about the future of the planet Talking about The Global Village	The Global Village	A blog on a town in Colombia The Global Village Photostory: It's not very green, is it?	An article on the future
Talking about conflicts and resolutions	Conversation about a *Conflict Resolution Programme*	Alfred Nobel Rests in Peace Literature in mind: *Pride and Prejudice* Aung San Suu Kyi	Writing about a person you admire
Talking about kindness Talking about presents	People talking about special presents Song: 'Put a Little Love in Your Heart'	The Kindness Offensive	Writing a summary
Talking about language, accents and translation	A TV programme on different accents People who speak English around the world	Lost in Translation Culture in mind: Artificial languages	A story
Talking about UN Goodwill Ambassadors	Opinion on politics and famous people	Celebrity Ambassadors Photostory: Isn't she that model?	A composition about the advantages and disadvantages of a given topic
Talking about TV talent shows Talking about music	An interview: talking about music and musical instruments	TV talent shows Literature in mind: *High Fidelity*	Mini saga Limerick Haiku
Talking about the Seven Wonders of the World Talking about trips	A holiday story Song: 'Over the Rainbow'	Extracts of a travel guide, a travel blog and a work of fiction	A description of your favourite place in the whole world
Talking about animal behaviour Talking about flower remedies	Flower remedies	Article: When animals are ill Advert: alternative medicine Culture in mind: Great breakthroughs in medicine	An article for a school magazine
Talking about films and movie therapy	A conversation about the film, *The Beach* and movie therapy	Movie therapy Photostory: What's so funny?	Synopsis of a film

Introduction

'If you can teach teenagers, you can teach anyone.' Michael Grinder

Teaching teenagers is an interesting and challenging task. A group of adolescents can be highly motivated, cooperative and fun to teach on one day, and the next day the whole group or individual students might turn out to be truly 'difficult' – the teacher might, for example, be faced with discipline problems, disruptive or provocative behaviour, a lack of motivation, or unwillingness on the students' part to do homework assigned to them.

The roots of these problems frequently lie in the fact that adolescents are going through a period of significant changes in their lives. The key challenge in the transition period between being a child and becoming an adult is the adolescent's struggle for identity – a process that requires the development of a distinct sense of who they are. A consequence of this process is that adolescents can feel threatened, and at the same time experience overwhelming emotions. They frequently try to compensate for the perceived threats with extremely rude behaviour, and try to 'hide' their emotions behind a wall of extreme outward conformity. The more individual students manage to look, talk, act and behave like the other members of their peer group, the less threatened and insecure they feel.

Insights into the causes underlying the problems might help us to understand better the complex situation our students are in. However, such insights do not automatically lead to more success in teaching. We need to react to the challenges in a professional way.[1] This includes the need to:

- select content and organise the students' learning according to their psychological needs;
- create a positive learning atmosphere;
- cater for differences in students' learning styles and intelligence(s), and facilitate the development of our students' study skills.

English in Mind second edition has been written taking all these points into account. They have significantly influenced the choice of texts, artwork and design, the structure of the units, the typology of exercises, and the means by which students' study skills are facilitated and extended.

The importance of the content for success

There are a number of reasons why the choice of the right content has a crucial influence over success or failure in the teaching of adolescents. Teachers frequently observe that teenagers are reluctant to 'talk about themselves'. This has to do with the adolescent's need for psychological security. Consequently, the 'further away' from their own world the content of the teaching is, the more motivating and stimulating it will be for the students. The preference for psychologically remote content goes hand in hand with a fascination with extremes and realistic details. Furthermore, students love identifying with heroes and heroines, because these idols are perceived to embody the qualities needed in order to survive in a threatening world: qualities such as courage, genius, creativity and love. In the foreign language class, students can become fascinated with stories about heroes and heroines to which they can ascribe such qualities. *English in Mind* treats students as young adults, offering them a range of interesting topics and a balance between educational value and teenage interest and fun.

As Kieran Egan[1] stresses, learning in the adolescent classroom can be successfully organised by starting with something far from the students' experience, but also connected to it by some quality with which they can associate. This process of starting far from the students makes it easier for the students to become interested in the topic, and also enables the teacher finally to relate the content to the students' own world.

A positive learning atmosphere

The creation of a positive learning atmosphere largely depends on the rapport between teacher and students, and the one which students have among themselves. It requires the teacher to be a genuine, empathetic listener, and to have a number of other psychological skills. *English in Mind* supports the teacher's task of creating positive learning experiences through: clear tasks; a large number of carefully designed exercises; regular opportunities for the students to check their own work; and a learning process designed to guarantee that the students will learn to express themselves both in speaking and in writing.

Learning styles and multiple intelligences

There is significant evidence that students will be better motivated, and learn more successfully, if differences in learning styles and intelligences are taken into account in the teaching–learning process.[2] The development of a number of activities in *English in Mind* has been influenced by such insights, and students find frequent study tips that show them how they can better utilise their own resources.[3]

The methodology used in *English in Mind*

Skills: *English in Mind* uses a communicative, multi-skills approach to develop the students' foreign language abilities in an interesting and motivational way. A wide range of interesting text types is used to present authentic use of language, including magazine and newspaper clippings, interviews, narratives, songs and engaging photostories.

1 An excellent analysis of teenage development and consequences for our teaching in general can be found in Kieran Egan: *Romantic Understanding*, Routledge and Kegan Paul, New York and London, 1990. This book has had a significant influence on the thinking behind *English in Mind*, and the development of the concept of the course.

2 See for example Eric Jensen: *Brain-Based Learning and Teaching*, Turning Point Publishing, Del Mar, CA, USA, 1995, on learning styles. An overview of the theory of multiple intelligences can be found in Howard Gardner: *Multiple Intelligences: The Theory in Practice*, Basic Books, New York 1993.

3 See Marion Williams and Robert L. Burden: *Psychology for Language Teachers*, Cambridge University Press, 1997 (pp. 143–62), on how the learner deals with the process of learning.

Grammar: *English in Mind* is based on a strong grammatical syllabus and takes into account students' mixed abilities by dealing with grammar in a carefully graded way, and offering additional teaching support.

Vocabulary: *English in Mind* offers a systematic vocabulary syllabus, including important lexical chunks for conversation and extension of the vocabulary in a bank at the back of the book.

Culture: *English in Mind* gives students insights into a number of important cross-cultural and intercultural themes. Significant cultural features of English-speaking countries are presented, and students are involved in actively reflecting on the similarities and differences between other cultures and their own.

Consolidation: Seven **Check your progress** revision pages per level will give teachers a clear picture of their students' progress and make students aware of what they have learned. Four **projects** give students the opportunity to use new language in a less controlled context and allow for learner independence.

Teacher support: *English in Mind* is clearly structured and easy to teach. The Teacher's Resource Book offers step-by-step lesson notes, background information on content, culture and language, additional teaching ideas and the tapescripts, photocopiable materials for further practice and extra lessons, taking into consideration the needs of mixed-ability groups by providing extra material for fast finishers or students who need more support, as well as an entry test.

Student support: *English in Mind* offers systematic support to students through: **Study help** sections and **Skills in mind**; classroom language; guidance in units to help with the development of classroom discourse and the students' writing; lists of irregular verbs and phonetics (at the back of the Student's Book); and a **Grammar reference** (at the back of the Workbook).

English in Mind: components

Each level of the *English in Mind* series contains the following components:

- Student's Book with accompanying DVD-ROM
- Audio CDs
- Workbook
- Teacher's Resource Book
- Testmaker Audio CD/CD-ROM
- DVD
- Classware DVD-ROM
- Website resources.

The Student's Book

Student's Book 4 has a **Welcome section** at the beginning. This is to allow teachers to check, reasonably quickly, some of the key areas of language which students may have covered in their previous learning. An alternative use of the Welcome section might be as diagnostic exercises, allowing teachers to gauge the strengths and weaknesses of their particular group of students before embarking on the material.

The units have the following basic structure, although with occasional minor variations depending on the flow of an individual unit:

- an opening **reading** text
- a **grammar** page, often including pronunciation
- two pages of **vocabulary** and **skills** work
- a **photostory**, a **Literature in mind** text, a **song** or a **Culture in mind** text, followed by **writing skills** work.

The **reading texts** aim to engage and motivate the students with interesting and relevant content, and to provide contextualised examples of target grammar and lexis. The texts have 'lead-in' tasks and are followed by comprehension tasks of various kinds. All the opening texts are also recorded on the Audio CDs, which allows teachers to follow the initial reading with a 'read and listen' phase, giving the students the invaluable opportunity of connecting the written word with the spoken version, which is especially useful for auditory learners. Alternatively, with stronger classes, teachers may decide to do one of the exercises as a listening task, with books closed.

Grammar follows the initial reading. The emphasis is on active involvement in the learning process. Examples from the texts are isolated and used as a basis for tasks, which focus on both concept and form of the target grammar area. Students are encouraged to find other examples and work out rules for themselves. Occasionally there are also **Look!** boxes which highlight an important connected issue concerning the grammar area; for example, in Unit 9 work on phrasal verbs has a **Look!** box showing how the parts can be separated in some phrasal verbs but not in others. This is followed by a number of graded exercises, both receptive and productive, which allow students to begin to employ the target language in different contexts and to produce realistic language.

Each unit has at least one **Vocabulary** section, with specific word fields. Again, examples from the initial text are focused on, and a lexical set is developed, with exercises for students to put the vocabulary into use. Vocabulary is frequently recycled in later texts in the unit (e.g. **photostories** or **Culture in mind** texts), and also in later units.

Pronunciation is included in every unit. There are exercises on common phoneme problems such as /iː/ in *seat* as well as aspects of stress (within words, and across sentences) and linking sounds. Vital areas are dealt with often in relation to a grammar area, for example, the pronunciation of contractions in third conditionals when conditionals are reviewed.

Language skills are present in every unit. There is always at least one **listening skills** activity, with listening texts of various genres; at least one (but usually several) **speaking skills** activity for fluency development. **Reading skills** are taught through the opening texts and also later texts in some units, as well as the **Culture in mind** sections. There is always a **writing skills** task, towards the end of each unit.

The final two pages of each unit have a **photostory** or a **song** (even-numbered units), or a **Culture in mind** or **Literature in Mind** text (odd-numbered units). The **photostories** are conversations between teenagers in everyday situations, allowing students to read and listen for interest and also to experience the use of common everyday language expressions. These **Everyday English** expressions are worked on in exercises following the dialogue. The photostories are expanded with videostories on the DVD / DVD-ROM, where students can follow the progress of the characters through a term at school. The **Culture in mind** texts are reading texts which provide further reading practice, and an opportunity for students to develop their knowledge and understanding of the world at large and in particular the English-speaking world. The **Literature in mind** texts are extracts from authentic literary sources that provide further reading practice.

Towards the end of each unit there is a **writing skills** task. These are an opportunity for students to further their control of language and to experiment in the production of tasks in a variety of genres (e.g. letters, emails, reports, etc.). There are model texts for the students to aid their own writing, and exercises providing guidance in terms of content and organisation. Through the completion of the writing tasks, students, if they wish, can also build up a bank of materials, or 'portfolio', during their period of learning: this can be very useful to them as the source of a sense of clear progress and as a means of self-assessment. A 'portfolio' of work can also be shown to other people (exam bodies, parents, even future employers) as evidence of achievement in language learning. Many of the writing tasks also provide useful and relevant practice for examinations such as Cambridge ESOL or Trinity Integrated Skills Examinations.

There is a **Check your progress** section after every two units. Here the teacher will find exercises in the Grammar and Vocabulary that were presented in the previous two units. The purpose of these (as opposed to the more formal tests offered on the Testmaker CD-ROM) is for teachers and students alike to check quickly the learning and progress made during the two units just covered; they can be done in class or at home. Every exercise has a marking scheme, and students can use the marks they gain to do some simple self-assessment of their progress (a light 'task' is offered for this).

Beyond the units themselves, *English in Mind* offers at the end of the Student's Book a further set of materials for teachers and students. These consist of:

- **Vocabulary bank:** extension of vocabulary from the units in the main body of the Student's Book for students to build on their vocabulary. This section is attractively illustrated and the words are taught either through definitions or pictures. This section is particularly useful for those students who want to learn more.
- **Get it right!** This section is based on the Cambridge Learner Corpus and concentrates on typical errors that students often make at this level. These errors are dealt with through a variety of exercises and activities which correspond with the grammar studied in the units in the Student's Book. They allow students to focus on the errors they make and give them the opportunity to correct them.
- **Projects:** activities which students can do in pairs or groups (or even individually if desired), for students to put the language they have so far learned into practical and enjoyable use. They are especially useful for mixed-ability classes, as they allow students to work at their own pace. The projects produced could also be part of the 'portfolio' of material mentioned earlier.

  Project 1, **A special person** can be done after students have finished Unit 7 of the Student's Book.

  Project 2, **Design a social initiative or a charity** fits in after students have finished Unit 5 of the Student's Book.

  Project 3, **A foreign country** should be done once students have finished Unit 9 of the Student's Book, and finally, Project 4, **Health** should be done after Unit 13.
- An **irregular verb** list for students to refer to when they need.
- A listing of **phonetic symbols**, again for student reference.

The DVD-ROM

The Student's Book includes a DVD-ROM which contains the listening material for the Workbook (listening texts and pronunciation exercises) in MP3 format and a range of carefully graded grammar and vocabulary exercises to provide further practice of the language presented in each unit. It also contains the 'Making Waves' videostories corresponding to the seven photostories in the Student's Book. These complement the photostories by dealing with the same themes and reflecting the same values, but they contain separate stories and scenes to them. They may take place before, at the same time as or after the photostories. There are four exercises for each videostory on the DVD-ROM, including a 'videoke' one in which students record their voices onto a short section of the videostory and can then play it back, either solo or as a pair with a friend. This provides a fun, sociable element, but also good practice of spoken English. The DVD-ROM also includes games for students to practise in an enjoyable and motivating way.

The Workbook

The Workbook is a resource for both teachers and students, providing further practice in the language and skills covered in the Student's Book. It is organised unit by unit, following the Student's Book. Each Workbook unit has six pages, and the following contents:

Remember and check: this initial exercise encourages students to remember the content of the initial reading text in the Student's Book unit.

Exercises: an extensive range of supporting exercises in the grammatical, lexical and phonological areas of the Student's Book unit, following the progression of the unit, so that teachers can use the exercises either during or at the end of the Student's Book unit.

Everyday English and **Literature/Culture in mind**: extra exercises on these sections in alternating units, as in the Student's Book.

Study help: these sections follow a syllabus of study skills areas, to develop the students' capacities as independent and successful learners. After a brief description of the skill, there are exercises for the students to begin to practise it.

Skills in mind page: these pages contain a separate skills development syllabus, which normally focuses on two main skill areas in each unit. There is also a skill tip relating to the main skill area, which the students can immediately put into action when doing the skills task(s).

Unit check page: this is a one-page check of knowledge of the key language of the unit, integrating both grammar and vocabulary in the three exercise types. The exercise types are: a) a cloze text to be completed using items given in a box; b) a sentence-level multiple-choice exercise; c) sentences to be completed with given vocabulary items.

At the end of the Workbook, there is a **Grammar reference** section. Here, there are explanations of the main grammar topics of each unit, with examples. It can be used for reference by students at home, or the teacher might wish to refer to it in class if the students appreciate grammatical explanations.

The audio for the Workbook is available on the Audio CDs as well as on the Student's Book DVD-ROM in MP3 format.

The Teacher's Resource Book

The Teacher's Resource Book contains:

- clear, simple, practical teaching **notes** on each unit and how to implement the exercises as effectively as possible.
- complete **tapescripts** for all listening and pronunciation activities.
- complete **answers** to all exercises (grammar, vocabulary, comprehension questions, etc.).
- **optional further activities**, for stronger or weaker classes, to facilitate the use of the material in mixed-ability classes.
- **background notes** relating to the information content (where appropriate) of reading texts. You can use these to set homework research tasks on the texts.
- **language notes** relating to grammatical areas, to assist less-experienced teachers who might have concerns about the target language and how it operates (these can also be used to refer to the Workbook **Grammar reference** section).
- a complete **answer key** and **tapescripts** for the **Workbook**.
- a **'Memo from Mario'** page at the end of each unit of teaching notes and ideas for further exploitation of the material in the Student's Book written by the well-known methodologist Mario Rinvolucri.
- an **entry test** which has been designed with two purposes. It can be used purely as a diagnostic entry test, or teachers can also use it for remedial work before beginning the **Welcome section** or after completing it.
- **photocopiable communication activities:** one page for each unit reflecting the core grammar and/or vocabulary of the unit. The communication activities recycle the key grammar and/or vocabulary in each unit. They are designed to activate the new language in a communicative context. They cover a range of fun and motivating activity types: board games; quizzes; information gap activities; descriptions; 'Find someone who ... ', etc.
- **photocopiable extra grammar exercises:** extra exercises for each unit, reflecting the key grammar areas of the unit. The grammar practice exercises cover specific areas of the key grammar from each unit. They are intended for fast finishers or students who need extra practice.
- **teaching notes** for the photocopiable communication activities which contain clear step-by-step instructions for all the activities. In addition, there are answers for the communication activities, where relevant, and answers for all of the grammar practice exercises.

Other resources

Testmaker Audio CD/CD-ROM: This allows you to create and edit your own tests, choosing from unit tests, which can be combined in unit pairs to match the course syllabus, or end-of-year tests. The tests offer 'standard' and 'more challenging' levels of testing, and can be created in A and B versions to avoid the sharing of answers. The listening test recordings are provided in audio CD format.

DVD: This contains both the 'Making Waves' videostories and the complete 'EiMTV' material from the original edition.

Classware DVD-ROM: This contains the Student's Book in digital format to project on a whiteboard or via a computer with projector. You can enlarge parts of the page for a clearer focus. The 'Making Waves' videostories and class listenings are also included, together with scripts.

Web resources: In addition to information about the series, the *English in Mind* website contains downloadable pages of further activities and exercises for students as well as interactive activities for students and wordlists with multiple translations. It can be found at this part of the Cambridge University Press website:

www.cambridge.org/elt/englishinmind

Introductory note from Mario Rinvolucri

As you read through the Teacher's Resource Book you will, at the end of each unit, find small contributions of mine that offer you alternative ways of practising a structure, of dealing with a text or of revising words.

- I want to stress that the ideas presented are simply alternatives to the ways of working proposed to you by the authors. I strongly recommend that you try the authors' way first.
- When you teach the book through for the second or third time you may be ready then to try something a bit different. The authors and I believe that options are important but options are not useful if they confuse you.
- Maybe you could think of my contributions as a sort of sauce with a slightly different flavour to be tried for variety's sake.

Mario Rinvolucri, Pilgrims, UK, guest methodologist.

Welcome section

This section is designed to serve as a review, giving students the opportunity to revise and practise language they already know, and it is also a tool for teachers to find out how much students know already and which areas students may need to do more work on before continuing with the course.

A

1 Read and listen

a As an introduction, ask students who the cleverest person they know is and why they are clever. Ask students if they have heard any stories about people with amazing mental abilities or seen any people on television doing incredible mental feats. Students read the text and answer the question. Tell them not to worry about understanding every word but to focus on the answer to the question. Check answer.

Answer

He was special because the two halves of his brain were not connected in the normal way and as a result he had amazing memory skills.

b ▶ CD1 T02 Ask students to read through the questions and check understanding. Students answer the questions. Encourage them to try to answer the questions without looking back at the text, but let them look back if necessary. Play the recording while students answer the questions. Ask students to correct the false answers. Allow them to compare their answers with a partner before checking answers in open class.

TAPESCRIPT

See the reading text on page 4 of the Student's Book.

Answers

1 T 2 T 3 T 4 T 5 F (He was given an Oscar by the writer of the film *Rain Man*.)
6 F (His fame made him more self-confident and he got used to being the centre of attention.)

OPTIONAL ACTIVITY

Divide the class into groups of three or four and tell them they are going to find out who has the best memory. Ask each student to write ten words of their choice (in English!) on a piece of paper without showing the others in their group. Students then take it in turns to show their words to the rest of their group for 30 seconds. Students must then write down all the words they remember, scoring one point for each word. When everybody has shown their words, the person with the highest total score is the winner. Alternatively this could be a whole-class activity with words written on the board by the teacher.

2 Past tense review

To remind students of the difference between the past continuous and past simple tenses, write the following sentences on the board.

I saw a parrot while I was waiting for the bus.

Ask students which action began first (*waiting for the bus*), which action interrupted another action (*I saw a parrot*) and which action continued after the interruption (*waiting for the bus*). Remind students that we use the past continuous to give background information and the past simple to describe specific actions.

Read through the text with students and check understanding of any difficult vocabulary: *diagnose, founded*. Ask students to complete the text using the correct form of the verbs in brackets. Allow them to check answers with a partner before open-class feedback.

Answers

2 were living 3 diagnosed 4 developed
5 began 6 was working 7 started 8 gave
9 had called

3 *be / get used to* + gerund vs. *used to* + infinitive

For a quick review of the difference between these two forms, write these sentences on the board:

1 *I used to live in France.*
2 *I am used to living in France.*

Ask students which sentence refers to the past (1) and which refers to the present (2). Elicit a possible context for each sentence and, if students have difficulty, explain that *used to* refers to a repeated or continuous past action which no longer exists, and *to be used to* means to be accustomed to or to find a situation normal. You may like to give further examples of each form to pay attention to the negative and interrogative forms, e.g. *He isn't used to eating a lot in the evening. / Are you used to getting up early? / They didn't use to watch television. / Did you use to have a skateboard?*

Students complete the exercise and check answers with a partner before open-class feedback.

Answers
2 used 3 I'm used 4 going
5 I'm completely used 6 have 7 used
8 be 9 going

OPTIONAL ACTIVITY

Give students three minutes to think of ways in which their lives have changed in the last five years. Divide the class into pairs and ask students to talk about how things have changed. Circulate and monitor, encouraging students to use *used to* and *get used to*. Listen to some of their ideas in open class as feedback.

4 Personality

Look at the adjectives with students. Ask them which of the adjectives are negative (*bossy, bad-tempered, insensitive*) and check the meaning of the remaining words.

Read through sentences 1–10 and check understanding. Students complete the exercise. Check answers.

Answers
2 determined 3 considerate 4 imaginative
5 insensitive 6 ambitious 7 bossy
8 independent 9 sensible 10 bad-tempered

OPTIONAL ACTIVITY

Divide the class into pairs and ask students to use the adjectives to describe people they know. Encourage them to give reasons for their choices and listen to some of the best descriptions in open class as feedback.

5 *make* and *do*

Write *make* and *do* on the board and give students a minute to think of phrases using each verb. Write some of their ideas on the board. Remind students that *make* is used to talk about constructing something and *do* is often used to talk about jobs or tasks. Students read the sentences and complete them with the correct form of *make* or *do*. Ask students to compare their answers with a partner. Check answers and tell students to write the phrases in their vocabulary notebook. Ask students to add other phrases with *make* and *do* to their list.

Answers
2 do 3 made 4 make 5 make 6 did
7 made 8 made

B

1 Read and listen

a As an introduction, write the words *Readers' problems* on the board and give students two minutes to work with a partner and think of the type of problems that appear in teenage magazines. Listen to some of their ideas in open class. Tell students they are going to read a letter to a teenage magazine. Students read and answer the question.

Answer
Sentence 1

b ▶ CD1 T03 Read through items 1–6 with students and check understanding. Students answer the questions. Play the recording while students read and find the pieces of advice. If necessary, play the recording again, pausing to check for understanding. Check answers.

TAPESCRIPT

See the reading text on page 6 of the Student's Book.

Answers
Sentences 1, 3, 4 and 6 are mentioned in the text.

2 *should / should have*

To introduce the topic, tell students about some imaginary problems that you have (e.g. your neighbours are very noisy / your car has broken down). Ask students to give you advice and write any sentences with *should* on the board. Repeat the exercise with past problems (e.g. You missed the bus this morning / A man in a shop was rude to you) and elicit sentences with *should have*. Clarify that *should* is followed by the bare infinitive and *should have* by the past participle. Students complete the exercise and check answers with a partner before open class feedback.

Answers
2 a 3 c 4 d

OPTIONAL ACTIVITY

For further practice of *should* and *should have*, divide the class into pairs and ask students to tell their partners some problems and ask for advice – *What do you think I should do / should have done?* Circulate and ensure students are using the forms correctly. If students have difficulty thinking of problems, you could write a few on the board:

My bicycle has been stolen.
I haven't got any money.
I can't concentrate on my homework.
My sister keeps taking my things.

Listen to any interesting answers in open class as feedback.

3 *wish*

a Write these sentences on the board:

1 *I hate this town. I wish I lived ...*
2 *I was stupid. I wish I hadn't ...*

Ask students to suggest ways of ending each sentence, e.g. *I wish I lived in a city / I wish I hadn't told him my secret.* Point out the tense of the verbs used after *wish* (1 uses the past simple to refer to the present and 2 uses the past perfect to refer to the past).

Students complete the exercise. Allow them to check their answers with a partner before open-class feedback.

Answers
2 past 3 past 4 present 5 present
6 past

b Look at the pictures and ask students to describe them. Students write a sentence with *wish* for each situation. Circulate to check they are using the forms correctly. Let them compare answers with a partner before listening to some of their ideas in open class.

Possible answers
1 I wish I'd gone to bed earlier.
2 I wish I'd brought my umbrella.
3 I wish I'd stopped sooner.

4 Problems

Ask students what they do if they have a problem. Do they talk to someone or deal with it themselves? Tell students they are going to read a short text about someone with a problem. Look at the multiple-choice options with students. Students complete the exercise. Check answers.

Answers
2 over 3 work 4 make 5 talked 6 go
7 sleep 8 come

5 Friends

Read through the poem with students and ask them which of the underlined phrases are positive (1,3,5) and which are negative (2,4,6). Do not discuss the meaning of phrases at this stage. Students match the phrases with the meanings. Check answers.

Answers
1 d 2 a 3 f 4 b 5 c 6 e

OPTIONAL ACTIVITY

Write these questions on the board:

1 *Have you ever told on anyone?*
2 *Do you get on well with your brother/sister/ cousins/neighbours?*
3 *Have you ever fallen out with someone?*

Ask students to discuss the questions with a partner and listen to some of the most interesting answers in open class.

C

1 Read and listen

Warm up

Books closed. Ask students if there is a lot of crime among young people in their country. What sort of crimes do young people commit? Is there a youth gang culture? Ask them if they think the situation is worse or better in the UK.

a Tell students they are going to read an interview with a man who is helping young criminals in the UK. If necessary pre-teach difficult vocabulary: *arrested, burglary, shoplifting, vandalism, deprived, broken families, mentors, hang out with.* Students read the interview and answer the question. Check answer.

Answer
His charity introduces young children to police officers who will act as their mentor and be a strong role model for them.

b ▶ CD1 T04 Play the recording while students read and answer the questions. Check answers. If necessary, play the recording again, pausing to check for understanding.

TAPESCRIPT

See the reading text on page 8 of the Student's Book.

Answers

1 Figures show there has been an increase in gang crimes.
2 Deprived inner-city areas.
3 Young children are assigned a police officer, who acts as mentor to them.
4 They go to football matches or go to the beach to do the normal things kids do with a strong role model.
5 Because the problem starts at an early age.
6 He plans to take the idea to other cities in the UK.

OPTIONAL ACTIVITY

Write these words on the board:

jobs money education prison family

Divide the class into five small groups and assign each group one of the five words. Tell students you are going to hold a class debate and they will have to argue that their concept is the best way to help young criminals. Encourage them to write down their ideas and give each group one minute to present their ideas before holding an open class debate. Finish with a vote to decide which is the best solution.

2 Present perfect and future passives

a To introduce this area, write this sentence on the board:

They have built a new library in my town.

Ask students to identify who is doing the action (*the subject – they*), and what is being done by the verb (*the object – a new library*). Ask students to identify the tense (*present perfect*). Point out that we are more interested in the object, i.e. the library, than the subject, and elicit how a passive construction would begin (*A new library …*). Ask students to complete the sentence and write the passive construction on the board (*A new library has been built in my town by them*). Ask students which part of the sentence can be omitted (*by them*).

Look at the example with students and check understanding of the exercise. Students work through the rest of the exercise before feedback in open class.

Answers

2 have given 3 has been chosen
4 will be taken 5 will spend 6 will tell
7 will apologise 8 will be helped

b Read through the sentences with students. If they have difficulty with this area, point out the main focus of each sentence and remind them how to start the passive sentence. Students complete the exercise. Circulate and help with any problems before checking answers in open class.

Answers

1 Our town has been chosen to host the next world swimming championships.
2 A lot of money will be spent on a new swimming pool.
3 A lot of tickets have already been sold.
4 Our town will be visited by more than 10,000 people.
5 A big opening ceremony will be held before the championships begin.
6 Lots of famous people have been invited to watch the championships.

3 Future predictions

Books closed. To introduce this area, write several activities on the board (e.g. read a book, watch TV, play Xbox, play football, text a friend) and ask students if they will do any of these activities at the weekend. Elicit different forms used for future predictions and write some example sentences on the board. Books open. Read through the sentences with students and ask them to order them. Let students compare answers with a partner before checking in open class.

Answers

1 I'll be famous before I'm 30.
2 I'll probably be in a successful rock band.
3 I might live abroad.
4 I'm not likely to have any children.
5 I probably won't get married.
6 I won't work in the family business.

4 Crimes

Look at the pictures with students and ask them to describe what is happening in each one. Help with vocabulary as required. Students match the words with the pictures. Check answers in open class.

Answers

1 B 2 E 3 F 4 A 5 D 6 C

OPTIONAL ACTIVITY

In pairs, students discuss which of the crimes are the most serious. What do they think the punishment should be for each crime? Listen to some of their ideas in open class.

5 Getting into trouble

Tell students they are going to read a text about a young criminal. Check understanding of difficult vocabulary: *offence, probation, community service.* Students complete the text and check answers with a partner before feedback in open class.

Answers
2 doing 3 broke 4 committing 5 getting
6 got 7 sent 8 put 9 do 10 pay

D

1 Read and listen

Warm up

Ask students if they ever argue with their parents. What type of things do they argue about? Do they have most arguments with their mum or their dad? Listen to some of their ideas in open class.

a Tell students that they are going to read a conversation between a girl and her mum. Students complete the exercise and compare their answer in pairs.

Answers
Dana is upset because her dad hasn't recorded her favourite programme.
Emily is upset because her mum has broken the computer.

b ▶ CD1 T05 Students read through the questions. Check any vocabulary problems. Go through the first item as an example, if necessary. Play the recording while students listen and read to answer the questions. Tell them not to worry if they do not understand every word at this stage. Check answers.

TAPESCRIPT
See the dialogue on page 10 of the Student's Book.

Answers
1 Emily 2 Dad 3 Dad 4 Mum 5 Emily
6 Mum

OPTIONAL ACTIVITY

Divide the class into pairs and ask students to discuss recent arguments they have had with their parents. Students could role play some of their arguments, taking it in turn to be the parents.

2 *make / let / be allowed to*

a To introduce this language point, write on the board:

My parents let me ...
My parents make me ...
I am not allowed to ...

Ask students to complete the sentences with their own ideas, then compare their sentences with their partners. Elicit some examples and point out the structure of *be allowed to* + verb, *let* + object + verb, *make* + object + verb. Remind students that *let* is the same in its infinitive, past and past participle forms.

Students complete the exercise. Circulate and help with any problems. Students check answers with a partner before open-class feedback.

Answers
1 makes 2 let 3 'm allowed to 4 makes
5 lets 6 is allowed 7 lets 8 makes

b In groups of three, students write and discuss rules in their family. Circulate and encourage them to use *make, let* and *be allowed to* in their discussions. Listen to some of their ideas in open class and find out who has the strictest parents.

3 Modals of deduction (past)

To introduce the language in this exercise, tell students that you arrived home last night and found a big box on your doorstep. Ask them to guess how it came to be there and what it was. Elicit sentences containing *might have*, e.g. *It might have been a present.* Tell students that you had ordered a CD on the internet and elicit *It must have been a CD.* Tell them the box was very big and elicit *It can't have been a CD.* Write all three sentences on the board and check students are clear that we use modal + *have* + past participle to talk about past possibility and probability. Finally, tell students that you opened the box and a man jumped out singing Happy Birthday! He was at the wrong address.

Ask students to complete the dialogue with modals of deduction. Circulate and monitor to check students are using the forms correctly. Allow them to compare answers with a partner before open class feedback.

Answers

2 can't have been 3 might have taken
4 might have thought 5 can't have eaten
6 must have been 7 might have been
8 can't have been 9 must have stolen

4 Television

Ask students to tell you the different types of television programme they watch and write some of their ideas on the board. If necessary elicit *quiz show* and the names of some quiz shows in their country. Divide the class into pairs and ask students to explain the rules of their favourite quiz show. Listen to some of their ideas in open class and help with vocabulary as necessary. Look at the words in the box with students and ask them to complete the text. During feedback, check understanding of the vocabulary.

Answers

1 viewing figures 2 celebrity 3 contestant
4 audience 5 viewers 6 Presenter
7 serial 8 episode

5 Anger

Remind students of the conversation between Emily and her mum in Exercise 1 and ask if they remember any of the phrases used connected to anger. Look at 1–8 and ask students to cover a–h. See if students can remember any of the endings before allowing them to look at endings and complete the exercise. Check answers.

Answers

1 h 2 a 3 f 4 b 5 g 6 c 7 d 8 e

1 Sport with a difference

Unit overview

TOPIC: New and unusual sports

TEXTS

Reading and listening: an article about chessboxing; an article about weird sports

Listening: an interview with two sportswomen

Writing: a composition about a sport

SPEAKING AND FUNCTIONS

A discussion about competition between sportsmen and sportswomen

Talking about unusual new sports

LANGUAGE

Grammar: relative clauses review; relative clauses with *which*

Vocabulary: sports

Pronunciation: intonation in questions

1 Read and listen

If you set the background information as a homework research task, ask the students to tell the class what they found out.

BACKGROUND INFORMATION

Berlin (population 3.4 million) is the capital city of Germany. It is famous for its diverse architecture, art scene, festivals, sporting events and nightlife. Berlin has a high quality of living and is renowned for its liberal lifestyle.

San Francisco (population 815,000) is a city in California, USA. It developed after the Gold Rush in 1848. It is famous for landmarks such as the Golden Gate Bridge and Chinatown, and for its liberal attitudes.

Chessboxing is a sport which combines chess and boxing. It originated in a graphic novel by Enki Bilal. Matches consist of a maximum of 11 rounds. Four-minute chess rounds alternate with three-minute boxing rounds. Opponents can win either with a knockout or a checkmate. World-class chess boxers have to be experienced boxers and chess masters. The current world champion is 18-year-old Leo Kraft from Belarus.

Warm up

Books closed. Divide the class into groups of three or four and give them two minutes to list as many sports or games which are played by two people as they can. Listen to some of their ideas in open class and write any interesting ideas on the board. Ask students if they have ever played chess or done any boxing. What are the differences between the two activities?

a Books open. Look at the words in the box with students and ask them to write them in the correct columns. Check answers and understanding of the words.

Answers

boxing: gloves, ring
chess: queen, board, checkmate
both: round, referee

b Read through the questions with students and ask them to read the text to find the answers. Encourage students not to look up every new word but just to focus on finding the answers to the questions.

Answers

1. **Chessboxing is a sport which combines chess and boxing. Players alternate one round of chess with one round of boxing.**
2. **He is German.**

c ▶ CD1 T06 Read through the questions with students and check understanding. Play the recording while students listen and answer the questions. After the first listening let students compare their answers with a partner. Check answers. If necessary, play the recording again, pausing to clarify any problems.

TAPESCRIPT

See the reading text on page 12 of the Student's Book.

Answers

1. **Because he is German and the fight is in Berlin.**
2. **Through checkmate or knockout.**
3. **It shows fighters can be smart.**
4. **He won the game of chess.**

Discussion box

In pairs or small groups, students discuss the question. Monitor and help as necessary, encouraging them to express themselves in English and to use any vocabulary they have learned from the text. Ask pairs or groups to feedback to the class and discuss any interesting points further.

2 Grammar

★ Relative clauses: review

a **Weaker classes:** Write these sentences on the board:

1 *That's the house ... I was born.* (where)
2 *I've got a friend ... plays the guitar.* (who)
3 *We met a boy ... mother is a film director.* (whose)
4 *I like stories ... have a happy ending.* (which/that)

Ask students to complete the sentences, and write the correct answers on the board. Remind students that these words are called *relative pronouns*. They link together two clauses and they refer back to someone or something mentioned earlier in the sentence. Now follow the procedure for stronger students.

Stronger classes: Ask students to complete the sentences. They then find the sentences in the text to check their answers. Point out that in sentences 2 and 3 the relative pronoun can be either *which* or *that*. Ask students to say what or who the relative pronoun refers to in each sentence (1 *Anti-Terror Frank*; 2 *a table*; 3 *exercises*; 4 *people*; 5 *Germany*).

Answers
2 which (or that) 3 which (or that) 4 whose
5 where

Language notes

1 All the examples in Exercise 2a are defining relative clauses – they give information that is essential to the meaning of the sentence. For this type of clause, *that* is commonly used instead of *which* to refer to things. We also sometimes use *that* to refer to people, especially in conversation.

2 In defining relative clauses, we often leave out *who*, *which* or *that* if it is not the subject of the clause, e.g.

Helena is the girl I met in Greece. (subject = *I*)
Here's the book you lent me. (subject = *you*)

b Students complete the rule.

Answers
who; which, that; where; whose

c **Weaker classes:** To clarify the use of non-defining relative clauses, write this sentence on the board:

John is a doctor.

Then add information:

John, who speaks German and Russian, is a doctor.

Point out that the information between the commas is additional and that the sentence makes sense without it. Now follow the procedure for stronger classes.

Stronger classes: Read through the explanation of defining (D) and non-defining (A) relative clauses and check understanding. Ask students to look back at the sentences in Exercise 2a and to say whether the information following the relative pronoun is defining or additional (*it is defining in all the sentences*). In pairs, students decide whether the sentences in 2c are defining (D) or non-defining (A). Point out the use of commas around non-defining clauses.

Answers
2 D 3 D 4 A 5 A

Language notes

In English we often express our feelings about something by ending a sentence with *which* + *be* + adjective, e.g.

I don't have to go to school next week, which is great!

I had three exams last week, which was terrible!

3 Grammar

★ Relative clauses with *which*

a Read the examples from the text and ask students to say what the pronoun *which* refers to in each case.

Answers
1 The opinion that boxers aren't very clever.
2 Winning the world championship.

b Students complete the rule.

Answers
which, whose

c Read through the example with the class. Students use *which* to complete the sentences in 2–6. Let students compare answers in pairs before getting feedback. Point out that all the relative clauses in this exercise offer additional information.

Answers

2 You need to be mentally and physically tough, which is why you need to prepare well.
3 Some people have been killed in boxing matches, which is terrible.
4 Chess is quite a complicated game, which means players have to concentrate a lot.
5 Two men sit in a boxing ring and play chess, which is quite strange.
6 Chessboxing is becoming more popular, which means we might start to see it on TV soon.

Grammar notebook

Remind students to note down the rules for relative clauses with *which* and to write a few examples of their own.

OPTIONAL ACTIVITY

For further practice of this area, write these sentences on the board and ask students to complete them in a suitable way. Invite individual students to read out their sentences as feedback.

1 *She's the girl who ...*
2 *Maths is a difficult subject, which ...*
3 *That's the boy whose ...*

4 Speak and listen

a Students look at the photos and name the sports. Ask them to list the sports in the three categories.

b Students add other sports to their three lists, referring back to the list they wrote in the warm up. Monitor and help students with any new vocabulary. Check that students are spelling and pronouncing words properly.

c In pairs, students discuss their lists. Encourage them to offer information and opinions about the sports they have tried and to give reasons explaining why they would/wouldn't like to try others. You may like to give them some examples of your own to get them started. For feedback, ask students to give some examples for each category. Find out which class member has done the most unusual sport.

d Tell students they are going to hear about two sportswomen: a snooker and pool player and an inline skater. Read the sentences with the class and pre-teach difficult vocabulary: *league, professional, undefeated.* Ask students to predict which of the two sportswomen says each of the sentences.

e ▶ CD1 T07 Play the recording. Students listen and check their answers. Tell them to listen specifically for sentences 1–6 and not to worry if they don't understand every word.

TAPESCRIPT

Man: Born in England, Allison Fisher was seven years old when she started playing snooker – traditionally, a game for men. By the time she was 14, she wanted to be a professional snooker player. Listen to what she has to say on the subject.

Allison: Because I started as a kid playing the game, being a girl just didn't seem to matter. It started to become important when I wasn't allowed to play in some league teams because I was a female!

Man: In her mid-twenties, she had become the number one women's player in the world. But she still couldn't play against men. Lots of people wondered if she could actually beat the top men players.

Allison: There was talk about me competing against the men and that created a lot of attention.

Man: In those days, the top professional men players were earning a lot of money, but Allison wasn't. But she knew that in the USA, there were women pool players who did make a lot of money. In fact, in America, women pool players were earning more money than male players! Allison thought about it.

Allison: I didn't know the game of pool, but I thought: how hard can it be?

Man: So, aged 27, Allison left her home and her family and moved to the USA, where she started playing pool. She soon found success – she won seven championships very quickly.

Allison: It was a very professional environment there – I loved it from the very beginning.

Man: Allison Fisher is still one of the top players on the USA pool circuit.

Part 2

Man: Brazilian, Fabiola da Silva is the most recognisable female inline skater in the world. Yet when she started, all her skating heroes were men.

Fabiola: You know, back in those days, there weren't so many girls skating, and the skaters I really admired were men.

Man: Fabiola began skating when she was 15. She skated with a group of friends who skated aggressively and after watching them she wanted to start skating that way too. She learned fast because she really liked it. She came onto the professional scene two years later, remaining undefeated for a long time.

Fabiola: I keep pushing the limits, you know.

Man: She has been the undisputed leader of the female inline skating scene for years now. But she knows that that might not always be the case.

Fabiola: All the girls on the tour are capable of beating me. I have my bad days too.

Man: Some years ago, she became famous when the inline skating authorities changed their rules so that she could compete against men. Fabiola – known as Fab to her friends and fans – has been in the men's top ten many times. Some of this, she attributes to her attitude in competition.

Fabiola: You know, every time I skate, I'm having fun, but I take what I do seriously. I always want to make sure I'm doing a good job.

Man: Which means she's probably going to go on being successful.

Answers
1 Allison 2 Fabiola 3 Allison
4 Allison 5 Fabiola 6 Fabiola

f ▶ CD1 T07 Read the questions with the class. Play the recording.

Weaker classes: Play the recording again while students listen and complete the exercise. Check answers, playing and pausing the recording as necessary to clarify any vocabulary problems.

Stronger classes: Ask students try to answer the questions from memory, based on the first listening. Play the recording again for them to check their answers.

Answers
1 She started playing snooker at seven years old. She became the women's number one in her mid-twenties.
2 She wasn't earning much money, so she moved to the USA where women players earned as much as, or more than, men.
3 She won seven championships in the USA.

g ▶ CD1 T07 Follow the procedure for weaker or stronger classes as in Exercise 4f.

Answers
1 She began skating aged 15 and turned professional aged 17.
2 She became famous when she started competing against men.
3 She takes what she does seriously and wants to do a good job.

Discussion box

In pairs or small groups, students discuss the questions. Monitor and help as necessary, encouraging them to express themselves in English and to use any vocabulary they have learned from the text. Ask pairs or groups to feedback to the class and discuss any interesting points further.

5 Vocabulary and speaking

✱ Sports

Warm up

Books closed. Refer back to the sports mentioned in Exercise 4 and ask students to give any names they know for equipment needed to play them. Write the vocabulary on the board. Students open their books and look at the picture on page 15. Ask them to name the sports equipment. If they don't know all the names, don't give them the answers at this stage.

a Students read texts 1–6 and decide which of the sports in the table in Exercise 5c they refer to.

b ▶ CD1 T08 Play the recording. Students listen and check their answers. Ask them if they can now name all of the sports equipment in the picture.

TAPESCRIPT

See the texts on page 15 of the Student's Book.

Answers
2 football 3 ice hockey 4 boxing 5 tennis
6 swimming

c Students use vocabulary from the texts in Exercise 5a to complete the table. Encourage them to try to complete the table from memory, before looking back at the texts. Check answers. Ask students if they can think of any other words to add to the table.

Answers
tennis: ball, net, racket; court
football: ball, net; pitch
ice hockey: skates, puck, sticks; rink
boxing: gloves, helmet; ring
surfing: board; sea
swimming: cap, costume, goggles; pool

Language notes

Students are often confused by the different names used to describe sports venues. This table may help them:

Sport	Place where it is done
football	pitch
cricket	pitch
hockey	pitch
rugby	pitch
tennis	court
basketball	court
badminton	court
golf	course

d In pairs, students choose a sport and their partner asks *yes/no* questions to guess what it is. Do an example with the whole class first, and encourage students to use as many words from Exercise 5c as possible. At the end, choose a few students to think of a sport for the whole class to guess.

Weaker classes: Before the pairwork stage, elicit possible questions and write them on the board for students to refer to during the activity.

e Write a football score on the board, for example *England 3 – Scotland 1*. Elicit sentences using the verbs *win, score, beat, lose*, e.g. *England won. Scotland scored one goal. England beat Scotland. Scotland lost 3–1.* Check understanding of *medal* and *referee*. Students complete the sentences and compare answers with a partner before feedback.

Answers
2 won 3 beat 4 score 5 get sent off
6 draw

Language notes
There are several different words for *0* in English. For football scores we say *nil*, as in *three–nil* (3–0) or a *nil-nil draw* (0–0). For tennis scores we say *love*, as in *forty-love* (40–0). When we are saying phone numbers we say *oh*, as in *two seven six five oh four* (276504).

f In groups, students discuss the questions in Exercise 4e. Encourage them to use the words from the box. Ask some students to give their opinions to the class and invite discussion.

Weaker classes: Students can write their ideas before speaking. Encourage them to look at their notes as little as possible.

Vocabulary notebook
Encourage students to start a new section called *Sport* in their notebook and to add these words. They may find it useful to note down translations, too.

6 Pronunciation
See notes on page 121.

Culture in mind

7 Read and listen

Warm up
Books closed. Ask students if they have ever taken part in any strange sports or games. Do they have any unusual sports at their school sports day? Are there any sports which are popular in their country but not common in the rest of the world? Divide the class into pairs and give students a few minutes to discuss their answers. Listen to some of their ideas in open class as feedback.

a Tell students they are going to read a text about weird sports. Write the names of the three sports on the board and ask students to guess what the sports involve.

Books open. Students skim through the article quickly to find the answers. There are quite a lot of difficult words in the text, but encourage them to concentrate on the task. Check answers in open class.

Answers
1 In Australia, Namibia and South Africa
2 Extreme ironing

b ▶ CD1 T10 Read questions 1–4 with students. Before students read the text again, pre-teach *courting, obstacle course, piggyback, performance art*. Play the recording while students read and listen to answer the questions. Pause where appropriate to check comprehension and help with difficult vocabulary. Check answers.

Answers
1 They are all a bit dangerous. They have all taken elements of one sport or tradition and mixed it with something else!
2 Wife-carrying
3 Sand boarding: standing on the board/lying on the board
Wife-carrying: piggyback/fireman's lift/Estonian style
4 Extreme ironing

Discussion box
In pairs or small groups, students discuss the question. Monitor and help as necessary, encouraging students to express themselves in English and to use any vocabulary they have learned from the text. Ask pairs or groups to feedback to the class and discuss any interesting points further.

OPTIONAL ACTIVITY

If you would like your students to do some further work on the vocabulary in the text, you can use this exercise. Write the following definitions on the board and ask students to find words and expressions with the same meaning in the text. The words are in the order of the texts. To make the exercise more challenging, you could write them on the board in a different order.

1 hill (*slope*)
2 moving (*weaving*)
3 joins (*combines*)
4 excitement (*thrill*)
5 places (*locations*)
6 lifting (*picking up*)
7 prize (*trophy*)

8 Write

a Ask students if they have ever seen a boxing match (either live or on television). Invite them to discuss briefly what happens at a boxing match and whether or not they think boxing is a good sport to watch. Students read the composition and decide whether it was written by a boy or a girl. Ask them to give reasons for their choice.

Possible answer
The writer seems to be a girl as she says '... seems to me that some people, especially men, ...'

b Write the words in the box on the board. Ask students which is used to give extra information (*Moreover*), which is used for contrast (*However*), which introduces an example (*for example*) and which introduces the ending of a composition (*To conclude*). Students read the composition again and add the words in the box.

Stronger classes: Ask students to use the words in the box to make sentences. Write some examples on the board and ask students what the purpose of the words is.

Answers
1 for example 2 However 3 Moreover
4 To conclude

Language note
You may want to make students aware of some more expressions used to give extra information (*furthermore, in addition, what's more*), to make a contrast (*on the other hand*), to introduce an example (*for instance*) and to introduce the end of a composition (*finally, in conclusion, to summarise*).

c Read through the paragraph titles with the students and ask them to decide which paragraph they refer to.

Answers
A Para 4 B Para 2 C Para 1 D Para 3

d Draw students' attention to the construction of the composition. Point out that it has a clear introduction and conclusion and that the writer's opinions are backed up by examples. Emphasise that it is important to plan a composition carefully before writing. Look at the mind map and ask students to think of more negatives, positives and opinions. They then prepare a similar mind map for a sport of their choice, and use this to organise their four paragraphs. The writing and checking stages could be set for homework.

Memo from Mario

Sport with a difference

1 We as a group

- Write the following gapped sentences on the board.

  We, as a group...

  have played .... different sports.

  have never tried ....

  have watched .... different sports live.

  have watched .... different sports on TV.

  have played .... hours of sport this month.

  have watched .... hours of sport this month.

  own .... items of sports equipment.

- Divide the class into groups of about six or seven. Get each group to appoint a secretary who will copy the sentences from the board. The groups should then ask each other questions to complete the gaps with the total figures for their group.
- When they have finished, the group secretaries report back to the class as a whole to compare results.
- As an optional extra, you could try to combine all the results onto the sentences on the board (or onto a poster).

RATIONALE

Getting students to think about themselves as a group rather than individually can help to build a group feeling.

This could be a good follow-up to section 5, when the students have already thought about the vocabulary.

2 Call my bluff

- This is based on a very old game, played on TV in the UK. Each group of three students will need a dictionary. (The groups could be larger than three, but this number seems to work best as everyone is more likely to contribute.)
- Explain that the students are going to give definitions of words. In each group of three, one definition must be correct and the other two invented. They should try to make the invented definitions plausible, as the class will vote for the one they believe to be correct.
- Divide the class into threes and give each group a piece of paper with the name of an unfamiliar object on it. Tell them not to let other groups see their paper until they have finished. They should look in the dictionary to find the correct definition and then work together to invent two more possible, but incorrect, definitions, using the following pattern.

  A .... is a thing which ....

  A .... is a person who ....

- While they are working, circulate and help as necessary. When the groups have finished, they should write their three definitions on the piece of paper and post them on the walls round the room. The students circulate, read the definitions and mark the one they believe to be correct – no dictionaries allowed! When they've finished, each group counts their votes and then reveals which definition is correct. The group with the most incorrect votes win.
- You can use any words the students are unlikely to know, but here are a few suggestions. Make sure they are in the dictionaries the students will use.

leash	*churn*	*heathen*	*chisel*	*yokel*
beehive	*drainpipe*	*dredger*	*pickaxe*	*midwife*

RATIONALE

Stimulating students' imagination and creative use of language whilst having fun.

2 People are people

Unit overview

TOPIC: Different personalities

TEXTS

Reading and listening: a questionnaire on personality; photostory: *You're both being a pain*

Listening: talking about funny people

Writing: a description of someone you've met recently

SPEAKING AND FUNCTIONS

Talking about jokes

Discussing important qualities in a friend

LANGUAGE

Grammar: *What* clauses; verbs + gerund/infinitive review

Vocabulary: personality

Pronunciation: sentence stress and rhythm

1 Read and listen

Warm up

Ask students to draw a horizontal line in their notebook with *sociable* at one end and *unsociable* at the other. Ask students to write their name somewhere on the line to indicate how sociable they are. Then they do the same for the students nearest to them in the class. Students compare their lines with the students whose names they have written. Do they have the same ideas of how sociable they are? Ask students what makes a person seem sociable or unsociable and write ideas on the board.

a ▶ CD1 T11 Tell students they are going to complete a questionnaire to find out how sociable they are. Check difficult vocabulary: *staffroom, relieved, awkward.* Play the recording while students complete the questionnaire. Encourage students not to look up every new word, but just to get the general idea.

TAPESCRIPT

See the text on page 18 of the Student's Book.

b Students turn to page 126, count up their scores and read the description. Give them time to compare their scores and to discuss the answers they gave to the questions. Ask students if they agree with the description, and if they think questionnaires are a good way of finding out about your personality.

c Students write another situation with three multiple-choice answers for their partner. Encourage them to discuss their answers briefly. If there is time, ask students to form new pairs to read and respond to each other's questionnaires.

Weaker classes: Students work together in pairs to write the description and the alternative answers for the questionnaire.

Stronger classes: Students could listen to each other's situation rather than reading it. You could organise this as a mingle activity with students standing up and circulating, asking as many people as possible in a given time period.

OPTIONAL ACTIVITY

Tell students that they are going to write a new questionnaire. In small groups, students choose a different adjective for their topic e.g. *Are you depressed/optimistic/pessimistic/friendly*? Ask groups to think of five *yes/no* questions for their questionnaire, e.g. *Are you friendly?; Do you like going to parties?; Do you smile and say 'Hello' to your teacher in the mornings?* Students read their questions to students from other groups and make a note of their answers. They then reassemble in their original group and compare results. Encourage them to draw some general conclusions (e.g. *Most students we interviewed are quite optimistic.*) and to present them to the class.

2 Grammar

* *what* clauses

a Write this sentence on the board: *What's nice about this T-shirt is its colour.* Explain that in this sentence, *what* means *the thing that.* Give another example, e.g. *What surprised me was that the door was locked.* Ask students to work out why *that* is not used in both sentences. If they can't decide, write this pair of examples on the board:

What I love about Kim is her sense of humour. / What I love about Kim is that she always makes you laugh.

Elicit that in the second example the *what* clause is followed by a new clause, with its own subject and verb. This new clause must be introduced by *that.*

Students complete the rule.

Answers
what; that

LOOK!

Read through the Look! box with students.

b Read through the sentences with the class. Ask students to join the sentences to make one. In feedback ask in which sentences 'that' can be replaced by a comma. (Sentences 1, 3, 4, 5)

Answers
2 ... what he told me.
3 ... him seem rude is that he never says 'please' or 'thank you'.
4 ... you should remember is that everyone makes mistakes.
5 ... I find really annoying is that he never stops talking.

Grammar notebook

Remind students to note down the rules for this structure and to write a few examples of their own.

OPTIONAL ACTIVITY

For further practice of this area, write these sentences on the board and ask students to match the beginnings and endings

1 *I don't know what ...*
2 *What I don't like is that ...*
3 *What you should do is ...*

a *buy a new car.*
b *she never phones me.*
c *you are going to do.*

Answers
1 c 2 b 3 a

3 Vocabulary

Personality

Warm up

Ask students to think about the types of personalities their friends have. Elicit adjectives to describe the characteristics that students look for in their friends. Write the adjectives on the board. You could also ask for adjectives describing characteristics they don't like.

a Students read the descriptions and decide which of the characters Matthew considers to be his friends. In some cases there will probably be some debate about the answers. Monitor and help with any difficult vocabulary. Students compare answers with a partner before feedback. Ask if they agree about the personality types, e.g. do they like bubbly people / intellectual people? Can careless or scatty people make good friends?

Weaker classes: You may want to ask students to translate the adjectives into their own language to check that they have understood the meanings.

Possible answers
1 Sophie, 2 Charlie, 3 Waseem, 5 Iago, 10 Brittany, 11 Chelsea 13 Stephan

b ▶ CD1 T12 Ask students to read through the sentences and choose the correct adjectives. Play the recording. Pause to check answers and ask students to repeat the adjectives.

Answers
1 sympathetic 2 smug 3 shallow
4 careless 5 witty 6 pushy 7 scatty

OPTIONAL ACTIVITY

Depending on the sensitivity of the class, you could ask students to work in pairs and use the adjectives to describe each other. Ask students which of the attributes they would look for in their ideal friend. Listen to some of their ideas in open class and try to build up a description of the perfect friend.

Vocabulary bank

Refer students to the vocabulary bank. Read through the words and phrases in open class and check understanding.

Vocabulary notebook

Encourage students to start a new section called *Personality* in their notebook and to add these words. They may find it useful to note down translations, too.

4 Pronunciation

See notes on page 121.

5 Speak

Read through the questions with the class and check understanding. In small groups, students respond to the questions, exchanging opinions and telling each other about their experiences. Encourage them to use adjectives from Exercise 3. Ask groups to report back and invite class discussion.

6 Listen

Warm up

To introduce the topic, ask students what type of things they find funny. Do they have any favourite comedy programmes on television? Who is the funniest person they know? Listen to some of their ideas and write any interesting vocabulary on the board.

a Ask students to look at the pictures. Ask them to guess what the jokes are about. Invite individual students to give their opinion.

b **▶ CD1 T14** Tell students they are going to hear three people talking about the funniest person they know. Play the recording while students listen and put the pictures in the order they hear about them. Tell students not to worry about difficult words, but to concentrate on the task. Let students compare answers with a partner before open-class feedback.

TAPESCRIPT

James: Clara, who's the funniest person you've ever met?

Clara: The funniest person I've ever met ... oh, I know. My uncle with his walnut jokes.

Kate: Walnut jokes? What's that all about?

Clara: Well, he really enjoys playing tricks on people, practical jokes, you know, that sort of thing. And he usually does it using walnuts.

James: What? Walnuts?

Clara: Yeah, I'll give you an example. Once his boss came to visit, and my uncle very carefully prepared some walnuts, I mean he opened them carefully with the help of a knife, but without breaking them, right?

Kate: Got you. And?

Clara: Well, then he took the nut out from the middle and put something else in, and used some glue to close the nut again. So, when his boss arrived, he offered him some walnuts. So he put this bowl of walnuts on the table, and then excused himself, and went out of the living room, but he didn't come back for quite some time.

James: OK, and?

Clara: Well, the boss didn't really know what to do, so he started to open a nut. And guess what he found?

James: No idea.

Clara: An almond!

Kate: Hahaha. That's funny. He must have been confused.

Clara: Well, he was at first. Then he decided to open another nut and guess what happened this time?

Kate: He found another almond?

Clara: No, not at all – he found a tiny toy car. And then the funniest thing was when he continued opening the nuts there was another one with a little note in it.

James: Really? What did it say?

Clara: 'I'm a walnut picker in the jungle and I've been taken prisoner. Please save me!'

James: Really? Ha ha ha hah.

Kate: How funny.

Kate: That reminds me of a friend of mine from my class, Jack. He never stops playing practical jokes on other people. And one day he played one on Mr Simmons, our maths teacher. Mr Simmons had to leave the room, and he left his laptop on his desk. So Jack installed this wireless mouse on Mr Simmons' computer, right?

Clara: So the teacher left the room, and Jack installed a wireless mouse. What did he do with Mr Simmons' mouse?

Kate: He unplugged it, but he left it on the desk. When Mr Simmons came back, he wanted to show us something – the laptop was connected to a projector, right? Well, guess what happened? Jack started moving the wireless mouse on the palm of his hands, and he clicked on various applications on Mr Simmons' computer. Mr Simmons was just sitting there, watching the screen of his laptop, trying to move the cursor where he wanted it to go, but of course it didn't work.

James: Did he get angry?

Kate: Well, I guess he wasn't too happy. It seemed he didn't like not having an explanation for what was going on. But then of course he found out, and he couldn't stop laughing.

James: That's a good one. You know what my sister did once? You need to know that my dad really loves his car, and he expects everyone to admire it all the time. And my sister hates playing this game. So one day, it was the first of April, she wrote this note, and she put it on my father's car. It said: 'Sorry I didn't see your car. I apologize for the damage. Please call me and I'll give you my insurance number.'

Kate: She didn't!

James: Yes, and there was a phone number and a person's name too. My sister and I had hidden behind a tree and we were watching Dad. You should have seen him. He went on going round and round the car, trying to find the damage. Even when we came from behind the bush laughing he still wouldn't stop looking at the car. He still wasn't sure the car was OK!

Kate: Have you ever heard of Groucho Marx?

James: Ah, I know, the comedian. He was very funny, wasn't he?

Kate: Exactly. When some people were talking about television, complaining that it would have a bad influence on people's education, he said: 'I think television is very educational. Every time somebody turns it on, I go into the other room and read a book.'

James: Ah, talking about books. Here's another one by Groucho Marx: 'Outside of a dog, a book is a man's best friend. Inside of a dog it's too dark to read.'

Clara: But you won't like another thing he said.

James: What's that?

Clara: 'There's one way to find out if a man is honest – ask him. If he says, "Yes," you know he is a liar.'

James: Ha ha. Very funny!

Answers
B C A D

c ▶ CD1 T14 Read through the questions with the class and check any difficult vocabulary: *walnuts, honesty*. Play the recording again while students answer the questions. Stronger classes may like to try to answer the questions before listening. If necessary, play the recording again with pauses during feedback.

d Ask students to compare answers in pairs before checking in open class.

Answers
1 Practical jokes, e.g. the walnut jokes.
2 An almond, a toy car and a note.
3 Jack's maths teacher.
4 A wireless mouse.
5 He was confused, then he found it very funny.
6 She hates it.
7 She left a note on his windscreen saying that his car had been damaged.
8 He said it was very educational – every time someone switched it on, he went into another room to read a book.
9 That if a man says he is honest, he is a liar.

Discussion box
In pairs or small groups, students discuss the questions. Monitor and help as necessary, encouraging them to express themselves in English and to use any vocabulary they have learned from the text. Ask pairs or groups to feedback to the class and discuss any interesting points further.

7 Grammar

★ Verbs + gerund/infinitive review

a **Weaker classes:** Write these sentence openings on the board:

I want ...
I don't enjoy ...

Give students a minute to make as many sentences as possible using these openings. Ask some students to read out their sentences. Make sure that when they want to add another verb, they are using *to* + infinitive after *want*, and the gerund after *don't enjoy*. Then follow the procedure for stronger classes.

Stronger classes: Ask students to circle the correct words to complete the sentences from the listening. Remind students that verbs of liking/disliking are usually followed by the gerund form. Other verbs, like *want* or *decide*, take *to* + infinitive.

Answers
2 playing 3 playing 4 to move 5 going

b Read through the rules with the class and check that students understand the meanings of the verbs. Ask them to complete the rules. If students need further practice, ask them to make example sentences using some verbs of each type.

Answers
a gerund, an infinitive; a gerund; an infinitive

c Ask students to discuss the differences in meaning with a partner. Feedback in open class.

Answers
1a = I stopped doing something else in order to drink my coffee.
1b = I was drinking my coffee and then I stopped doing it.
2a = I bought the book in the past – I remember that I did this.
2b = I remembered what I had to do, so I bought the book (I didn't forget).

d Students complete the rule.

Answers
different

e Ask students to look at the pictures and tell you what they can see. Students match the sentences with the pictures. Clarify the difference between the two forms. Point out that sentence 1 means 'We opened the window in an attempt to make the room cooler, but it didn't work.' Sentence 2 means 'I wanted to open the window. I tried to do it, but it wasn't possible.'

Answers
1 B 2 A 3 C 4 D

Read the sentences with the class and ask students to complete the rule.

Answers
gerund, infinitive

Language notes

Students may have difficulty distinguishing between the different meanings of *try*. Encourage them to translate the sentences, as they may use different verbs in their own language. To help them see the difference, ask them to think of cures for a headache *(Try drinking water. Try taking an aspirin.)*, then ask them to try to do difficult things *(Try to say the alphabet backwards. Try to say 'big brown bottle' without moving your lips.)*.

f Read through the sentences and check understanding of *charming* and *self-centred*. If necessary, go through the first sentence as an example. Students complete the sentences and compare answers with a partner before feedback. Check answers.

Answers
2 to help 3 to invite 4 seeing 5 surfing
6 to talk 7 being 8 going 9 to phone
10 to give

Grammar notebook

Remind students to note down the rules for these structures and to write a few examples of their own. You could ask them to write the verbs from the exercise into this table:

Verb + gerund	Verb + *to* + infinitive	Verb + gerund OR + infinitive	
		Same meaning	*Different meaning*

OPTIONAL ACTIVITY

Write these prompts on the board and ask students to complete them so that they are true for them. Divide the class into small groups and ask students to compare their answers. Encourage them to ask each other further questions. Monitor and check students are using verbs correctly. Invite individual students to tell the class about one of their colleagues.

1 *I enjoy ...*
2 *I hate ...*
3 *I can't stop ...*
4 *I remember ...*
5 *I tried ...*

Photostory: You're both being a pain

8 Read and listen

Warm up

Write these questions on the board: *Do you ever have arguments? Who do you argue with most: members of your family or your friends? What was the last argument you had about?* Students ask and answer the questions in pairs. Ask some pairs to report back to the class.

a ▶ CD1 T15 Students look at the photos, identify the people and describe what they are doing. Ask them to guess the answers to the questions, but don't comment on their answers at this stage. Play the recording. Students read and listen to check their answers.

TAPESCRIPT

See the dialogue on page 22 of the Student's Book.

Answers
Nick and Amy are fighting because Nick says Amy's backpack is in the way. Jack thinks they should sort it out and make friends again. Lily thinks they are both being a pain.

b Students read the text again and find the answers to the questions. Allow them to check answers with a partner before open-class feedback. Encourage students to correct the false sentences.

Weaker classes: Before students look at the questions, you may want to play the recording again, pausing as necessary to clarify any problems. Then read through the questions with the class and check that the meaning is clear.

Answers
1 F (She always leaves it on the floor.)
2 T
3 T
4 T
5 F (He wants them to reach an agreement about the argument.)

Discussion box

In pairs or small groups, students discuss the question. Monitor and help as necessary, encouraging students to express themselves in English and to use any vocabulary they have learned from the text. Ask pairs or groups to feedback to the class and discuss any interesting points further.

9 Everyday English

a Ask students to locate the expressions 1 to 6 in the story on page 22 and decide who says them.

Weaker classes: Check answers at this stage.

Answers
1 Nick 2 Lily 3 Nick 4 Amy 5 Jack 6 Jack

Students then match the expressions with the situations. Go through the first item with them as an example, if necessary. Check answers.

Answers
a 3 b 6 c 1 d 5 e 2 f 4

b Ask students to read through the sentences and complete the answers. Go through the first sentence with them as an example if necessary.

Answers
1 Mind out 2 I'd have thought 3 don't look at me 4 and so on 5 No chance 6 can do without

OPTIONAL ACTIVITY

These optional activities can be used after every *Everyday English* exercise in the Student's Book.

Weaker classes: They can act out the dialogues. Make sure they are saying them with the correct intonation and expression and in the right context.

Stronger classes: They can write their own short dialogues using the expressions. They can then act them out in front of the class. Make sure they are saying them with the correct intonation and expression and in the right context.

Vocabulary notebook

Encourage students to start a section called *Everyday English* and to note down the expressions from Exercise 9. They may find it useful to note down a translation for each expression too.

10 Improvisation

Books closed. Divide the class into pairs. Ask them to write down as many expressions from Exercise 9a as they can remember. Circulate and check they are writing the expressions correctly. Read through the instructions with students. Give them two minutes (or more if necessary) to prepare a short role play. Invite some of the groups to act out their role play for the rest of the class and hold a vote on which was the most entertaining and which included the most expressions from Exercise 9a.

11 Making Waves (DVD Episode 1)

a Look at the photo with students and ask them to name the people. What can they remember about Nick, Amy, Jack and Lily from the photostory? Ask students to work in pairs and discuss the questions.

b Ask students to match the phrases and the definitions. Allow them to compare with a partner, but do not give answers. Tell students they are going to watch a DVD in which the phrases appear and ask them to listen for the phrases and to check the meaning.

Answers
1 c 2 e 3 d 4 a 5 b

c Play episode 1 of the DVD and ask students to answer the questions. Check answers and also refer back to the answers from Exercise 11b.

Answers
The others think that Nick is out of order. Although he compliments Lily on her interview with the principal, he then says it's thanks to him that the show went well.

12 Write

Students can do the preparation for this in class and the writing can be set for homework.

a Refer students to the box and ask them to write the adjectives in the two lists. Allow them to use a dictionary for help.

Answers
personality: disorganised, cheerful, honest, lazy
appearance: smart, tall, handsome, wavy, plump, slim, scruffy

b Encourage students to add another four words to each list and then compare their lists with a partner. Ask some pairs to give you their examples and write them on the board.

c Tell students they are going to read an email in which a girl gives a description of someone she met at a party. Students read to identify the topics of the first four paragraphs. During feedback, deal with difficult vocabulary in the email: *gossip, caught my attention, exaggerating.*

Answers

first paragraph:	a general description of the party
second paragraph:	basic facts about Harry
third paragraph:	Harry's appearance
fourth paragraph:	Harry's personality

d Point out to students that the third paragraph contains unnecessary information and ask them to decide which sentences could be left out.

Answers
He's average height. His nose is quite small.

e Students look at the descriptions of Harry's eyes and smile in paragraph 3. Draw attention to the simile (*like the colour of the ocean you see in those holiday postcards*) and the use of adjectives (*gorgeous, bright blue, warm, friendly*). Students write their own descriptions of someone's hair and mouth. Ask different students to read out their descriptions.

f Students find the examples of behaviour in paragraph 4. Check answers and explain that these details, like the descriptions in Exercise 12e, are very important if we want to make a description interesting.

Answers
He said loads of nice things about Olivia. He listened to her problems and he gave her some good advice.

g Ask students to write three or four sentences describing someone (real or imaginary) who is generous and imaginative. Remind them to give examples of the person's behaviour to illustrate his/her qualities. Ask some students to read out their description, and ask the class to say whether they would like to meet this person.

h Introduce the writing task and ask students to plan their email, using Olivia's email as a model. Encourage them to:

- organise their writing as outlined in Exercise 12c.
- use interesting descriptions of appearance.
- include examples of the person's behaviour to show their character.
- make sure their writing is informal.

Students could do the writing for homework. In a subsequent lesson, give them the opportunity to read each other's descriptions and decide which is the most interesting.

OPTIONAL ACTIVITY

As an extension of Exercise 12b, write the words *Personality* and *Appearance* on the board and ask students to add as many adjectives as possible to the two lists in two minutes. Write their suggestions under the headings on the board.

Vocabulary notebook

Encourage students to start two new sections called *Personality* and *Appearance* in their notebook and to add the adjectives from Exercise 12a. They may find it useful to note down translations, too.

Check your progress

1 Grammar

a
2 My friend, who wants to become a psychologist, loves helping people.
3 This is the book that our teacher was talking about.
4 Many experts will attend the conference where new theories will be presented.
5 Our neighbour, whose daughter lives in Portsmouth, is going to the UK soon.

b
2 What makes him seem friendly is that he's always singing.
3 What you should remember is that noone is perfect.
4 What I find really annoying is that Paul always interrupts when I speak.
5 What I'll never forget is that she gave me a really nice smile.

c 2 phoning 3 to have 4 apologising/to apologise 5 to invite

2 Vocabulary

a 2 a 3 f 4 e 5 b 6 c

b 1 sympathetic 2 smug 3 careless 4 charming 5 witty

The mystery word is 'pushy'.

How did you do?

Students work out their scores. Check how they have done and follow up any problem areas with revision work.

Memo from Mario

People are people

1 Computer matchmaking

- Give the students four slips of paper each. Ask the students to write short descriptions of imaginary people (two boys and two girls) suitable to be posted on a computer dating site. Tell them to give the people names, ages, use some of the vocabulary from section 3 and to include some likes and dislikes.
- When they have finished, make groups of four students and ask them to read the 16 descriptions and decide who should meet up with who. Then make pairs and get them to choose one of the couples they have made and take on their characters. Now change partners within the group. Students should now pretend they have been on a date with the other half of the couple and recount to their new partner how it went. They should give their first impressions and how they see the 'date' now. Tell them they can be as polite or rude as they like.

RATIONALE
Taking on a new personality can release some of the constraints students might feel if talking about real people.

2 My aunt's cat

- This is based on an ancient children's game.

Get the students to do this in pairs. Two heads are usually better than one.

Tell them to write *My aunt's cat is a(n)............... cat* at the top of a blank page and then write all the letters of the alphabet down the left-hand side of the page. They should then try to write an adjective starting with each letter to fill in the gap in the sentence. You could tell them to 'cheat' on the letter X and use an adjective starting with EX.

The first ones to finish could try to write a second adjective for each letter.

Examples: *My aunt's cat is an adventurous cat. ... a beautiful cat.*

RATIONALE
This kind of simple game revises a lot more vocabulary than is used on the page, especially if you ask them to try and think of adjectives that other students may not have thought of. This will cause them to reject the most obvious and maybe find more interesting possibilities.

3 Time travellers

Unit overview

TOPIC: Time

TEXTS

Reading and listening: a quiz about popular TV series *Doctor Who*; an extract from the *The Time Machine* by H.G. Wells

Reading: advice about revising for exams

Listening: an interview about *Doctor Who*

Writing: an informal email

SPEAKING AND FUNCTIONS

Using expressions with *time*

Talking about revising for exams

Discussing time travel

LANGUAGE

Grammar: reported speech review; reporting verbs review

Vocabulary: expressions with *time*

Pronunciation: schwa /ə/

1 Read and listen

If you set the background information as a homework research task, ask the students to tell the class what they found out.

BACKGROUND INFORMATION

Doctor Who is an extremely popular BBC science fiction series which originally ran between 1963 and 1989. The Doctor travels through time and space in a time machine, accompanied by a human helper. He fights a variety of monsters and evil beings, the most famous of which are the Daleks. From time to time the Doctor 'regenerates' and takes on a new body (so that the part can be played by a different actor). The show was successfully re-launched in 2005 and is popular with both children and adults.

Warm up

Write *science fiction* on the board and ask students to think of as many science-fiction films or TV programmes as possible. Make a list of their suggestions on the board. Ask students each to choose their favourite. They then find somebody in the class who has not seen the programme/film and explain it to them. Monitor and help with vocabulary if necessary.

a Look at the photo. If students are familiar with *Doctor Who,* ask them to briefly describe the programme. If not, ask them to imagine the type of things that might happen in this show. Read through the extract from a TV guide with the class and check difficult vocabulary: *charismatic, enthusiastic.* Students answer questions 1–4.

Answers

1 18 months ago 2 Time Lord 3 assistant
4 *The Eleventh Hour*

b ▶ CD1 T16 Read through the questions and check for any difficulties with vocabulary. Ask students to try to guess some of the answers, but do not comment on them at this stage. Play the recording. It is a long dialogue, so you may need to break it down into stages. Students listen for the answers to the questions and then compare answers with a partner. Check answers with the class. Play the recording again, pausing and asking questions to clarify other content in the dialogue.

TAPESCRIPT

Presenter: And just in case you need reminding. *Doctor Who* returns to BBC on Saturday. And I, for one, am very excited … Well, we thought he might never make it, but Matt Smith will finally take over as the new doctor on Saturday. To celebrate this great moment in British TV history, I have the biggest *Doctor Who* fan in the world here with me in the studio. Laura Littleton, welcome to the show.

Laura: Thank you. It's good to be here.

Presenter: Now Laura, believe it or not, I was talking to a young woman the other day and she didn't believe me when I told her I used to watch *Doctor Who* when I was a child growing up in the 1970s. She had no idea of the history of the show.

Laura: Well, I think that's very true of many teenagers. The thing is – the show originally ran from 1963 to 1989. Then it stopped until 2005, when a new series was launched. Teenagers usually think that it was broadcast for the first time in 2005.

Presenter: And how do you explain the success of this show? I know there are a lot of people who love science fiction but this show seems to appeal to everyone.

Laura: Well, I'm not sure that I would describe it as pure science fiction. Although the basic idea behind the programme is very sci-fi, one of the things that has made the show so popular is the way it changes genre so often. So, for example, one show might be comedy and the next might be real horror. You always get something different.

Presenter: Now one thing I've never really understood is who exactly is the Doctor? I mean, I know he's a Time Lord but what exactly does that mean?

Laura: OK, the Time Lords are an alien race who live on the planet Gallifrey. These Time Lords have the ability to travel through space and time and change the ways of the universe. Now the Time Lords said that they would never change anything in the universe, but Doctor Who doesn't agree with that, so he travels about and changes things.

Presenter: Naughty man!

Laura: Well, not really. He only does it because he wants to fight evil and help people who need help.

Presenter: Of course.

Laura: Now to help him get about the universe, the Doctor has a time-travel machine called the Tardis. From the outside this looks like a tiny old-fashioned blue police telephone box. But of course, inside it's huge. And that's because the Tardis is dimensionally transcendental.

Presenter: Wow. What's that exactly?

Laura: Well, no one's really sure. I asked a scientist once and he said that it was a fancy way of saying it's bigger on the inside than the outside.

Presenter: One of the best things about *Doctor Who*, is, of course, the great monsters he has to face. Which are your favourite ones?

Laura: That's an almost impossible question to answer. How can I choose? There are the Ice-men and the Sea Monsters and the Cybermen and of course, the Daleks. I mean they're all great. But one of the best new monsters must be the Weeping Angels.

Presenter: The Weeping Angels?

Laura: Yes, they're these stone statues that move when noone's looking at them. So they creep up on people and crush them to death.

Presenter: I don't think I've seen them but they do sound very scary. My favourites though will always be the Daleks. Now when I was a kid and I heard that, I used to hide behind my sofa.

Laura: I think we all did. The Daleks were pretty scary monsters.

Presenter: Now another thing that I never quite understood is how the Doctor can change his appearance.

Laura: Well, the original Doctor was played by William Hartnell but one day he told the show's producers that his health was getting worse and that he couldn't play the Doctor any more. Now they didn't want to lose their show just because they were losing their star, so they had to think of a way of saving the programme. So they came up with the great idea that every time a Time Lord gets old or wounded in a battle his body transforms so that he looks like a new person. This meant they could change the actor and continue with the series.

Presenter: And how many Doctors have there been?

Laura: Since William Hartnell there have been ten other official Doctors.

Presenter: And what about Matt Smith? Have you any word on whether he'll be any good?

Laura: Well, I've actually had a sneak preview and I must say, he's excellent.

Presenter: And his assistant?

Laura: Yes, Karen Gillan looks like she'll do a great job. She seems to be very much a classic assistant.

Presenter: Which is?

Laura: Well the Doctor's assistant is almost always a young woman from present-day Earth, although there have been a few assistants from the past and the future too.

Presenter: Well, it's all very exciting and I must say that I for one will be glued to my TV set this Saturday evening. Laura, thank you so much for sharing all this with us. Will you be watching the new series too?

Laura: I most certainly will.

Answers

1 a 2 c 3 a 4 b 5 a 6 c 7 d 8 c

OPTIONAL ACTIVITY

Doctor Who is capable of travelling back through time. Ask students which era they would like to visit and why. In pairs, students discuss what different things they would find if they visited another period of time.

2 Grammar

Reported speech review

a **Weaker classes:** If students need to be reminded of the rules of reported speech, write these sentences on the board:

I live in London.
I'm playing football this evening.
I've been to France three times.
I'll go to the shop.

Say the sentences and ask students to report what you said. Help them as much as necessary and write the answers on the board:

You said (that) you lived in London.
You said (that) you were playing football this evening.
You said (that) you'd been to France three times.
You said (that) you would go to the shop.

Remind students how tenses change when we are reporting speech. Then follow the procedure for stronger classes.

Stronger classes: Students read the sentences and write down what was said in each case. Check their answers.

Answers

2 **I can't play the Doctor any more.**
3 **It is a fancy way of saying it's bigger on the outside than the inside.**
4 **We will never change anything in the universe.**

OPTIONAL ACTIVITY

To remind students of the rules of reported speech, ask them to write down answers to these questions:

What did you do yesterday?
What are you going to do at the weekend?
Have you ever met a famous person?

Two of their answers should be true and the other false.

Choose different students to say one of their answers.

Other students report what was said and decide if the answer was true or not. Encourage students to correct any errors in reported speech themselves.

b Ask students to complete the table. They can compare answers with a partner before getting feedback.

Stronger classes: If students are confident with the structures, ask them to think of an example for each of the tenses in reported speech.

Answers

Direct speech	Reported speech
present continuous →	past continuous
present perfect →	past perfect
past simple →	past perfect
can / can't →	*could / couldn't*
will / won't →	*would / wouldn't*
must →	*had to*

c Ask students if they remember which other words often change when we use reported speech. Give them some time to discuss this with a partner before asking them for examples.

Answers

pronouns (e.g. *I, you, mine, ours*); possessive adjectives (e.g. *my, your*); some time expressions (e.g. *now, tomorrow, this afternoon*).

Language notes

1 Remind students that in some cases we don't have to change the tense or the time expression when reporting speech. If the statement is still true when we report it, we can leave it in the original tense, e.g. *David told me he can't swim. Kate said she's going to Italy this summer.*

2 If we are reporting something that has just been said, the reporting verb can be in the present simple and the reported statement can be left in its original tense, e.g. *That was Sarah on the phone. She says she doesn't want to go to the cinema.*

d Students write the sentences in reported speech. Remind them that quotation marks are not used in reported speech and *that* is optional after the reporting verbs *say* and *tell*. Check answers and ensure that students are using the correct tenses.

Answers

2 **The Doctor said (that) they had to get to the Tardis before it was too late.**
3 **The Doctor said (that) they would only know what year it was outside when they arrived.**
4 **The Doctor said (that) he had a plan and he knew how they could kill the Ice-men.**
5 **Romana told the Doctor (that) he was getting the time wrong.**
6 **Chronotis told the Doctor (that) he had heard so much about him.**
7 **The Doctor said (that) they didn't know what was going on.**
8 **The Doctor announced that there wouldn't be enough time.**

Language notes

If we are reporting what was said by an unknown speaker, we use the impersonal *they*, e.g. *Somebody phoned about the car. They said we could pick it up tomorrow.*

Grammar notebook

Remind students to note down the rules for reported speech and to write a few examples of their own.

3 Vocabulary

* Expressions with time

▶ CD1 T17 Explain to students that there are many English idioms that use *time*. Ask them to give you any examples they may already know and write these on the board. Then ask them to circle the correct words in sentences 1–9. They should guess the ones they don't know, or look them up in a dictionary. Play the recording for students to check their answers.

TAPESCRIPT/ANSWERS

1 Come on! Quickly! We're running out of time!
2 My father's always busy. He never has time to relax.
3 I'm not in a hurry. Take your time.
4 Our maths teacher often complains that we give him a hard time.
5 I got home just in time to avoid the rain.
6 I'm not late. I'm exactly on time. Look at the clock.
7 Come on! Let's get started – we've wasted a lot of time already.
8 I think you should take time off and go on holiday. You've worked too hard.
9 Annie's a very relaxed person. She spends a lot of time meditating.

Language notes
Students may have difficulty distinguishing between *on time* and *in time*. Explain that we use *on time* if something happens exactly at the expected time (*The 2:30 train arrived on time* = at 2:30). We use *in time* if something happens before the expected time (*We arrived in time for the film* = we arrived before the start of the film). *Just in time* refers to something happening very close to the expected time.

Vocabulary bank
Refer students to the vocabulary bank. Read through the words and phrases in open class and check understanding.

Vocabulary notebook
Encourage students to start a new section called *Time* in their notebook and to add these expressions. They may find it useful to note down translations, too.

*** OPTIONAL ACTIVITY**
Write these sentences on the board. In pairs, students complete the sentences, using the correct expression with *time*.

1 *If we don't leave now, we won't be ... time to meet the others.* (in)
2 *Read the question carefully and ... your time. Then you will make fewer mistakes.* (take)
3 *Rajeev is very healthy. He ... a lot of time doing sport.* (spends)
4 *Come on! The plane leaves soon. We're ... out of time.* (running)
5 *What a surprise! You're usually late, but today you're exactly ... time.* (on)
6 *You can't work all weekend! You need some time ... .* (off)

4 Pronunciation

See notes on page 121.

5 Speak

Divide the class into pairs and give each student a letter, A or B. Ask A students to look at questions 1–4, while B students turn to page 126 and read their questions. They then ask each other their questions. Monitor and encourage students to answer in full sentences using the expressions with *time*, and to expand on their answers. Ask a few pairs to tell the class about their partner's answers.
Weaker classes: Weaker students may benefit from having some time to practise saying the sentences to themselves to work on pronunciation and intonation before asking their partner.

6 Read

Warm up

Books closed. Write *revision* on the board. Ask students how they revise for exams. Do they set a timetable for themselves and do three hours revision every night? Or do they find it more difficult? Divide the class into pairs and ask them to discuss why revising is a difficult process. Listen to some of their ideas in open class.

a Books open. Tell students they are going to read some advice on how to focus on work. Pre-teach difficult vocabulary: *procrastination, be into, time to kill, get down to, lose your cool*. Students read the text and decide which piece of advice they like best. Allow them to discuss their choice with a partner before listening to some of their thoughts in open class.

b Students read through the statements. Clarify any problems with understanding. Ask students to read the text and match the statements with the sections. Check answers.

Answers
1 A 2 E 3 B 4 C 5 D

Discussion box

In pairs or small groups, students discuss the questions. Monitor and help as necessary, encouraging them to express themselves in English and to use any vocabulary they have learned from the text. Ask pairs or groups to feedback to the class and discuss any interesting points further.

7 Grammar

★ Reporting verbs review

a Write the verbs *say* and *tell* on the board. Then ask students to look through the text in Exercise 6 and find some more reporting verbs (*encourage, persuade, claim, advise, recommend, refuse, suggest, promise*). Draw attention to the verbs in the tables and check that all the meanings are clear. Tell students that different reporting verbs have different patterns; for example, *tell* is followed by an object, but *say* is not. Also point out that the same reporting verb can follow different patterns; for example *I recommend that you go to bed early* or *I recommend going to bed early*. Ask students to complete the tables, referring to the text to help them. Check answers and elicit some example sentences for each of the verb patterns. Point out the importance of learning not only the verbs themselves, but also the grammatical forms that follow them.

Answers

say **claim** recommend suggest deny **promise**	that…
tell warn	someone that
deny **recommend** (not) **suggest** (not)	doing…
warn	someone not to do
advise **encourage** **persuade**	someone (not) to do…
promise (not) **refuse**	to do

b Read through the sentences with students and check understanding of *lifeguard* and *vase*. Students complete the sentences and compare answers with a partner before feedback in open class. Ensure students use the correct tense in their answers.

Answers

1 warned, persuaded 2 is refusing / refuses 3 denied 4 suggested 5 told, persuaded, encouraged

c Check that students understand the meaning of speech types a–h. Ask them to match the sentences with the speech types.

Answers

2 b 3 a 4 c 5 e 6 g 7 h 8 f

d Students rewrite the sentences using the reporting verbs from Exercise 7a. Their answers to Exercise 7c will help them to choose the appropriate verb, and they should look back to the table in Exercise 7a to check the pattern. Explain that more than one answer is possible in some cases. Circulate to check that students are creating sentences correctly. Check answers with the class.

Answers

2 He promised not to be late. / He promised that he wouldn't be late.
3 He claimed that his father had won over fifty golf competitions.
4 The doctor warned him/her that he/she was going to get really ill if he/she didn't eat more healthily.
5 She denied working too hard. / She denied that she worked too hard.
6 They recommended trying the new café. / They recommended that I/we try the new café.
7 The doctor advised me to take a break sometimes.
8 She encouraged Steve to jump.

Grammar notebook

Remind students to note down the patterns for reporting verbs and to write a few examples of their own.

Literature in mind

8 Read

If you set the background information as a homework research task, ask the students to tell the class what they found out.

BACKGROUND INFORMATION

Herbert George (H.G.) Wells (1866–1946) was an English novelist, and is most famously known as the father of science fiction. His most famous novels are *The Time Machine*, *The War of the Worlds*, *The Island of Doctor Moreau* and *The Invisible Man*.

The Time Machine was published in 1895. It tells the story of a man who invents a time machine and travels forward in time to 802,701 AD where he encounters a society split between the peaceful Eloi and the apelike subterranean Morlocks. He also travels forward 300 million years into the future to witness the final days of Earth. The book was made into a film in 1960 and again in 2002.

a Books closed. Write the words *science fiction* on the board and ask students what science fiction novels or films they know. In open class, discuss what *science fiction* actually is (a story that couldn't happen in the world we know, with elements of technology and invention). Ask students to open their books and look at the cover of the book and photo of the film. Read the short summary and discuss whether students think the book sounds interesting.

b ▶ CD1 T20 Read through the sentences with students. Play the recording while students listen and place sentences in the order they appear in the extract. The text contains some new vocabulary, but tell students not to worry about difficult words and to concentrate on the task. Ask them to compare answers with a partner before feedback. Play the recording again, pausing as necessary for clarification.

TAPESCRIPT

See the reading text on page 30 of the Student's Book.

Answers

Sentence order: 2, 5, 1, 3, 7, 6, 4

c Ask students to read the sentences and help with any difficult vocabulary. Students read the text again and decide why the statements are incorrect. Ask them to compare answers with a partner before open class feedback.

Answers

1 It has two levers.
2 It takes five and a half hours.
3 It is hazy and dark.
4 He finds it incredibly unpleasant.
5 He loses sight of the laboratory, 'The dim outline of the laboratory seemed to fall away from me.'
6 The snail speeds past too fast to be seen.
7 He is very interested (see final sentence).

Discussion box

In pairs or small groups, students discuss the questions. Monitor and help as necessary, encouraging them to express themselves in English and to use any vocabulary they have learned from the text. Ask pairs or groups to feedback to the class and discuss any interesting points further.

9 Write

a As an introduction to this exercise, tell students to imagine that they are going to write an email to a friend. Write this on the board:

You haven't written for a very long time.
You want to go and visit your friend.
You want an answer soon.

Ask students for some ideas about what they could write to express these three ideas in an email or letter. Also ask them how they would end the email. Elicit some suggestions from students but do not comment at this stage. Students read the questions and then read the email quickly to find the answers.

Answers

1 Because she's been very busy with exams.
2 The summer holidays.
3 The week of the 10th–15th of August.
4 Reply to her request as soon as possible.

b Remind students that this is an informal email. Explain that the underlined expressions are not incorrect, but they are too formal for an email to a friend. Ask students to choose the less formal expressions.

Answers

2 ... it's OK with you ...
3 ... the last time I was there.
4 ... can you let me know ...
5 ... write soon.

c Tell students they are going to write Alex's reply to Sally. Before they write, ask them to choose the most suitable expressions from 1–5.

Answers
1 b 2 a 3 a 4 b 5 a

d Read through the information with students. Ask them to write the reply to Sally's email. After planning, they could complete the writing at home. In a subsequent lesson, encourage students to read each other's emails.

Weaker classes: Work with the class to build up a list of possible sentence openings to help students with the main body of their emails. For example:

Para 1 It was great to get your email ...
I'd love to see you ...
Para 2 Of course you can stay ...
The problem is ...
I can't change these plans because ...
How about ...?
Para 3 I hope ...
Let me know ...

OPTIONAL ACTIVITY

Write this on the board:

1 *pleasure give would see me it to great you* (It would give me great pleasure to see you. Formal)
2 *love you I'd see to* (I'd love to see you. Informal)
3 *decision me please your of inform* (Please inform me of your decision. Formal)
4 *think me let know what you* (Let me know what you think. Informal)

Ask students to write the words in their notebook in the correct order, and to decide if the sentences are formal or informal.

Memo from Mario

Time travellers

1 Personalising vocabulary

- Exercise 3 is a good example of a coursebook exercise that the students can personalise. This can help them to remember the expressions.
- After doing the exercise as in the book, ask the students to write sentences like the ones in 3, but true for them. You could give them some examples from your own experience. For example:

  I always try to be on time for my gym class.

  I hate wasting time waiting for a bus.

  When I was a teenager, I used to give my mum a hard time over clothes.
- When they have finished they could compare their sentences with another student.

RATIONALE

Making the vocabulary their own, bringing the words and phrases into their lives, helps to make the language up-close and personal, rather than something distant and for 'the other'.

2 Your own interview questions

- Tell the students they are going to be interviewed and their answers will be reported to another student. Ask them to write down 10 interesting open-ended questions they would like to be asked. They can be about anything, past, present or future. You might like to give some examples. *What's the best holiday you've ever had? Do you collect anything? What? Where in the world would you like to visit? Why?* etc.
- Then put the students in pairs and tell the interviewer to ask the questions the interviewee wrote. Change over and repeat.
- Now change partners and report the answers from the interview to another student.
- To round up, ask for a few reports of things that the students thought interesting about the person they interviewed.

RATIONALE

Knowing that the information given out will be reported to other people, the student is given complete control of what that information is.

4 In and out of fashion

Unit overview

TOPIC: Crazes and fads

TEXTS
Reading and listening: an article about past toy crazes
Listening: an interview about flash mobs; song 'Accessory'
Writing: a formal letter to a newspaper

SPEAKING AND FUNCTIONS
Talking about toy crazes
Talking about flash mobs and discussing ideas for inventing one
Discussing the relationship between fashion and pop music

LANGUAGE
Grammar: *would* and *used to*; adverbs and adverbial phrases
Vocabulary: common adverbial phrases
Pronunciation: /æ/ *accident* and /e/ *excitement*

1 Read and listen

If you set the background information as a homework research task, ask the students to tell the class what they found out.

BACKGROUND INFORMATION

The Magic Eye originated as a series of books in the 1990s. They contain colourful patterns which contain hidden 3D images. These are technically known as autostereograms and the hidden image can only be seen if the reader focuses his eyes beyond the image at the right distance. The books were an immediate success and spent 73 consecutive weeks on *The New York Times* bestseller lists.

Pac-Man is a computer game which was first released in Japan in 1980. It is considered one of the classic computer games of all time. Pac-Man is chased around a maze by four ghosts known as Shadow, Speedy, Bashful and Pokey. In September 1999, David Race from the USA took three hours 41 minutes to achieve the maximum possible score of 3,333,360 points.

Yo-yo. This toy consists of a piece of string tied at one end to a spool. The string is pulled, causing the spool to move up and down on the string. It became popular as a toy in the 1920s and then again in the 1960s, since when many yo-yo tricks have been developed and World Championships are held every year. The eleven-time, double-handed world champion Shinji Saito – considered the best player in the world – is Japanese.

Warm up

Ask students if anyone has a hobby which they have become addicted to, i.e. something they do every day, often several times, or for hours without stopping. Perhaps give an example of your own. Discuss interesting comments in class, helping with vocabulary if necessary.

a Ask students to describe what they can see in the photos and ask if they have played with any of the things shown. Use the photos to pre-teach the words *Magic Eye, Pac-Man* and *yo-yo.*

b Read through the three sentences and explain the meaning of *swept the world.* Students read the texts quickly to identify the main topic. When you check the answer, ask them to say the word that means 'a fashion that sweeps the world' *(craze).*

Answer
3 Each of the objects was, at some time, the latest fashion and swept the world.

c ▶ CD1 T21 Play the recording while students read and listen. Students answer the questions and compare answers with a partner before feedback. Play the recording again, pausing as necessary to clarify any problems.

TAPESCRIPT
See the texts on pages 32–33 of the Student's Book.

Answers
1 Pac-Man 2 Magic Eye 3 yo-yo

d Read through the definitions with the class and help with any vocabulary difficulties. Give students time to read the texts closely and to check their answers with a partner before feedback.

Answers
1 all the rage 2 crazes 3 latest 4 'in'
5 eagerly 6 addictive 7 caught on
8 heyday

Discussion box
In pairs or small groups, students discuss the questions. Monitor and help as necessary, encouraging them to express themselves in English and to use any vocabulary they have learned from the text. Ask pairs or groups to feedback to the class and discuss any interesting points further.

2 Speak

a In open class, elicit possible ways of marketing a product, e.g. TV advertisements, paying famous people to use it, giving away free samples. Tell students that they are going to re-market one of the three products in Exercise 1 to today's teenagers. Ask them to work together in pairs or small groups to answer the questions and decide what they would do to make the object popular again. Students work together to create a short presentation (no more than about three minutes) for the rest of the class.

b Groups present their ideas to the rest of the class. Ask them to come to the front of the class and encourage them to use the board to help present their main arguments. Take a class vote on which was the best presentation.

3 Grammar

★ *would* and *used to*

a To revise *used to*, ask students to think back to when they were eight years old. How were their lives different? Write this on the board:

1 *(music) I used to like ... , but now I like ...*
2 *(reading) I used to read ... , but now I read ...*
3 *(TV) I used to watch ... , but now I watch ...*
4 *(personality) I used to be ... , but now I'm ...*

Ask students to complete the sentences and elicit answers in open class. Ask students to think of another example of their own. Now focus on the three sentences in the book. Students look back at the text and complete the sentences.

Answers
1 would 2 used to 3 used to

b Students look back at the examples in Exercise 3a and complete the rule. Clarify the difference between habits or repeated actions and states, drawing attention to the verbs that are used to describe a state or situation. Go back to the four examples on the board and ask students in which of the four sentences we could replace *used to* with *would* (sentences 2 and 3).

Answers
used to, would; used to

c Look at the example with the class. Students read the sentences and cross out *would* when it is not possible to use it.

Answers
It is not possible to use *would* in sentences 1, 2, 5, and 7.

d Ask students to think of things they used to play with when they were young children. Write some examples on the board. In pairs, students talk about the toys they played with in their childhood. Encourage them to use *would* and *used to.* Ask a few pairs to give some examples as feedback, and allow discussion on any interesting points.

Grammar notebook
Remind students to note down the rules for these structures and to write a few examples of their own.

4 Listen

If you set the background information as a homework research task, ask the students to tell the class what they found out.

BACKGROUND INFORMATION
Flash mobs. The first flash mob was organised in Manhattan in 2003 by Bill Wasik, senior editor of *Harper's Magazine*. They have since taken place all over the world. They are usually organised over the internet or by sending text messages on mobile phones. Flash mobs started as a bit of fun, but have since been used to make political statements, with people appearing suddenly in large groups to make protests.

a Students look at the photos. Ask for their ideas about what might be happening in each photo and what they might have in common. Introduce the term *flash mob*, but don't explain it at this stage.

b ▶ CD1 T22 Tell students that they are going to listen to an interview with a man who is connected with the photos. Read through the sentences with the class and check that students understand *make a stand* and *pillow fight*. Play the recording. Students listen and answer the questions. Let them check their answers with a partner before feedback in open class.

TAPESCRIPT

Presenter: Can you believe that it was nine years ago today that the world witnessed its very first ever flash mob when more than 100 people congregated at Macy's department store in New York to look at a rug on June 3rd 2003? Far from being a passing fad, these sudden impromptu gatherings have become more and more common as they have become more and more imaginative. Of course, networking devices such as Twitter and Facebook have made it even easier for people to advertise their events and send out invitations. To celebrate this historic date, I have invited social commentator Ian Hicks to join me and talk about his three favourite flash mobs of the last nine years. Ian, welcome to the show.

Ian Hicks: Thank you.

Presenter: So Ian, what is it that attracts you to flash mobs?

Ian Hicks: Well, I suppose the greatest attraction is the fun of it all. I mean it's great to see so many people, complete strangers that is, all meeting up for a common purpose and having such a good time together. Also, I think in this modern age when we're becoming more and more isolated from each other, flash mobs are a sign that the spirit of society is still alive. And I also like the imagination of the organisers. I think some flash mobs these days should be looked on as works of modern art, moving sculptures, if you like. So there are lots of things which are great about flash mobs – but yes, first of all, the fun!

Presenter: Which brings us to the question of the best three flash mobs ever.

Ian Hicks: Well, in third place I've chosen the great pillow fight flash mob that took place on March 22nd 2008 in over 25 cities all over the world. I mean, this was a truly international event and involved thousands of people. In New York alone, there were more than 5,000 people involved. To date, this remains the largest flash mob ever. I was involved in the London one and I've never laughed so much. I hadn't had a pillow fight since I was a kid and I'd forgotten how much fun they are. It brought out the eight-year-old child in hundreds and hundreds of people that day and it was fantastic.

Presenter: It certainly sounds like you had a good time. So what have you got in second place?

Ian Hicks: Well, in second place I've chosen another flash mob that I took part in and that is the silent disco which happened in April 2006. There were about 4,000 of us and we all arrived at London Victoria station and at the set time we all suddenly started dancing to music from our iPods. It was the most amazing sight with all these people just dancing, and of course, no one could hear what anyone else was listening to. This one was interesting because the officials actually started to try and break it up and move people on. They said we were causing a disturbance to the travellers. Luckily it was all very peaceful. London Transport said they would take steps to stop it happening again but I'm happy to say they didn't and there have been many more of these discos since.

Presenter: Which brings us to your favourite flash mob of all time.

Ian Hicks: Yes, my number one. And this is one that I wasn't involved in but I would have loved to have been there. I'm going to have to choose the one you referred to in your introduction and that's the Macy's department store flash mob of 2003. Imagine, you're working in a shop when suddenly about 100 people turn up to ask you about a $10,000 rug and then leave as quickly as they arrived. And then realising much later that you had taken part in the very first flash mob. And that, of course, is the reason why this is my number one. Because it is the grandfather of all flash mobs that followed. Without this one, we may have never had any of the others.

Answers
1 a 2 b 3 b 4 b 5 a 6 c

Discussion box
In pairs or small groups, students discuss the questions. Monitor and help as necessary, encouraging them to express themselves in English and to use any vocabulary they have learned from the text. Ask pairs or groups to feedback to the class and discuss any interesting points further.

5 Speak

a Students work in small groups and think of a fun flash mob event. Monitor to help with any difficult vocabulary as they discuss their ideas.

b Ask each group to describe their event. Make a note of each one on the board. Students discuss the events and decide which they think is the best.

6 Grammar

✱ Adverbs and adverbial phrases

a Ask students to complete the sentences from the listening text. Ask which word is an adjective *(sudden)* and which is an adverb *(suddenly)*.

Answers
suddenly; sudden

b Students complete the sentences in the rule.

Answers
adjectives; adverbs

c Explain that instead of adverbs, we can use adverbial phrases of three or four words to say how someone does something. Students look at the adverbial phrases in Exercise 6d and decide which types of words are used to complete them.

Answers
We use adjectives with expressions in A.
We use nouns with expressions in B.

d Students complete the lists using the words in the box. Elicit example sentences with some of the phrases from each list.

Answers
A: in an *exciting* way, in a *horrible* way, in a *different* way
B: with *difficulty*, with *excitement*, with *interest*

e Students work individually or in pairs, choosing suitable words to complete the sentences. Point out that there is often more than one possibility.

Answers
1 excitement 2 a friendly way 3 difficulty 4 fear 5 a fun way / an interesting/ exciting way 6 a different way

Grammar notebook

Remind students to note down the rules for this structure and to write a few examples of their own.

OPTIONAL ACTIVITY

Write these situations on the board:

Tell your grandmother her cat has died.
Talk to your friend's little brother.
Talk to your favourite film star.
Walk home on your own late at night.
Do your homework.

Divide the class into pairs and ask students to choose an adverb to describe how they would act in each situation. Circulate to check that they are using adverbial phrases correctly. Listen to some of their ideas in open class as feedback.

7 Vocabulary

★ Common adverbial phrases

a Check that students know the meaning of *intentionally.* Ask them to match the phrases with the definitions. Tell them to guess the meaning of unknown phrases and to use a dictionary to check, if they have time. They could work on this in pairs.

After checking the answers, say the phrases and ask students to repeat them.

Answers
2 f 3 a 4 h 5 d 6 b 7 c 8 g

b Read through the sentences with the class and check any difficult vocabulary, e.g. *broke out.* Students complete the sentences with the phrases in Exercise 7a.

Answers
1 on purpose 2 in secret 3 in a row
4 in private 5 by accident 6 in a hurry
7 in public 8 in a panic

OPTIONAL ACTIVITY

Write these questions on the board:

1 *Have you ever broken anything by accident?*
2 *Have you ever broken anything on purpose?*
3 *When did you last react to something in a panic?*
4 *Do you like speaking in public?*
5 *When did you last do something in a hurry?*

In pairs, students discuss the questions. You may like to give them an example of your own to get them started. Encourage students to use the adverbial phrases from Exercise 7 in their answers. Listen to some of their answers in open class.

Vocabulary bank

Refer students to the vocabulary bank. Read through the words and phrases in open class and check understanding.

Vocabulary notebook

Encourage students to start a new section called *Adverbial phrases* in their notebook and to add these words. They may find it useful to note down translations, too.

8 Pronunciation

See notes on page 121.

9 Speak and listen

If you set the background information as a homework research task, ask the students to tell the class what they found out.

BACKGROUND INFORMATION

Jordyn Taylor (born 1992) is a pop and R&B singer from California. She released her first album, *Strong* in 1997 aged 15. 'Accessory' (2009) was a big hit for her and featured on the soundtrack of the film *Confessions of a Shopaholic* which was adapted from the *Shopaholic* books by Sophie Kinsella. The film took over $106 million at the box office. Jordyn's other songs include 'Lovin' You', 'Strong' and 'Female Intuition'. For further information see the *Did you know?* box on page 37 of the Student's Book.

Books closed. Write the following on the board: *Chanel, Dolce Gabbana, Jimmy Choo* and ask them what they have in common – they are all famous (and expensive!) fashion brands. Ask students if they know of any other designers that are 'in' at the moment. Do they like these brands?

a Books open. Teach the words *fashion accessory* and get students to think of as many different kinds of fashion accessories as they can in two minutes e.g. shoes, sunglasses, handbags, etc. Write their ideas on the board and briefly ask them if they like to accessorise what they wear with such items.

b Tell students they are going to hear a song called 'Accessory'. Ask students to match the words in italics with the pictures on the page.

c ▶ CD1 T25 Tell students they are going to listen to a song called 'Accessory'. Look at the words in the box and check understanding of difficult vocabulary: *scoop up*. Students complete the lyrics with the words. Encourage them to guess if they are not sure. Play the recording for students to listen and check their answers. Allow them to compare answers with a partner and play the recording again if necessary. pausing as required to check answers.

TAPESCRIPT

See the song on page 36 of the Student's Book.

Answers
1 match with 2 scoop; up 3 go with
4 goes with 5 carry; round 6 comes in
7 go without

d Read through the definitions 1–7 with students and ask them to match the verbs from exercise 9c with the correct meanings. Stronger classes might try to complete the exercise without looking back at the lyrics. Check answers in open class.

Answers
1 comes in 2 carry round 3 go/goes with
4 match with 5 go with 6 scoop up
7 go without

Discussion box

In pairs or small groups, students discuss the questions. Monitor and help as necessary, encouraging students to express themselves in English and to use any vocabulary they have learned from the text. Ask pairs or groups to feedback to the class and discuss any interesting points further.

Did you know?

Read the information in the box with students. Ask students what they think of Jordyn Taylor and if they know any other songs by her, or any other songs which are about fashion.

10 More speaking

a Look at the photo of Lady Gaga with students and ask individuals to describe what they see. Look at the ideas for what she is trying to say and ask students to think of another idea. Listen to some of their thoughts and write any good ideas on the board.

b Divide the class into small groups. Ask students to think of four famous rock/pop stars and to discuss their image and what their style says about them. You may like to give them an example of your own to get them started. As students discuss, circulate and help with any difficult vocabulary. Encourage students to give detailed descriptions. Listen to some examples in open class as feedback and invite whole group discussion.

c Read through the statements and check understanding. Groups discuss and grade each sentence 0–3. Make sure all members of the groups have a chance to give their opinion. As feedback ask groups to give their scores and try to reach group agreement on the grade for each sentence.

11 Write

The planning for this exercise can be done in class and the letter can be set as homework.

a Tell students they are going to read a letter to a newspaper. Pre-teach *witnessed, overreacts, mini-riot.* Ask students to read the letter quickly and then look at the notes which another person has made on this letter. Students answer the questions.

Possible answers

1 No
2 He/She disagrees strongly with it. He/She thinks the arguments are ridiculous, the opinions are intolerant and the letter is potentially dangerous.
3 He/She thinks flash mobbing is a form of art, and that people have the right to decide for themselves how to spend their time. He/She thinks flash mobs are nothing to be afraid of.

b Make it clear that the second letter is written by the person who made the notes on the first letter. Students read the second letter to find out which of the notes the writer has forgotten to include.

Answer

He/She hasn't mentioned note 6.

c Students read the third letter and underline the main points. Check these in open class. Students look at each point and decide whether they agree or disagree. Ask them to write notes on each point.

Answers

Young people ... fall for whatever the commercial world wants to sell them.
(The things people buy are) just crazes that cost money and do no good to young people today.
... the only things young people are interested in are fads and electronic communication.
(I hope that) parents and teachers soon become more aware of all the dangers of the modern world.

d Tell students they are going to write a letter to the editor of the newspaper giving their point of view about the third letter. Encourage them to:

- start with *Dear Sir* and finish with *Yours sincerely.*
- use their notes from Exercise 10c.
- give examples to support their opinions.

Check your progress

1 Grammar

a
2 The alien shouted that they were approaching the Earth.
3 The commander announced that their spaceship would be landing soon.
4 My girlfriend promised that she'd be at the club by five o'clock.
5 Steve denied that he'd broken my mobile. / Steve denied breaking my mobile.
6 Our teacher recommended that we repeated the phrases twice a day before the test. / Our teacher recommended repeating the phrases twice a day before the test.
7 Lucy encouraged Sophie to enter the competition.

b 2 would 3 would 4 used to 5 would 6 used to 7 used to

2 Vocabulary

a 2 Take 3 in 4 on 5 waste 6 take 7 spend

b 2 on 3 in 4 in 5 by 6 in

How did you do?

Students work out their scores. Check how they have done and follow up any problem areas with revision work.

Memo from Mario

In and out of fashion

1 Things I remember

- Tell the students about something you had as a child which you hated. For example, a colleague of mine told her students the following.

  When I was a child I used to have a silver bangle which my grandmother had given me. I hated it. But every time we visited my grandmother, I would have to wear it. I would try to avoid it, I would hide it but my mother always found it. Even now I can't stand wearing metal bangles.
- When you've finished, invite the students to ask questions about what you've told them. (*Why did you hate it? Where did you hide it?* etc.) Then tell them about something you loved as a child and follow the same pattern.
- Ask the students to think for a minute about things they loved and hated as a child. Then put them in pairs to talk about them.

RATIONALE
Telling the students something true about yourself is important in building up a good relationship with them. We often ask students to reveal things about themselves, so we should be prepared to do the same.

2 How can that be the answer?

- To introduce this activity you could remind the students of the octopus which 'predicted' the results of the 2010 World Cup matches as an example of random predictions. If you like, you could set a situation such as a TV panel game and give prizes to the best answers.
- You will need two slips of paper for each student and two bags. Give each student two slips of paper.
- On the first slip they should write a question, personal or general, referring to the future: for example, *Shall I get a good job after I leave school?* or *Will global warming be reduced this century?* Collect the pieces of paper and put them in bag one.
- On the second slip the students should write a phrase that they have learnt from Units 3 and 4 and put them in bag two.
- The students now take one slip from each bag, without looking at them.
- In groups of four, each student should first read out the question slip and then the word or phrase on the other slip as the answer to the question on the first slip. The group should discuss and suggest ways in which the word or phrase could be the answer to the question.

RATIONALE
This gives the students the opportunity to explore their own and other students' new vocabulary in a variety of situations. The discussion will often require some very creative thinking.

5 Do something

Unit overview

TOPIC: Making a difference

TEXTS

Reading and listening: an article about comedian Eddie Izzard's marathons

Reading: articles about different fundraising events

Listening: an interview about young people's ability to influence politics

Writing: a formal letter asking for sponsorship

SPEAKING AND FUNCTIONS

Talking about raising money for charity

Talking about teens and their power without the vote

Discussing the age young people are allowed to do things

Talking about different ways of fundraising

LANGUAGE

Grammar: conditionals review; mixed conditionals

Vocabulary: ways of getting involved

Pronunciation: contractions in third conditionals

1 Read and listen

If you set the background information as a homework research task, ask the students to tell the class what they found out.

BACKGROUND INFORMATION

Eddie Izzard (born 1962) is a British comedian and actor. He has released many best-selling DVDs including *Unrepeatable* and *Glorious* and also appeared in *Ocean's Twelve* and *Ocean's Thirteen*. In 2010 he ran 43 marathons to raise money for charity.

Trafalgar Square is a square in central London. It is a popular tourist attraction and is home to Nelson's Column. The square is used for political demonstrations and gatherings such as the celebration of New Year's Eve.

Warm up

Ask students if anyone has ever done something for charity. Perhaps give an example of your own. Discuss interesting comments in class, helping with vocabulary if necessary.

a Ask students to describe what they can see in the pictures and to answer the questions. Point out the map of the United Kingdom. Ask students how far they think the man has run.

b Students read the text quickly to check their answers to Exercise 1a. Tell them not to worry about difficult vocabulary, but just to concentrate on the task. Check answers with the class.

Answers

The man is finishing his 43rd marathon in less than two months. He ran the marathons to raise money for charity.

c ▶ CD2 T02 Play the recording while students read and listen. Students answer the questions and compare answers with a partner before feedback. Play the recording again, pausing as necessary to clarify any problems.

TAPESCRIPT

See the reading text on page 40 of the Student's Book.

Answers

1 He ran 43 marathons in less than two months and he had only had five weeks of training.
2 He ran for six days out of seven.
3 They joined him on his run.
4 Because it was very painful. He had to have his feet bandaged, lost several toenails and had many blisters.
5 He started slowly at first. But, more importantly, he wanted to make a difference to people's lives.

Discussion box

In pairs or small groups, students discuss the questions. Monitor and help as necessary, encouraging them to express themselves in English and to use any vocabulary they have learned from the text. Ask pairs or groups to feedback to the class and discuss any interesting points further.

2 Grammar

✱ Conditionals review

a Books closed. Write *Four types of conditionals* on the board and elicit as much information as possible from students: the names of the conditionals, an example of each and explanations of when they are used. Students then open their books, look at the four examples and complete the table. Write the table on the board and ask students to help you fill it in. Draw attention to example A and remind students that the two clauses can be reversed, with the *if* clause coming first or second.

Answers

	Example sentence	*If* clause	Main clause
Zero conditional	A	present simple	present simple
First conditional	B	present simple	*will* + infinitive
Second conditional	C	past simple	*would(n't)* + infinitive
Third conditional	D	past perfect	*would(n't) have* + past participle

b Read through the descriptions with the class. Students decide which conditional each sentence describes. Check answers. Refer back to the examples in Exercise 2a and use these for further explanation if necessary.

Answers
1 third 2 zero 3 second 4 first

Language note
It is common to use imperatives in conditional sentences, for example: *If he phones, tell him I'm out. If the baby cries, give her some milk.*

c Students decide which conditionals are used in the sentences. During feedback, ask them to explain why a certain conditional is used in each case, referring back to the explanations in Exercise 2b.

Answers
1 second 2 zero 3 first 4 third

Language notes
Students may make the mistake of thinking they should use *will* in the *if* clause, as it has a future meaning, e.g. **If it will rain, I will take my coat.*

You could point out some other sentence types where we use the present simple to refer to the future, for example:
When I see him, I'll call you.

OPTIONAL ACTIVITY

Write these sentence openings on the board:

If I hadn't eaten three hamburgers,
If I forget my mother's birthday,
If an alien walked into the classroom,
If I miss the bus,
If I had known you were coming,

Ask students to complete the sentences with suitable endings and compare answers with a partner. Monitor to ensure that students are using the correct forms. Listen to some of their ideas in open class.

Grammar notebook
Remind students to note down the rules for conditionals and to write a few examples of their own.

3 Vocabulary

✱ Ways of getting involved

Write the words *petition, demonstration, leaflets, donation* and *voluntary work* on the board and elicit the meanings. Refer students to the leaflet and ask them to try to complete the sentences using the words in the box. If they find this difficult, tell them to look back at the text in Exercise 1a for help. Stronger students should complete the exercise first and then look back at the text to check. After going through the answers with the class, say the full expressions and ask students to repeat them.

Answers
1 sign 2 Join 3 Hand out 4 Make 5 raise 6 Do

OPTIONAL ACTIVITY

If students are interested in charities, put them into small groups and ask them to create a poster for a fund-raising activity for a charity of their choice. Monitor to help with vocabulary. Display their work on the walls and let students circulate to read the posters.

Vocabulary bank
Refer students to the vocabulary bank. Read through the words and phrases in open class and check understanding.

Vocabulary notebook
Encourage students to start a new section called *Charities* in their notebook and to add these expressions and any interesting words from the text in Exercise 1a. They may find it useful to note down translations, too.

4 Listen

a Books closed. Write these words on the board: *to vote, an election, the government, to run a country.* Make sure the meanings are clear and ask students what links the words (politics). Ask students if they know any other words connected to politics.

b ▶ CD2 T03 Books open. Tell students they are going to hear a girl talking on a radio show discussing whether teenagers should have the right to vote. Before they listen, ask students what their opinions on the subject are. Play the recording. Students listen for the information. During feedback, ask students what they heard on the recording to make them choose their answers.

TAPESCRIPT

Presenter: They're interested in music, fashion and cool gadgets, they use every opportunity they can to chill out or surf the web, and the last thing they're interested in is? Right! POLITICS! Who are they? That's right: TEENS! Well, if you think that's true, you'll be surprised at what our guest today has to say. It's 15-year-old Emma Wilkins, and her hobby is … what most people would agree is a complete turn-off for teens. Yes, well guessed, she's interested in politics. Hi, Emma – it's great to have you on the show!

Emma: Thanks, and yes, I'm very interested in politics.

Presenter: Why's that? No friends? Bored with your life? Fed up with teachers and parents? Or is it just what some people would call a teenage fad that will go away as soon as she has her first boyfriend?

Emma: No, it's not and I'm actually having a lot of fun in life. But what I would like to tell all those kids out there who may be listening to this show is that there aren't enough adults who are standing up for your rights! Simply because they're interested in their rights, not yours.

Presenter: But in all fairness, and – I must admit – I'm absolutely fascinated with what you're saying and the passion you're saying it with – is there any point in teens becoming involved in politics? I mean the power's with the adults, and not with the teens, isn't it? Teenagers can't vote, so what difference does it make if they get involved in politics?

Emma: Well, that's the point! As you say, elections happen without the involvement of 15-year-olds because 15-year-olds can't vote and they don't form part of a government. Actually I am sure that if young people had the vote, this government wouldn't have won the last election. But that's not the point. The point is that teens may not have the vote, and yet, they still have a lot of power … if they were only aware of it.

Presenter: What do you mean, teens have a lot of power? Can you give us some concrete examples?

Emma: Young people basically have three different kinds of power: number power, economic power, and persuasion power.

Presenter: Hang on, hang on, hang on. You're sounding more and more like a politician, but – I must admit – a very passionate one!

Emma: Let me just explain. The first power is number power. Did you know that teens are almost 15% of this country's population? They have money, in fact billions, to spend. So all we need to do is become aware of this power, and spend it on meaningful things. We all hear every day about the environment, and how bad things are. Well, what I'm saying is stop complaining. Think and do something, but do the right things, for example buy stuff that makes a difference to our environment. Recycled stuff rather than plastic bottles and aluminium cans, that sort of thing! So it's number power and economic power we are talking about.

Presenter: OK, I've got you. You're saying there are lots of teens with lots of money out there but now – how are you going to get all those teens involved? How are you going to make them believe that they should stop complaining, think and do something, but do the right thing as you have just said. Do they really want to listen?

Emma: They do, because we have energy, and we have passion, and we have a sense of what's right. We're talking persuasion power here – and we have the tools to do it, and to do it well and fast and efficiently: the internet, our blogs, text messaging, Twitter, Facebook, etc. We can use all those, and we will! If there are things we want to change, we need to find others who want to change them too – together we can do something about it. Together we have power!

Presenter: You're talking all those electronic tools, but you also told me before the show that you actually decided to become involved in politics after doing something really old-fashioned – reading a book?

Emma: That's right. The book's called *Teen Power Politics*, and when I got it as a present from a friend I wasn't very impressed at first. A book, you know, and I really wasn't very much into reading, and then politics? Not my cup of tea, I thought. But then I got hooked, and I must say in many ways this book has changed my life. It's full of great cartoons and quotes, and it's not boring at all. It has great examples of very real – and not perfect – young people who have changed things through protest, through teaming up with others, and through simply asking the right questions at the right time and raising their voice so they could be heard.

Presenter: Fascinating, Emma. Let me ask you a question. If you could change one thing...

Answers

1 Politics.
2 Because they have economic and number power.
3 A book about politics.

c **▶ CD2 T03** Read through the sentences with students and check any difficult vocabulary: *stand up for, rights, corrupt, campaigns, at ease with.* Play the recording again. Students listen and choose the correct endings to the sentences. Check answers.

Answers

1 a 2 b 3 b 4 b 5 b

Discussion box

In pairs or small groups, students discuss the questions. Monitor and help as necessary, encouraging them to express themselves in English and to use any vocabulary they have learned from the text. Ask pairs or groups to feedback to the class and discuss any interesting points further. If this issue is of particular interest to your students, arrange a debate. Divide the class into two halves (one half in favour of giving 15-year-olds the vote and the other half against). You could also ask one student to be the neutral leader of the debate. Students present their arguments. At the end, you can make a decision about which side won the debate.

5 Pronunciation

See notes on page 122.

6 Grammar

★ Mixed conditionals

a **Weaker classes:** Write these sentences on the board:

If I had found a holiday job, I would have earned some money.

If I had found a holiday job, I .... now.

Point out that the first example is a normal example of the third conditional – we are imagining a situation in the past which did not happen. Focus on the second example and ask students if they can suggest an ending. Point out that although the *if* clause is the same, we are talking about now in the main clause. Elicit or supply a suitable ending, e.g. *I would have plenty of money now / I wouldn't be so poor now)* and write it on the board. Point out to students that this sentence does not follow the normal pattern for conditional sentences – it is a mixture of third and second conditionals. Follow the procedure for stronger classes.

Stronger classes: Students read the example sentences and answer the questions. Ask them to decide whether we are talking about the past or the present in the first and second clause of each sentence (*1: present in the first clause, past in the second; 2: past in the first clause, present in the second).* Explain that these are mixed conditionals, which are variations on the structures that students have learned.

Answers

1 No 2 Yes 3 No 4 No

b Read through the rules with the class and ask students to complete them. Check answers.

Answers

past, third; past perfect, second

c Students match the *if* clauses with the main clauses. Do the first sentence as an example if necessary. Students compare answers with a partner. Check answers and point out that there is no difference in meaning if the clauses are reversed.

Answers

1 e 2 a 3 f 4 b 5 c 6 d

d Students work in pairs to combine the two sentences to make mixed conditionals. You may want to go through the exercise quickly with the whole class before they begin. Check answers in open class.

Answers

2 If I really understood maths, I wouldn't have failed the test.
3 If I hadn't spent all my money on CDs, I would have some money today.
4 If I spoke Spanish, I would have understood what they said.
5 If I could swim, I would have been able to save the young girl.

Grammar notebook

Remind students to note down the rules for mixed conditionals and to write a few examples of their own.

7 Speak

a Read through the list of actions with the class to check understanding. In pairs, students discuss and guess the legal age when young people can do each of these things in the UK. Tell them they are not expected to know the information – just to give the ages that they think are likely. Ask different pairs for their ideas, and then give them the actual answers.

Answers
buy a pet 12
work part-time 13
be legally responsible for a crime they commit 10
drive 17
buy a lottery ticket 16
become a Member of Parliament 21
leave school 16
give blood 18
borrow money from a bank 18

b Students work together to discuss the age when young people can do these things in their own country. There will probably be some disagreement on this. If possible, research the answers yourself prior to the class and give the information after students have had time to exchange ideas. Alternatively, you could ask students to find the answers themselves as a homework activity and to report back in the next lesson.

c Read through the examples with the class. Ask concept-check questions to ensure that students are clear about the meanings. Working individually, students think about consequences of changing the age limits and make similar sentences. Monitor to check progress and ensure that students are using the forms correctly.

d In small groups, students compare their ideas. Get feedback from some individuals and write some of the most interesting ideas on the board. With weaker classes, let students read their answers. Stronger classes can try to remember their sentences without referring to their notes.

Culture in mind

8 Read and listen

If you set the background information as a homework research task, ask the students to tell the class what they found out.

BACKGROUND INFORMATION

Twitter is a social networking website which allows users to send and receive messages called 'tweets'. Messages must be of 140 characters or less. Twitter started in July 2006 and now has 190 million users, sending an average of 65 million 'tweets' a day. Twestival has raised over $1.75 million for charity since 2009.

J.K. Rowling (born 1965) is a children's author famous for the seven *Harry Potter* novels, which have sold over 400 million copies and made her the twelfth richest woman in Great Britain. She uses her wealth well by giving large sums of money to various charities.

a As an introduction, ask students if they have ever done anything for charity. Listen to some of their ideas in open class. Tell students they are going to read about some unusual charity events. Read through items 1–3. Students read the text quickly to answer the questions. They can compare answers with a partner before feedback.

Answers
1 626 2 over $250,000
3 The Children's Voice

b ▶ CD2 T06 Read through the questions and check understanding of *humanitarian* and *handwritten*. Students listen and read the text again and answer the questions. There is a fair amount of new vocabulary in the text, but encourage students to work without help from you or a dictionary at this stage. Ask them to underline any words or phrases they don't understand. Let students compare answers with a partner and discuss possible meanings of new words together before feedback.

TAPESCRIPT

See the reading texts on page 44 of the Student's Book.

Answers
1 It was raining too heavily to play.
2 It has organized events like 'Twestival', 'Tweetsgiving' and 'Tweet-a-thon'.
3 She produced six copies for important people in her life and a seventh for charity. (It also matched the number of *Harry Potter* novels)

Discussion box

In pairs or small groups, students discuss the question. Monitor and help as necessary, encouraging students to express themselves in English and to use any vocabulary they have learned from the text. Ask pairs or groups to feedback to the class and discuss any interesting points further.

9 Write

The planning for this exercise can be done in class and the letter can be set as homework.

a Look at the text and tell students it is a letter asking for sponsorship for a charitable event. Read through the questions with students. Students read the letter and find answers to the questions.

Answers
1 James MacDonald.
2 A charity called Have a Heart.
3 A half-marathon.
4 Sponsorship of individuals by members of the public and institutional sponsorship by companies or organisations.
5 It's to a business.

b As an example of a formal letter, this is a good opportunity to draw students' attention to the layout of the letter. Ask students to read the letter again and answer questions 1–4.

Answers
1 In the top right corner.
2 Dear Sir/Madam,
3 No, he doesn't.
4 Yours faithfully, (Because he doesn't know the name of the recipient.)

c Ask students to plan how to raise money for a charity of their choice. If they have done the optional activity in Exercise 3, they might like to refer back to their poster. Students work in small groups to decide on the charity and how they hope to raise money. Encourage them to make notes.

d Tell students they are going to write a letter to a company asking for their support. Ask them to organise their letter in paragraphs, using their notes from their group discussion. In a subsequent lesson, encourage students to read each other's letters and decide which charity would be most successful.

OPTIONAL ACTIVITY

If you would like to give your students practice in writing summaries, you could ask them to write a summary of each of the four paragraphs in James MacDonald's letter. If students find this difficult, give them an example for the first paragraph and show them how to pick out the main points to put in the summary.

Memo from Mario

Do something!

1 Matching conditionals dictation

- You will need to prepare two sheets. On one write a list of the first part of conditional sentences, on the other write the second half. Make sure the two halves are in different orders on the sheets. Put the sheets on the wall on opposite sides of the room.
- You could use sentences from the unit or make up your own. Below are some suggestions.
- Before you start, make the rules very clear. No pens/pencils to be taken to the walls. No shouting to the secretary.
- Put the students in groups of three, A, B and C. Student A is the secretary and must remain seated. Student B should go to the first sheet, read a sentence part, return and dictate it to the secretary. At the same time, Student C goes to the second sheet, reads a sentence part and returns to dictate. Together they must decide if the two parts go together to make a conditional sentence. If they do, the secretary writes them together, if not, he or she writes them on separate lines, to wait for a second part that goes.

If I was older...	I could receive email on it.
If I had a time machine...	they can concentrate better.
If the car breaks down...	I'll never get to sleep.
If the fire had started on the ground floor...	nobody would have been injured.
If I didn't have to study for a test...	I'll probably see that new film.
If people understand the need...	I would have pictures to show you.
If people take a nap after lunch...	more people would have been injured.
If I go to the cinema...	you can call me.
If the fire hadn't burnt so fiercely...	I'd be watching TV now.
If my mobile was more modern...	they will help.
If that dog goes on barking...	I'd visit the future.
If I hadn't broken my camera...	I wouldn't still be at school.

- You could use fewer sentences to make the activity shorter or tell the students they only need to get eight that match and then they can finish any other phrases any way they like.

RATIONALE

Dictation doesn't have to be boring. Student–student dictation can be very useful. This activity also involves movement, which can raise the energy level in the group. If you really want to wake them up, make it a race for the first trio to get five correct sentences.

2 Writing a group poem

- You will need four slips of paper for each student.
- Write the word *Charity* on the board.
- Ask the students to shout out sentences beginning with the word *charity*.
- Add the verbs they use, and any others you think of, to the board.
  ... is / begins / means / helps / makes / doesn't...
- Give out four slips of paper to each student. Ask them to write four affirmative or negative sentences on the slips.
- Put the students in groups of four and ask them to create a simple poem from the group's sentences, by putting the sentences in groups of four to make four verses and then writing *Charity is* after every verse. The title of the poem is *Charity is...*
- Have the students read out their poems to the class or put them on a poster to display for other classes to read.

RATIONALE

Working round the topic of Unit 4 will recycle vocabulary. The original idea was inspired by the poem 'Love is' by Adrian Henri, one of the Liverpool poets of the 1960s and 1970s.

6 Our world

Unit overview

TOPIC: Global issues

TEXTS

Reading and listening: a blog about an eco town in Colombia; photostory: *It's not very green, is it?*

Listening: the Global Village

Writing: a magazine article about the future

SPEAKING AND FUNCTIONS

Talking about eco communities and the future of the planet

Discussing global trade

Discussing the impact of flying

LANGUAGE

Grammar: future continuous; future perfect

Vocabulary: global issues

Pronunciation: /ð/ *the* and /θ/ *thing*

1 Read and listen

If you set the background information as a homework research task, ask the students to tell the class what they found out.

BACKGROUND INFORMATION

Colombia (population c. 46 million) is a country in South America. It is the second most populous country in South America after Brazil. It has the fourth largest Spanish-speaking population in the world after Mexico, the USA and Spain. Colombia has a varied landscape, including the Andes Mountains, Amazon rainforest and Caribbean and Pacific coastlines.

Gaviotas is an eco-town set up in 1971 in Colombia. Gaviotans have planted millions of trees, thus regenerating an indigenous rainforest. They farm organically and use wind and solar power. Every family enjoys free housing, community meals, and schooling. There are no weapons, no police and no jail. It has been a centre of innovation, creating ecological solutions specific to its environment. Residents have invented a water pump powered by a child's see-saw and have made their own solar panels. The community is almost entirely self-sufficient and even has its own hospital.

Warm up

Draw a picture of the Earth on the board and elicit examples of problems facing the planet. Write these on the board, grouping different ideas together in topic areas. In open class, discuss ways in which we might avoid these problems in the future.

a Ask students to describe what they can see in the photos. Read through the instructions with students and ask them to read the text quickly to find the information. Remind them not to worry about the meaning of every word. Check answers.

Answers

1 She went to Gaviotas.
2 At first she thought there would be nothing to do; after visiting she thought it was a very interesting, successful town.
3 That in twenty years' time we will all live in towns like Gaviotas.

b ▶ CD2 T07 Check that students understand the statements. Play the recording while students read. Pause as necessary to check comprehension and clarify any difficulties. Students decide if the statements are true or false and correct the false ones. They can compare answers with a partner before feedback in open class.

TAPESCRIPT

See the reading text on page 46 of the Student's Book.

Answers

1 F (She wasn't keen at first.)
2 T
3 F (He says we will have used up all of our resources by 2050.)
4 T
5 T
6 F (They need to import 30% of their energy and food.)
7 F (There are no police.)

Discussion box

In pairs or small groups, students discuss the questions. Monitor and help as necessary, encouraging them to express themselves in English and to use any vocabulary they have learned from the text. Ask pairs or groups to feedback to the class and discuss any interesting points further.

2 Grammar

★ Future continuous

a **Weaker classes:** Books closed. Ask students what they are doing now and elicit an example sentence, e.g. *I'm sitting in the classroom now.* Ask about a time in the past (e.g. *at 8 o'clock this morning*), eliciting a sentence in the past continuous. Remind students that we use continuous tenses to refer to an activity in progress at a particular point in time. Now write this sentence on the board:

At 12 o'clock tonight I .... sleep ....

Ask students to try to complete the sentence *(will be sleeping).* Give them the answer if they are unable to guess. Tell them this tense is called the future continuous. Students then follow the procedure for stronger classes.

Stronger classes: Ask students to look at the example, and establish that it refers to the future. Read through the rule with the class, using the time line to show that the action (living) will already be in progress at a given time (20 years from now) and will continue after that time. Point out the similarities between the future continuous and other continuous tenses. Ask students to complete the rule.

> **Answers**
> *will*, *be*, present participle / *-ing* form of the verb

★ Future perfect

b **Weaker classes:** Write this sentence on the board:

By 2050 we will have used up our planet's resources.

Ask students if the action will take place before, in or after 2050 (before). Ask them if we know exactly when (no, we don't – we only know it will be some time before 2050). Students then follow the procedure for stronger classes.

Stronger classes: Ask students to look at the examples. Read through the rule and ask them to complete it. Emphasise that the future perfect action is something that will be completed before a given time in the future. Compare this with the future continuous, where the action will still be going on.

> **Answers**
> *will*, *have*, past participle

c Read through the sentences with the class and check for any difficulties with vocabulary. Students complete the sentences, using the future continuous or future perfect. Ask them to compare answers with a partner before feedback in open class.

> **Answers**
> 1 have used up 2 have died out 3 be living
> 4 be looking

d Read through the prompts with the class. Ask them to complete the sentences with the correct tense. Check their answers in open class.

> **Answers**
> 2 By 2017 politicians will have decided on an undersea policy.
> 3 In 2024 engineers will be building homes under the sea.
> 4 In 2050 people will be living under the sea.
> 5 By 2055 half the world's population will have moved to a home under the sea.

Grammar notebook

Remind students to note down the rules for the future continuous and future perfect and to write a few examples of their own.

3 Vocabulary

★ Global issues

a Students complete the sentences, using the words in the box. Tell them to guess unknown words and to use dictionaries to check, if they have time. Check answers. Then say the words and ask students to repeat them.

Weaker classes: Check answers in open class at this stage.

> **Answers**
> 1 species 2 resources 3 waste
> 4 atmosphere 5 temperatures 6 starvation

Students match the underlined phrasal verbs with meanings a–f. Remind them that phrasal verbs cannot be translated literally into other languages and that the two or three words together have a different meaning from when they are used separately.

> **Answers**
> 1 b 2 e 3 d 4 f 5 c 6 a

b Students work with a partner and discuss the sentences. Encourage them to agree on one sentence which they both find the most worrying, and then to order the other sentences in order of importance.

c Put students into small groups and ask them to compare lists. Ask a representative from each group to give feedback, and encourage further class discussion on interesting points.

OPTIONAL ACTIVITY

If students are interested in this area, divide the class into six groups. Ask them to choose one of the six sentences and to prepare a presentation describing the problem and offering possible solutions. Ensure that each of the six areas is covered by at least one group. After preparation, students give their presentation and invite questions and comments. You could ask the class to vote on which was the best presentation.

Vocabulary notebook

Encourage students to start two new sections in their notebook called *Global issues* and *Phrasal verbs* and to add these words together with examples. They may find it useful to note down translations, too.

4 Read and listen

Warm up

Ask students to guess how many people live in the world and how many live in Asia, Africa and Europe. What percentage of people do they think have an internet connection / own a car / have a bank account / have electricity in their houses? Invite students to offer their guesses, but don't comment on them at this stage.

a Tell students they are going to look at some statistical information from a website. Read through the first paragraph of the text with them and make sure they understand the concept of viewing the world as a 'village' of 100 people. In groups, students read the text, discussing and guessing the missing information together. Ask them to fill in their answers in pencil.

b ▶ CD2 T08 Play the recording while students listen, read and complete the gaps with the correct information. Students compare answers with a partner. Then play the recording again, pausing if necessary for clarification. Check answers in open class and invite students to comment on the information.

TAPESCRIPT

The Global Village

If we could turn the population of the Earth into a small village community of 100 people, keeping roughly the same proportions we have today on our planet, it would be something like this:

Welcome to our Global Village, the village Earth. In our village there are 100 people. 51 people are women and 49 are men.

61 people are from Asia. 12 people are from Europe. 14 people are from North and South America. There are 13 people from Africa.

13 people don't have enough to eat, or are actually dying from hunger.

More than 40 people in the village live without basic sanitation, and 16 people live without water that can be drunk.

Roughly 14 adults in the village can't read or write. Only seven have had a secondary school education. Eight people have a computer, and four are connected to the internet.

Eight people have a car, and 10 per cent of the houses are powered by electricity.

Some people keep their food in a refrigerator, and their clothes in a wardrobe; they have a roof over their heads, and they have a bed to sleep in. These people represent about 75 per cent of the entire population of the village.

Six people in our village own 59 per cent of the entire wealth of all the people in our community. 47 people live on two dollars or less a day. 25 people struggle to live on a dollar a day or less. If you have a bank account, you're one of the 30 wealthiest people in the village.

Of all the money that the village spends every year, about 5.5 per cent is spent on weapons and war, roughly 3.4 per cent is spent on schools and university, and something like 2.6 per cent is spent on keeping people healthy.

Next year, there will be 105 people in the village.

Work with passion,
Love without needing to be loved,
Appreciate what you have,
And do your best for a better world.

Answers

1 men **2** Asia **3** Europe **4** America **5** Africa **6** eat **7** education **8** connected **9** wardrobe **10** population **11** a dollar **12** wealthiest **13** war **14** education **15** healthy **16** have **17** better

Discussion box

In pairs or small groups, students discuss the questions. Monitor and help as necessary, encouraging them to express themselves in English and to use any vocabulary they have learned from the text. Ask pairs or groups to feedback to the class and discuss any interesting points further.

OPTIONAL ACTIVITY

Do some work on estimating numbers. Ask students to look through the text and underline six examples of approximate numbers *(More than 40 people, Roughly 14 adults, about 75 per cent, two dollars or less, about 5.5 per cent, something like 2.6 per cent).* Then ask students to look again at the text and decide if these sentences are true or false. Ask them to correct the false sentences.

1 *Roughly half the population haven't got enough food.* (False. 13% of people don't have enough to eat.)
2 *Something like 90% of houses haven't got enough electricity.* (True)
3 *Somewhere in the region of 12% of people own a car.* (False. 8% own a car.)
4 *Approximately a third of the village have a bank account.* (True)
5 *A quarter or so of the people in the world haven't got a bed to sleep in.* (True)
6 *More or less half the people live on $2 or less a day.* (True)
7 *More than 95% haven't got a computer.* (False. 92% haven't got a computer.)
8 *Fewer than 15% can't read.* (True)

5 Pronunciation

See notes on page 122.

6 Speak

a Set a time limit of three minutes for this activity. Students write as many examples as they can for each category. Ask some pairs for examples and ask a few follow-up questions, for example: *Where is that programme from? Which is your favourite American show? Have any of these groups done a tour in our country? Do we produce (name of product) here?*

b Read through the examples with the class. In pairs, students discuss the items listed in Exercise 6a, estimating the percentage that comes from abroad and supporting their estimates with reasons and/or examples. Students compare their answers in class discussion.

c Divide the class into pairs and ask students to draw up a list of advantages and disadvantages. Circulate and help with vocabulary as necessary. Invite students to express their opinions in an open class debate.

OPTIONAL ACTIVITY

You could ask students to do some research on the internet to find out further interesting information on this topic, e.g. the percentage of locally made programmes on TV or the percentage of certain foodstuffs which are imported. Ask them to report their findings in English in the next lesson.

Photostory: It's not very green, is it?

7 Read and listen

Warm up

Ask students what they can remember about the last episode of the story (*Nick and Amy had an argument about Amy leaving things lying around. Jack and Lily tried to calm them down and get them to make friends again.*)

a ▶ CD2 T11 Pre-teach *carbon footprints, sponsored*. Students read the text and answer the questions. Play the recording. Check answers in open class. If students ask questions about vocabulary, write the words on the board but don't explain their meaning.

TAPESCRIPT

See the story on page 50 of the Student's Book.

Answers

Sandra's dad flying to New Zealand to watch a cricket match.

b Students read the text again and find the answers to the questions. Allow them to check answers with a partner before open class feedback. Encourage students to correct the false sentences.

Weaker classes: Before students look at the questions, you may want to play the recording again, pausing as necessary to clarify any problems. Then read through the questions with the class and check that the meaning is clear.

Answers

1 He thinks it's cool. Amy thinks it will cause a lot of pollution.
2 To do a sponsored triathlon.
3 She feels he has a good reason for going; she might also feel embarrassed.

8 Everyday English

a Ask students to locate the expressions 1 to 6 in the story on page 50 and decide who says them.

Weaker classes: Check answers at this stage.

Answers

1 Jack 2 Nick 3 Amy 4 Jack 5 Nick 6 Amy

Students then match the expressions with the situations. Go through the first item with them as an example, if necessary. Check answers.

Answers
a 5 b 2 c 4 d 6 e 1 f 3

b Ask students to read through the sentences and complete the answers. Go through the first sentence with them as an example, if necessary.

Answers
1 Whatever 2 give me a break 3 let's face it 4 Are you out of your mind? 5 Hang on a minute 6 It's none of your business

OPTIONAL ACTIVITY

See Unit 2, Exercise 9 Everyday English, Optional Activities.

9 Improvisation

Divide the class into groups of three. Ask them to write down as many expressions from Exercise 8a as they can remember. Circulate and check they are writing expressions correctly. Read through the instructions with students. Give them two minutes (or more if necessary) to prepare a short role play. Invite some of the groups to act out their role play for the rest of the class and hold a vote on which was the most entertaining and which included the most expressions from Exercise 8a.

10 Making Waves (DVD Episode 2)

In open class, ask students to tell you what they remember from episode 1 of the DVD. Look at the photograph and ask individual students to describe what they see.

a Divide the class into pairs and ask students to discuss the question. Listen to some of their ideas in open class, but do not comment at this stage.

Answer
Mary is upset because she has seen Lily getting out of a car, which seems hypocritical when she is campaigning for everyone to walk or cycle to school.

b Read through the phrases and the sentences with students and check understanding. Ask them to complete the sentences. Tell students they are going to watch the DVD to check their answers.

Answers
1 running late 2 How dare you 3 Bring it on 4 up for it

c Watch episode 2 of the DVD. Divide the class into pairs and ask students to discuss the question. Listen to some of their ideas in open class and check the answers to Exercise 10b. Play the DVD again, pausing as necessary to clarify language.

11 Write

The planning for this exercise can be done in class and the article can be set for homework.

a Ask students to read the article quickly and to say whether the writer is optimistic or pessimistic.

Answer
The writer is optimistic.

b Students read the article again and find which of the topics are covered. Ask them to say a little about the writer's opinions on these topics. Do they agree with them?

Answers
The writer covers:
scientists' warnings concerning the Earth's future, his/her own beliefs about what the future will be like, peace vs. war, people's lifestyles, what people will eat / hunger in the world.

c Tell students they are going to write a magazine article entitled *Our life – 50 years from now.* Read through the writing guide with the class and encourage them to follow this procedure for their article. In a subsequent lesson, encourage students to read each other's articles and discuss their predictions in open class.

Check your progress

1 Grammar

a
2 If I spoke French, I would have got the job.
3 If she had passed her driving test, she'd be happy now.
4 If I had had enough money, I would have bought a bigger motorbike.
5 I would have gone to the club if I liked dancing.
6 I wouldn't be tired if the dog hadn't barked all night.

b 2 be doing 3 be flying 4 have finished 5 have discovered 6 be thinking 7 have fallen

2 Vocabulary

a 1 leaflets 2 petition 3 demonstration 4 donation 5 volunteer 6 stop it

b 2 up 3 of 4 up 5 up 6 about

How did you do?

Students work out their scores. Check how they have done and follow up any problem areas with revision work.

Memo from Mario

Our world

1 My life in the future

- Here are two suggestions to give the students a chance to talk about their own hopes and dreams. Which you use depends on the time you have available.

A Write these sentences on the board.

- *By the time I'm 30...* (Choose a suitable age for your students.)

I'll be living in a different place.

I'll be managing my own company.

I'll be in a stable relationship.

I'll have visited lots of places in different countries.

I'll have completed an advanced course.

I'll have taken part in campaigns to save the planet.

I'll be writing a book about my life.

I'll be driving an electric car.

I won't be studying English.

- Ask the students to copy the sentences, putting *certainly / probably / possibly / it's unlikely that / there's no way that* into each statement, according to what they think about their future. You could give some personal examples and encourage the students to ask you follow-up questions.
- Now put the students in pairs or small groups to compare their sentences and ask follow-up questions.
- **B** Write *By the time I'm 30...* on the board and then write the beginnings of future sentences: *I'll ... / I'll be ... / I'll have ...* Give the students some personal examples to start them thinking.
- Ask the students to complete the sentences for themselves. Then mingle, or work in groups, to compare ideas and ask follow-up questions.

RATIONALE

Talking about hopes and dreams can be a very positive experience for students.

2 A simple gap filler

- Here's a suggestion for when you have a few minutes to spare. You can also use it for students who finish an activity before the others are ready.
- It's probably best to demonstrate this with the whole group the first time and then let them play in pairs.
- Ask the students to draw a 3x3 grid. Have one yourself for the demonstration. Explain that they are going to try to make as many three-letter words as they can on the grid, sideways, upwards, downwards and diagonally. Start by calling out a letter. Everyone puts that letter anywhere they like in their grid. Then ask a student to call out another letter which everyone puts in their grid. Then ask more students to choose letters until all the squares on the grid have been filled. Everyone (including you) counts up the words they have managed. Then put students in pairs to continue. Obviously they must not let their partner see their paper. As well as getting the letters that they want, they will also sometimes name a letter just to make their partner's life difficult. There's more to this game than appears at first.

7 Peacemakers

Unit overview

TOPIC: Conflicts and resolutions

TEXTS

Reading and listening: an article about Alfred Nobel; an extract from *Pride and Prejudice* by Jane Austen

Reading: an article about Aung San Suu Kyi

Listening: a conversation about a conflict resolution programme

Writing: writing about a person you admire

SPEAKING AND FUNCTIONS

Talking about Nobel Peace Prize winners

Discussing ways to resolve a conflict

Discussing characters from *Pride and Prejudice*

LANGUAGE

Grammar: past perfect passive; past perfect continuous

Vocabulary: conflicts and solutions

Pronunciation: linking sounds

1 Read and listen

If you set the background information as a homework research task, ask the students to tell the class what they found out.

BACKGROUND INFORMATION

The Nobel Peace Prize is one of six Nobel prizes (the others are for Physics, Chemistry, Economics, Medicine and Literature) awarded every year in Scandinavia. The winner is decided by a group of five people who form the Norwegian Nobel Committee. The prize can be won by an individual or an organisation.

Martin Luther King Jr (1929–1968) was a church minister and leader of the American civil rights movement which opposed racial discrimination against black Americans. King won the Nobel Peace Prize in 1964. Martin Luther King Day (January 15th) was established in his honour, following his assassination in 1968.

Nelson Mandela (born 1918) is a South African politician. He became leader of the African National Congress in 1961 and tried to end racial inequality (apartheid) in his country. He was put in prison for his political activities in 1963 and stayed there for 27 years. He became President of South Africa in 1994 and won the Nobel Peace Prize in 1993.

Aung San Suu Kyi (born 1945) is a supporter of democracy in Myanmar. She won the Nobel Peace Prize in 1991. For more information about her, see page 59 of the Student's Book.

Kofi Annan (born 1938) is from Ghana. From 1997 to 2006 he was the Secretary-General of the United Nations. He and the UN itself were joint winners of the Nobel Peace Prize in 2001 for 'their work for a better organised and more peaceful world'. During his term of office he was deeply committed to strengthening the role of the UN in promoting international peace and security.

Lech Walesa (born 1943) was a Polish electrician who became a trade union and human rights activist in Poland. In the 1980s he led the Solidarity trade union which opposed government repression, and after the fall of the Communist regime he became President of Poland from 1990 to 1995. He won the Nobel Peace Prize in 1983.

Mother Teresa (1910–1997) was an Albanian-born Catholic nun who founded the Missionaries of Charity in India. Her work for the poor in Calcutta led to her winning the Nobel Peace Prize in 1979.

The First World War is also called World War I and the Great War. It lasted from August 1914 to November 1918. The Allied Powers (led by Britain, France, Russia until 1917, and the United States after 1917) defeated the Central Powers (led by the German Empire, the Austro-Hungarian Empire and the Ottoman Empire).

Warm up

Books closed. Ask students to imagine that they have to give some prizes for special achievements: the class prize for music, the class prize for acting and the class prize for peace. Give students a short while to decide who they would give the prizes to and discuss interesting answers in open class. Ask students if they know of any real prizes in these three fields.

a Ask students to look at the photos and elicit anything they know about the people. (The photos, top row left to right, show Mother Teresa, Aung San Suu Kyi, Martin Luther King Jr, and bottom row left to right, Nelson Mandela, Lech Walesa and Kofi Annan.)

b Pre-teach *explosive, fortune, dynamite*, and *obituary.* Students read the questions and then read the text quickly to find the answers. Encourage them to look for the answers and not to spend time looking up new words.

Answers
1 By making explosives, including dynamite.
2 He saw his own obituary and he didn't want to be remembered only as the man who had invented a destructive weapon.

Discussion box
In pairs or small groups, students discuss the question. Monitor and help as necessary, encouraging them to express themselves in English and to use any vocabulary they have learned from the text. Ask pairs or groups to feedback to the class and discuss any interesting points further.

c ▶ CD2 T12 Read through the text with the class, pausing where necessary to check comprehension and help with difficult vocabulary: *landmines, sea mines, blast, weapon of mass destruction, promote, abolish, grave.* Then read the additional sentences (1–5). Ask students to look back at the text and to add the sentences in the appropriate spaces (A–E). Play the recording for students to check their answers. During feedback ask them to explain why they chose a certain sentence to fill each gap.

TAPESCRIPT
See the reading text on page 54 of the Student's Book.

Answers
A 5 B 1 C 4 D 2 E 3

d Students read the text again and number the events 1–8 in the order in which they occurred.

Stronger students: Let students try to order the sentences from memory before looking back at the text to check their answers.

Answers
Order of events: 7, 1, 3, 6, 8, 4, 2, 5

OPTIONAL ACTIVITY
Write these sentences on the board. Ask students to decide if they are true or false and then to look back at the text and check their answers. Ask them to correct the false sentences.

1 *Alfred Nobel was the first winner of the Nobel Peace Prize.* (False. He created the prize.)
2 *Alfred was the first member of his family to develop explosives.* (False. His family had been developing explosives for many years when he joined the company.)
3 *Dynamite was safer than nitroglycerine.* (True.)
4 *Alfred Nobel was not a rich man.* (False. He had a great fortune.)
5 *Alfred Nobel is still alive.* (False. He is dead.)

2 Grammar

Past perfect passive

a Books closed. Ask students how many past tenses they can think of. Elicit *past simple, past continuous* and *past perfect.* Write these sentences on the board and ask students which tenses are underlined.

Dan Brown <u>wrote</u> The Da Vinci Code. (past simple)

She <u>*was cooking*</u> *dinner when I got home.* (past continuous)

When I opened the door, I realised somebody <u>*had stolen*</u> *my computer.* (past perfect)

Write *passive* on the board and ask students to change the three sentences into the passive by changing the underlined verbs:

The Da Vinci Code *was written by Dan Brown.*

Dinner was being cooked when I got home.

When I opened the door, I realised my computer had been stolen.

Books open. Ask students to complete the sentences from the text in Exercise 1.

Answers
1 had been 2 had been

b Ask students to read through the rule and choose the correct options. Check answers. Refer back to Exercise 2a to show students examples of the use of this tense.

Answers
be, past participle

BACKGROUND INFORMATION
The League of Nations was an international organisation founded after the Paris Peace Conference of 1919. The League's main goals were to stop war through collective security, to settle disputes between countries through negotiation and to improve global welfare.

c Tell students they are going to read a text about the First World War. Elicit what they already know about this war. Pre-teach difficult vocabulary: *peace treaty, railway carriage, vast amounts, opposing armies.* Students read the text and circle the correct verb forms. Ask them to compare answers with a partner before feedback.

Answers
1 was signed 2 were sent 3 had been killed
4 had been spent 5 had been destroyed
6 was taken 7 had been discussed
8 was fought

d Students complete the sentences with the correct form of the verbs.

Answers
1 had been destroyed 2 had been sold
3 was killed 4 was held 5 had not / hadn't been repaired 6 had been painted

Grammar notebook

Remind students to note down the rules for the past perfect passive and to write a few examples of their own.

OPTIONAL ACTIVITY

Write these sentences on the board. In pairs, students complete the sentences with a verb in the past perfect simple.

1 *When I got home, somebody had broken my window.*
My window ...
2 *I realised the decorators hadn't painted my front door.*
My front door ...
3 *They had kept their cat in the house for five years.*
Their cat ...
4 *Johnny's Dad had given him a new bike*
Johnny ...

Answers
1 My window had been broken.
2 My front door had not / hadn't been painted.
3 Their cat had been kept in the house for five years
4 Johnny had been given a new bike.

3 Listening

Warm up

In open class, ask students what the disciplinary procedures are in their school. Do they think the system works well? Are there any parts of it that they would change? Invite individuals to give their opinions and write any interesting vocabulary on the board.

a Read through the sentences with students. Divide the class into pairs and ask students to discuss the meanings of the underlined words. Check answers.

Possible answers
1 ended amicably 2 causes aggression
3 keeping away from physical conflict
4 when two or more people hit each other
5 knocked against 6 intervene 7 points of view 8 possible courses of action

b ▶ **CD2 T13** Tell students they are going to hear a discussion with an American teenager called Jackson, and his friend, Olivia. Check understanding of *conflict resolution programme.* Ask students to read through the questions and then play the first part of the recording, several times if necessary. Students listen and answer the questions.

TAPESCRIPT

Presenter: A study carried out among US teenagers shows that a growing percentage of them see fighting as the only acceptable way to resolve disagreements. 33 per cent of junior and senior high school students said that when they were really angry there was no way they could control themselves. 41 per cent said that if they were challenged, they would fight and that avoiding fights was a sign of weakness. And what is most alarming is that one in three high school students said they had been in a physical fight in the past year.

Olivia: I can't listen to this any more. It's exactly the same at our school.

Jackson: Really? Well, it's not like that at ours. Probably because we've got this conflict resolution programme.

Olivia: A what programme?

Jackson: Yeah, that's what I thought when I first heard about it. But it's really cool, you know.

Olivia: What is it all about, then?

Jackson: Well, it's basically what the name says. A programme we're doing with a psychologist that helps us to resolve conflicts.

Olivia: So, how does it work, I mean how does the psychologist work with you?

Jackson: Well, for example, we had this situation recently where one of my friends got into a fight with another boy.

Olivia: What was the fight about?

Jackson: Well, he was standing in line at the canteen, and the other boy bumped into him, which wasn't really his fault as someone else had pushed him. There wasn't much of a reason really, but suddenly they were really angry and if one of the teachers hadn't stepped in, who knows, there might have been some serious fighting. And it's not the first time something like this has happened.

Olivia: Uh huh. So what did the psychologist do?

Jackson: Well, the first thing he taught us was that conflicts and disagreements are a normal part of life ...

Olivia: Right.

Answers
1 That fighting amongst US teenagers is increasingly seen as an accceptable way to resolve disputes.
2 He thinks the programme works well, and he likes it.
3 Two boys who got into a fight in the lunch queue.
4 That they are a normal part of life.

c ▶ CD2 T14 Read through the instructions with the class and check understanding. Play the recording and ask students to put the steps in the correct order. Check answers. You may want to play the recording again, pausing as necessary for clarification.

TAPESCRIPT

Jackson: ... but they don't have to lead to violence. And then he told us about this six-step process for resolving conflicts. The first step is all about 'Setting the stage'.

Olivia: What does that mean?

Jackson: Well, the two kids who have a conflict have to agree that they will try to work together to find a peaceful solution, and accept certain ground rules, for example there is no name-calling, shouting, or interrupting. And of course the whole class takes part in this process.

Olivia: So what's the second step?

Jackson: It's called 'Gathering perspectives'. Each person describes the conflict from his or her perspective or point of view, without interruption. The other kids listen and then ask questions. In the conflict I mentioned, for example, it turned out that the two guys had been having similar problems for some time.

Olivia: Right. What about step three?

Jackson: Well, that's about 'Finding common interests'. Again, in this case, it turned out that neither of the boys actually likes violence at all.

Olivia: I see. What's the fourth step then?

Jackson: 'Creating options' – this is about taking time for each kid to try to think of solutions to the problem where both people gain something – think win–win!

Olivia: Win–win?

Jackson: Yeah. Too often we assume that for one person to win, the other person has to lose. But it's also possible to think creatively and come up with a solution that both people feel good about. What's important in this step is that you hear all the opinions, but nobody is allowed to say 'This doesn't work' or 'That's not a good idea.' That's all for the next step. In step five , we 'Evaluate options'. We all discuss the different solutions that have been suggested.

Olivia: And the final step?

Jackson: Is about 'Creating an agreement'. The kids involved agree what they will do to solve their conflict. And it's fascinating because conflicts can actually be positive – if we learn how to solve them, we understand others and ourselves better.

Olivia: So how did the two boys from the lunch line solve their conflict?

Jackson: Well, the solution was that the two of them became kind of assistants in the lunch break. They had to make sure that there were no more fights in the line. This meant there were far fewer conflicts, and a month later, because they had been working together so well, they actually became really good friends.

Answers
1 Set the stage 2 Gather perspectives
3 Find common interests 4 Create options
5 Evaluate options 6 Create an agreement

4 Grammar

✱ Past perfect continuous

a Look at the example with the class and focus on the verb *had been working*. Tell students that this tense is called the past perfect continuous. Draw attention to the form (*had + been + -ing*). Ask: *Did they work before or after they became friends?* (Before.) *Did their work happen at a particular time or was it an extended action?* (An extended action.) Students read through the rule and circle the correct options.

Answers
continuous, before

b Ask students to read quickly through the text in Exercise 1 to find another example of the past perfect continuous. Ask them which happened first – Alfred joining the company or the development of explosives (the development of explosives). Draw attention to the time expression *for many years* and point out that the action of developing explosives continued for an extended period of time.

Answer
When Alfred joined the Nobel family company, it had been developing explosives for many years.

c To clarify the difference between the past perfect and the past perfect continuous, write these sentences on the board:

I recognised the hotel. I had stayed there in 2004. When I arrived, I met Isobel. She had been staying at the hotel for a few days.

Point out that both forms of the past perfect refer to an event that happened earlier than another event in the past. Ask students if they can say why the second example is different from the first. Elicit the point that we use the past perfect continuous to express continuous or repeated activities up to a point in the past. Students work in pairs to read through the sentences and decide which is the correct verb form. During feedback, you may find it useful to draw a timeline on the board to show when different actions took place.

Answers
1 was going 2 had been travelling
3 had received 4 had been looking

d Students complete the sentences, using the correct tense. Ask them to compare answers with a partner before feedback.

Answers
1 had been sleeping 2 had been crying
3 was shopping 4 had been waiting
5 was crossing 6 had been thinking

Grammar notebook

Remind students to note down the rule for the past perfect continuous and to write a few examples of their own.

* OPTIONAL ACTIVITY

Divide the class into small groups. Read out the following situations and give the groups a short time to think of a reason for the situation. Their reason must include the past perfect continuous. Encourage them to use their imagination and give a point for the best idea.

Example: *Why was Sally standing at the bus stop looking angry?*

She had been waiting for twenty minutes.

1 *Why was Tony's face wet?*
2 *Why did Bill's feet hurt?*
3 *Why was Kate carrying two heavy bags?*
4 *Why were Ian's knees dirty?*
5 *Why did Sue have blue fingers?*

If students enjoy the activity, you could ask them to think of some different situations and ask the class.

5 Vocabulary

* Conflicts and solutions

Warm up

To introduce the topic, ask students if they have ever had a serious argument with one of their friends or a member of their family. Ask them to discuss with a partner. What was the argument about? Did they make friends again? Did they go to somebody else for advice? Listen to a few examples in open class.

a Read through the two sentences with students and ask them to fill the gaps. Make sure they understand that we *resolve a problem* or *find an answer/solution to a problem.*

Answers
resolve, find

b Tell students that they are going to read a page from a website which helps people resolve conflicts. Ask students to read the webpage and then to match the underlined expressions with the definitions. Students compare answers with a partner before feedback.

Answers
1 b 2 g 3 c 4 d 5 f 6 e 7 a 8 h

c ▶ CD2 T15 Ask students to complete the sentences, using the underlined expressions. Point out that they will need to change the form of some of the verbs. Play the recording for students to check their answers.

TAPESCRIPT/ANSWERS

1 He's a bit upset because he's fallen out with his best friend.
2 Can you help me with my maths homework? I keep getting stuck.
3 Let's reach a compromise. If you change your mind and let me go to the party, I'll be back by 11 o'clock instead of 12!
4 I get angry at home because my parents always take my brother's side.
5 The presidents of the two countries are meeting to try and resolve the conflict that started last month.
6 Annie can help you with any problems you've got. She's really good at sorting things out.
7 Haven't you and your brother made up yet? I'm tired of seeing the two of you fighting all the time!
8 There are many countries in the world that always stay neutral when a war starts.

Vocabulary bank

Refer students to the vocabulary bank. Read through the words and phrases in open class and check understanding.

Vocabulary notebook

Encourage students to start a new section called *Conflicts and solutions* in their notebook and to add these words. They may find it useful to note down translations, too.

OPTIONAL ACTIVITY

For further practice of the vocabulary in this exercise, photocopy and hand out the following sentence parts, or write them on the board. Ask students to match 1–6 with a–f.

1 *She's very good at creating problems*
2 *The only way to resolve this conflict*
3 *I'm trying to find a solution to this problem*
4 *Jane and Fred fell out again last week, and*
5 *Why do you always have to take someone's side?*
6 *They failed to end the argument because*

a *but I keep getting stuck.*
b *they only made up yesterday.*
c *Why can't you stay neutral?*
d *but not so good at sorting them out.*
e *they couldn't reach a compromise.*
f *is to find out who started it.*

Answers
1 d 2 f 3 a 4 b 5 c 6 e

6 Pronunciation

See notes on page 122.

7 Speak

Read the text with the class. In groups, students discuss ways of resolving the conflict. Ask different groups to present their solutions to the class and encourage others to comment and ask questions. Encourage the class to try to come to agreement about the best way of resolving the problem.

OPTIONAL ACTIVITY

If you have a strong class, you could ask pairs to write a dialogue between Evie and Jake, first arguing and then resolving their conflict. Invite different pairs to act out their dialogue for the class.

Literature in mind

8 Read

If you set the background information as a homework research task, ask the students to tell the class what they found out.

BACKGROUND INFORMATION

Jane Austen: (1775–1817) was born in Hampshire, England. She wrote six classic novels between 1811 and 1817: *Sense and Sensibility, Pride and Prejudice, Mansfield Park, Emma, Northanger Abbey* and *Persuasion*. Her work is recognised for its definition of character and the insights it offers into the 18th-century middle and upper classes. Her books are still extremely popular throughout the world. In a major BBC poll in 2005, *Pride and Prejudice* was voted the second most popular British novel (first was *The Lord of the Rings* by J.R.R. Tolkien). The photo on this page is from the 2005 film of *Pride and Prejudice* starring Keira Knightley and Matthew Macfadyen.

a Ask students if they have heard of Jane Austen. Tell them they are going to read an extract from one of her novels, *Pride and Prejudice*. Students look at the cover of the book and read the summary of the story to decide if they think they would like to read the book. Discuss students' ideas and help with vocabulary if necessary.

b ▶ CD2 T17 Ask students to read the extract. Tell them it includes some difficult language and encourage them not to worry about the meaning of individual words. Play the recording while students read the extract for a second time and complete the exercise. Allow them to compare answers with a partner before checking answers in open class. Play the recording again, pausing as necessary to clarify language.

Answers
1 hastily 2 with composure 3 heightened 4 to rejoice 5 spared me the concern 6 might have been suppressed 7 perfectly comprehend 8 tempted me to accept it

Discussion box

In pairs or small groups, students go through the questions in the box and discuss them. Monitor and help as necessary, encouraging students to express themselves in English and to use any vocabulary they have learned from the text. Ask pairs or groups to feedback to the class and discuss any interesting points further.

OPTIONAL ACTIVITY

Divide the class into pairs. Ask students to use their own words to 'translate' the extract into more simple language. Tell them that they should try to explain the meaning without repeating any of the words in the text. As feedback, work together as a group to create a modern English version of the extract.

9 Write

The planning for this exercise can be done in class and the writing can be set as homework.

a Ask students to read the text quickly and match the paragraphs (1–4) to the topics (a–d).

Answers
a 4 b 2 c 3 d 1

b Students read the last paragraph of the text again and discuss the writer's admiration for Aung San Suu Kyi.

Possible answers
The writer admires her because she has acted with great courage for the good of her people, although this was dangerous for her personally. She held on to her ideals and tried to achieve them through peaceful means. The writer describes what is special about Aung San Suu Kyi and shows how her behaviour and beliefs fit with the values that he/she believes in.

c Students think of somebody that they admire. Read through the notes with the class and tell students to plan their composition using the same paragraph structure as in the sample text. Encourage them to think about why they admire the person they have chosen and to express this in the final paragraph. This task could be extended into a class presentation, with students putting their writing on the walls, passing them round for cross-reading or giving oral presentations based on their texts.

Memo from Mario

Peacemakers

1 Both of us

- Write on the board: *By the time we were 15 both of us had… neither of us had…* (Choose a suitable age for your group.)
- Put the students in pairs to complete both sentences in as many ways as they can. They should ask each other questions to establish what they have in common. After a few minutes, get the students to mingle to see if anyone else has any of the same sentences. Ask some students to report back on the most interesting things they found out about their partners.

RATIONALE
This activity should produce a great deal of grammar practice without the main focus being on grammar. The language is being used to find out what students have in common. This can also help to build relationships within the group.

2 Continuous dictation

- Choose a short passage to dictate to your students. There is an example below.
- Put the students in groups of three. Ask them to choose one person to act as secretary for the group. This person must remain seated and is the only one allowed to write.
- The other two members of the group are to listen to your reading, memorise what they can and then go back and dictate it to the secretary. You should be far away enough from the secretaries for them not to be able to hear you.
- Start reading the passage in a fairly quiet voice. Read the passage over and over. You will have to concentrate quite hard to keep your reading natural!

The staff of a friend's small hotel wanted a pay rise. They demanded twenty per cent but the talks got stuck when my friend offered only two. I was called in to try to sort things out when they all refused to compromise. Obviously I couldn't take sides – a referee has to remain neutral if he wants to resolve an argument – but I felt my friend was being too hard. When I said so, we fell out over it and nearly got into a physical fight. In the end, the staff were happy with twelve per cent, but it was months before my friend and I made up again.

RATIONALE
Cooperation is the key to this activity. It also makes a dictation exercise more interesting.

3 My hero stories

- As a follow-up activity to the writing in exercise 9c, ask the students to tell a partner about the person they wrote about. They should not read out what they have written, but tell the story, maybe using the notes they wrote before completing their essay. Tell them that they will be repeating the stories they hear to another student. If you decide to allow the listeners to make notes, they should not be more than one or two key words.
- When they finish telling each other, they should change partners and tell their new partner what they heard from the first. Then they tell a third partner about what they heard from the second, so that many students in the group hear about the people other students have written about.

RATIONALE
Knowing that they are going to re-tell the story to another student makes for attentive listening. Sharing stories like this gives the writer a wider audience.

8 Kindness matters

Unit overview

TOPIC: Kindness

TEXTS

Reading and listening: an article called The Kindness Offensive

Listening: people talking about special presents; song 'Put a Little Love in Your Heart'

Writing: a summary

SPEAKING AND FUNCTIONS

Talking about kindness

Talking about the best presents you've ever got

Discussing birthdays and presents

LANGUAGE

Grammar: dummy *it*; modal verbs review

Vocabulary: making an effort

Pronunciation: linking sounds: intrusive /w/ and /j/

1 Read and listen

If you set the background information as a homework research task, ask the students to tell the class what they found out.

BACKGROUND INFORMATION

The Kindness Offensive began in September 2008. Its purpose is to 'Practise random kindness and senseless acts of beauty'. They have had extensive media coverage in the UK. Their YouTube channel received more than two million hits in its first few months of operation.

Moscow State Circus is a group of mainly Russian circus performers based in the UK. They tour regularly in the UK and abroad. The current circus production consists of a cast of twenty-five performers, including clowns, trapeze artists, aerial acrobats, jugglers and contortionists.

Wembley Stadium is a football stadium in London. Since 1923 it has been home to the England football team and the FA Cup is played there. The stadium was rebuilt in 2007 at a cost of £798 million.

Warm up

Books closed. Ask students to write down the names of two people they know who are kind, i.e. people who always try to help others and make other people happy. Ask them to think of examples of kind actions that these people have done. They could discuss their answers in pairs or small groups. Listen to a few examples in open class.

a Ask students to look at the photo on page 60 and answer the questions, guessing what the situation might be. Students read through the text quickly to check their answers. Tell them not to worry about the meaning of every word, but to concentrate on the task.

b ▶ CD2 T18 Read the questions with the class. Play the recording. Students read and listen to the text and then answer the questions. If needed, play the recording again, pausing as necessary to clarify vocabulary and help with comprehension. Let students check their answers with a partner before open class feedback.

TAPESCRIPT

See the reading text on page 60 of the Student's Book.

Answers

1 They live in North London.
2 They carry out random acts of kindness for total strangers.
3 He thinks people are taught to mistrust each other.
4 People didn't think they were genuine.
5 They think they are treated badly.

OPTIONAL ACTIVITY

Students work in pairs and think of a random act of kindness that they can do at some point over the next few days. In a subsequent lesson, ask students if they have done their act of kindness and how it was received.

Discussion box

In pairs or small groups, students discuss the questions. Monitor and help as necessary, encouraging them to express themselves in English and to use any vocabulary they have learned from the text. Ask pairs or groups to feedback to the class and discuss any interesting points further.

2 Grammar

Dummy *it*

a Ask students to look back at the text in Exercise 1 to complete the sentences. During feedback, write the sentences on the board and ask students what *it* refers to in each one. Point out that *it* in these sentences refers to something which comes later in the sentence. We usually use *it* to refer to something which has come before.

Answers
1 It is, to
2 It is, to

b Students match the two parts of the sentences to make statements that they agree with. Give students an example of your own to get them started and make it clear that many different answers are possible. Let students compare answers with a partner and listen to a few examples in open class as feedback.

Answers
Students' own answers

c Look at the example with the class and point out the structure of the sentence (*It's / It isn't* + adjective + *to* + infinitive). Ask students to transform the other sentences, using the same structure. Check answers.

Answers
2 It's fun to be kind to people.
3 It's important to help other people.
4 It's crazy to give things to people for free!
5 It's normal to be a bit suspicious sometimes.

d **Weaker classes:** To help students think of examples, write these words on the board: *transport, clubs, sport, cinemas, music, shops.* Ask students questions about the facilities in the town where they live (e.g. *Is it easy to get from one place to another? Is it difficult to find a music shop? Is it normal to go to clubs at the weekend?*). Then follow the procedure for stronger classes.

Stronger classes: Ask students to write some sentences describing the place where they live using the structure *It ... to ...* Ask them to read their answers to a partner before listening to some examples in open class and comparing opinions. If students dislike certain things, they may enjoy discussing possible ways of improving them.

Grammar notebook

Remind students to note down the rules for this structure and to write a few examples of their own.

OPTIONAL ACTIVITY

For further practice of dummy *it*, write these sentence openings on the board and ask students to work in pairs and complete them. Listen to some of their ideas in open class as feedback.

1 *It's hard ...*
2 *It's easy ...*
3 *It's difficult ...*
4 *It's horrible ...*
5 *It's exciting ...*

3 Vocabulary

Making an effort

a Ask students to find the expressions in the text which match the definitions. As you check answers, ask students questions to ensure they are clear about the meaning of the expressions, e.g. *When do you go to great lengths? How do you know if someone is doing something half-heartedly?* Say the expressions and ask students to repeat them.

Answers
1 goes to great lengths
2 a bit half-hearted
3 struggling
4 trial and error
5 find it easy
6 get a lot out of it
7 do it properly

b Students complete the text with the expressions from Exercise 3a. Point out that they may need to change the form of some verbs to make them grammatically correct.

Answers
1 struggled
2 half-hearted
3 didn't find it easy
4 go to great lengths
5 trial and error
6 did ... properly
7 get a lot out of

c Students discuss their learning experiences using the expressions in Exercise 3b. To get them started, you may like to give an example of the way you learned something. Encourage students to correct each other's sentences if necessary. Ask a few pairs to tell the class about their partner's answers.

OPTIONAL ACTIVITY

It is very useful to carry out a needs analysis on your students. To find out how they feel about various aspects of the language, write these words on the board: *grammar, vocabulary, spelling, pronunciation.* To find out how they feel about classroom activities, write this: *listen to recordings, read texts, speak to partners, repeat words,* etc. Ask students to use the structure *It ... to ...* and the vocabulary from Exercise 3 to make sentences, e.g. *It's hard to learn phrasal verbs. I struggle to understand listening texts.* When students have thought of some sentences, ask them to discuss their opinions in small groups, then expand into an open class discussion.

Vocabulary bank

Refer students to the vocabulary bank. Read through the words and phrases in open class and check understanding.

Vocabulary notebook

Encourage students to start a new section called *Making an effort* in their notebook and to add these expressions. They may find it useful to note down translations, too.

4 Pronunciation

See notes on page 123.

5 Listen and speak

a Ask students to describe what they can see in the photos. Students complete the sentences with the verbs in the box. Then ask them to match two sentences with each photo. Don't check answers yet.

Answers
1 lend 2 learning 3 got 4 had 5 making 6 kept
Football shirt: Sentences 4, 6
Bicycle: Sentences 1, 3
Guitar: Sentences 2, 5

b **CD2 T20** Tell students they are going to listen to three people talking about a special present that they remember. Students listen and check their answers to Exercise 5a.

TAPESCRIPT

Sally: A long time ago, when I was just a little girl aged about seven, my father came home one day and told us that we had to move house the next day – his company was sending him to work in another city, it was really urgent and we had to go straight away. He said we should start to pack our things and also say goodbye to people. I was really upset and the first thing I did was to go to the house next door where a little boy called Alan lived. I think Alan was about a year older than me but we had always been friends. I told him what was happening. He didn't say anything, he just turned round and went back into his house and he closed the door. I was even more unhappy! The next morning my mum, dad and I were putting things into the family car while the removal company were putting our furniture and everything into the lorry. Suddenly Alan came out of the house – he was carrying a football shirt, it had the colours of his favourite team and it was his favourite thing, and he gave it to me and told me to keep it. He said I should look at it every day. 'You'll always remember me when you look at it,' he said. And he ran away again. I kept it, for a long time, and I even wore it sometimes, but then I must have lost it somewhere, perhaps when we moved house again. I never saw Alan again and I guess now I'll never know what happened to him. But that shirt was one of the best presents I ever got.

Graham: A few years ago I was working in a small café as a waiter. I wasn't a very good waiter and it wasn't the work I really wanted to do but I was very poor. I didn't have a car, I had a bicycle, I used to go to work on it but then one day it got stolen and I couldn't buy another one, I just didn't have enough money , and I didn't know anyone who could lend me one either, so I had to walk. Well, the next day the café wasn't busy and I was telling the other waiter about the bicycle, then when I turned round there was an elderly couple there at the table and they asked me for two coffees. When I brought the coffees, they said that they'd heard me talking about the bike and they were sorry to hear about my problem. I just thought, 'Well, that's nice,' so I smiled and said thanks and then brought them their bill. When they'd finished, the man asked me if the bill included a tip. I said 'No', and he just said 'OK'. Another customer came in and I went to serve her. The couple left. When I went back to their table, I looked at the money and they'd left £150 on the table with a note saying 'Get yourself a new bike!' I ran to the door but they'd gone. I bought a bike with the money. The couple never came back to the café, so I never got to say 'Thank you' to them, but clearly they weren't worried about that. Amazingly kind – and probably the best present I ever got, it was so unexpected.

Eve: Well, on my tenth birthday my grandfather and grandmother gave me a guitar. I was really, really surprised when I got it. I just thought 'They must be joking! I don't want this!' – I mean, I had never, ever said that I wanted one or had ever said that I was interested in learning to play one. So I smiled sweetly and said 'Thank you very much' like my parents had always told me to do! And my grandmother smiled back and said: 'Try it. Who knows? You might like it.' I said 'OK, why not?' and my granny then just showed me how to play three chords on it, just very simple things. I thought it was really cool – it was me making those musical sounds! Then my dad got me a 'teach-yourself' book and I started playing more and more. Now I love it – I mean, I've never been any good really, and I never will be, I guess, but I still enjoy picking it up now and again and playing, it's so relaxing. And now the guitar reminds me of my grandparents too – so it was just a wonderful present.

c ▶ CD2 T20 Give students time to read through the sentences and check understanding. Play the recording again while students choose the correct answers. Students compare answers with a partner before feedback.

Answers
1 b 2 a 3 c 4 a 5 b 6 b

d Give students an example by describing in some detail a present which was special for you. Students think of the best present they have received and answer the three questions, making notes in preparation for the next exercise.

e In small groups, students talk about the best present they have received. Encourage students to describe their present without referring to their notes. Discuss any interesting answers in class.

6 Grammar

★ Modal verbs review

a Students read the sentences from the listening text. Draw attention to the pronouns in italics and ask students to try to remember which of the three presents they refer to. Remind students of the importance of using pronouns in sentences to avoid repetition of nouns.

Answers
2 G 3 S 4 G 5 S 6 B

b Write a few sentences with modal verbs on the board, e.g. *You must be tired. We should buy a new car. He couldn't speak English.* Ask students to identify the modal verbs and to think of some other examples. Remind students that a modal is always followed by the infinitive of another verb and that its form doesn't change. Ask students to circle the modal verbs in sentences 1–6 in Exercise 6a.

Answers
1 should 2 must 3 'll (will) 4 might
5 must 6 couldn't

Language note

Students may think that forms of *be, have* and *do* are modal verbs. These are auxiliary verbs and are used to form tenses. Modal verbs like *can, may, should,* etc. have no infinitive, no continuous form, no passive form, no *-s* ending for the third person singular. Questions are formed by inverting the modal and the subject *(Must I ...? Can we ...?)*. Students often make errors with modal verbs, so you may like to write these sentences on the board and ask students to tell you why they are wrong.

1 *I must to go.*
2 *I don't can come this evening.*
3 *Do I must do my homework now?*
4 *He cans play the piano.*

c Students work in pairs to match the sentences in Exercise 6a with the uses of the modal verb. Give them time to discuss their answers. Check answers and elicit other examples for some of the modals.

Answers
b 6 c 4 d 2 e 1 f 5

d Students choose the correct modal verb for each sentence. Ask them to compare answers with a partner. During feedback, encourage students to explain why the second option is not correct.

Answers
1 should 2 won't 3 can't 4 can
5 May 6 might 7 would 8 must

Grammar notebook

Remind students to note down the rules for this structure and to write a few examples of their own.

7 Speak

a Students complete the questions with a modal verb and check their answers with a partner before feedback in open class.

Answers
1 would 2 will 3 would/could 4 will

b Students work with a different partner and discuss the questions. In feedback, discuss the questions further with the whole class.

8 Speak and listen

If you set the background information as a homework research task, ask the students to tell the class what they found out.

BACKGROUND INFORMATION

Annie Lennox (born 1954) has been a popular singer since 1979 when she had her first hit with the Tourists. She had massive success with the Eurythmics in the 80s and 90s before going solo in 1992.

Al Green (born Arkansas, USA, 1946) is a soul singer and preacher. His most popular hits are 'Let's Stay Together' and 'I'm Still In Love With You'. He has sold more than 20 million records in his 40-year career.

a Tell students that they are going to listen to a song called 'Put A Little Love in Your Heart'. Ask them to read quickly through the lyrics and decide what the message of the song is.

Answer

3 Let's look after each other.

b ▶ CD2 T21 Play the recording while students listen and put the verses in the correct order. Students compare answers with a partner. Play the recording again.

TAPESCRIPT

See the song on page 64 of the Student's Book.

Answers

1 Think of your fellow man ...
2 You see it's getting late ...
3 And the world will be a better ...
4 Another day goes by ...
5 If you want the world to know ...
6 Take a good look around ...
7 I hope when you decide ...

c Read the sentence with students and check understanding. See if they can complete the sentence without looking back at the song. If not, students look back at the lyrics to complete the sentence.

Answer

wait and see

d Explain that there are several phrases in English which follow the verb and verb pattern. Read through the sentences and ask students to complete them. Check answers and elicit the meanings of the phrases.

Answers

1 go 2 think 3 take 4 pray

Did you know?

Read through the information in the box with the class. Ask students if they know any of the artists mentioned and invite them to give any interesting information they may know about them. Ask if they have seen any big concerts live or on TV.

9 More speaking

Warm up

Write on the board: *The world is perfect!* In open class, ask students if they think the statement is true. Why / Why not? Listen to some of their ideas and invite debate.

a Read through the sentences and check understanding. Divide the class into pairs and ask students to decide which of the statements they agree with. Listen to some of their ideas in open class.

b Ask students to write four more sentences. Remind them that they should use the past simple in the second part of the sentence. Circulate and help with vocabulary. Let students compare their sentences with a partner and discuss which are their best sentences.

c Ask individuals to read sentences in open class. Write any interesting ideas on the board and invite further discussion. Hold a class vote to decide on the best idea.

10 Write

a Ask students what they can remember from the text about 'The Kindness Offensive' in Exercise 1. Students read the summary quickly to get a general impression of its quality. Discuss their opinions in open class. Without going into details, they should recognise that the text is far too long and rambling to be a good summary and that the general effect is very confusing.

b Students read the summary again and check the questions. Point out that they should decide not only if the summary is factually correct, but also if the writer has focused on key points and used his/her own words. Discuss the summary in more detail and help students to identify some of the problems, for example:

- It isn't clear who, or what, 'The Kindness Offensive' actually is. While the information in the summary isn't factually wrong, it is not well organised and it lacks clarity.

- In paragraph 2, there is no mention of why they the four friends felt there was a need to start their organisation or of how they got it going. There is also too much unimportant information (e.g. about asylum seekers).
- In paragraph 3 the writer is not concise enough (e.g. 'to make themselves well-known or famous') and the repetition of the word 'people' three times in one sentence does not help with clarity.

c Tell students they are going to re-write the summary in Exercise 10a. Go through the guide with them to make sure they are aware of what needs to be included. If there is time, you may want to work through the first two steps of the guide with the class. Discuss the main ideas of the text together and write notes on the board. Then give students time to underline key points, and again give feedback before asking them to write their summary. Set a target length of about 150 words. Remind students to use their own words as far as possible and to use quotation marks if they quote directly from the text.

Language note

Quotation marks can be either double ("...") or single ('...'). Tell students that it doesn't matter which style they choose, but they should be consistent throughout their piece of writing.

OPTIONAL ACTIVITY

For further practice of summary writing, ask students to choose one of the longer reading texts from an earlier unit, and write a summary of it. Tell them they should write 150–200 words and use the guide in Exercise 10c to help them.

Check your progress

1 Grammar

a 2 had been eaten 3 had left 4 had been written 5 had seen

b 2 had been waiting 3 had eaten 4 had been sitting

c 2 would 3 May 4 can't 5 might

2 Vocabulary

a 2 f 3 a 4 e 5 b 6 c

b 2 error 3 lengths 4 struggled 5 heartedly 6 properly

How did you do?

Students work out their scores. Check how they have done and follow up any problem areas with revision work.

Memo from Mario

Kindness matters

1 Explain it

- After doing section 6, set up this situation: *You have arranged to study with a friend at his/her house. When you arrive at the set time, you find the windows of the house are open, the front door is closed, but when you ring the bell, nobody answers.* How can you explain this?
- Put the students in pairs or small groups to come up with as many explanations for this as possible. After a few minutes, ask each group to report their best reason to the class. Other students could question their logic or disagree, giving reasons. (*That's not possible, if ... had happened, ... would be...* etc.) You could also ask them what they would do in the situation.

Other possible situations:

A man driving a car runs through a red light.

A child is sitting on the pavement outside a shop, crying.

A man is sitting on the roof of his house, wearing pyjamas.

A car is parked in the middle of a football field.

RATIONALE
This activity can be serious or not, depending on the students. They have control. Their explanations require creative thinking and using the language as a means of expressing their ideas.

2 The happiness collector

- Write each sentence of this story on a separate slip of paper. There is another story below to use if you think your students will prefer it. You will need enough copies to give one slip to every student in the group. If the group is small, give students two or three slips.

A teacher asked a class of young students to do a project.

The project was to collect happiness.

After a week the children brought their projects to class.

Each child talked about what they had done.

One girl had brought a large paper sack with her.

She said, 'This is the result of my project.'

Everybody wanted to see what was in the sack.

But the girl didn't open the sack.

She only gave the teacher a small box.

The teacher opened the box.

She smiled.

The girl took out a camera.

She took a photo of the smiling teacher.

She put the camera in the sack.

Then she showed them what was in the box.

It was a picture of a smiling face.

She had discovered that when people see a smiling face, they smile.

- Mix up the slips and give them out. Tell the students that they should read their sentence, but must not show it to anyone else. They are to put the story into the correct order. Put the students in groups so that each group has the entire story. Ideally, they could stand in a circle and organise themselves in the same order as the sentences in the story.

An urban legend

Farmer Fleming was a poor Scottish farmer.

One day he heard a cry for help coming from a nearby bog. He ran to the bog.

There was a terrified boy struggling to free himself from the mud. Farmer Fleming saved the lad from what could have been a terrifying death.

The next day, a fancy carriage pulled up to the Scotman's poor house.

An elegantly dressed nobleman stepped out and introduced himself as the father of the boy Farmer Fleming had saved. 'I want to repay you,' said the nobleman. 'You saved my son's life.'

'No, I can't accept payment for what I did,' the Scottish farmer replied.

At that moment, the farmer's own son came to the door of the family hovel. 'Is that your son?' the nobleman asked.

'Yes,' the farmer replied proudly.

'I'll make you a deal. Let me take him and give him a good education. If the lad is anything like his father, he'll grow to a man you can be proud of.'

And that he did. In time, Farmer Fleming's son graduated from St Mary's Hospital Medical School in London.

He went on to become known throughout the world as the noted Sir Alexander Fleming, the discoverer of penicillin.

Years afterward, the nobleman's son was stricken with pneumonia. It was penicillin that saved him.

The name of the nobleman's son was Winston Churchill, who became prime minister of the United Kingdom.

Someone once said what goes around comes around.

RATIONALE
This activity requires some attentive listening and cooperation.

9 Language

Unit overview

TOPIC: Languages and translation

TEXTS

Reading and listening: an article about mistakes in translation; a text about artificial languages

Listening: a TV programme on different accents

Writing: a story called *Misunderstandings*

SPEAKING AND FUNCTIONS

Talking about language, accents and translation

Discussing the merits of artificial languages

LANGUAGE

Grammar: phrasal verbs review

Vocabulary: meanings of phrasal verbs; understanding language

Pronunciation: words ending in *–ough*

1 Read and listen

If you set the background information as a homework research task, ask the students to tell the class what they found out.

BACKGROUND INFORMATION

Tajikistan (population c. 7 million) is a country in Central Asia bordered by Afghanistan to the south, Uzbekistan to the west, Kyrgyzstan to the north and China to the east. It was part of the Soviet Union until it became independent in 1991. Mountains cover 90% of the country.

Swansea (population 169,880) is a coastal city in Wales, UK. It is the second most populous city in Wales after Cardiff. It was an industrial centre in the 19th century, famous for its copper factories. Swansea is the wettest city in the UK with an average of 67cm of rain a year.

Wales (population c. 3 million) is a country situated to the west of England, and forms part of the UK. It is a bilingual country with 20% of Welsh people speaking Welsh as well as English. This number has grown considerably in recent years. It was a major producer of coal until the late 20th century when the industry went into decline.

Warm up

You could introduce the topic by writing a list of ten or so words on the board, some of which are very similar in English and the native language of your students, others of which are false friends (words which look the same but actually have different meanings). Ask students to point out the false friends and ask them to imagine possible misunderstandings which could arise from their use. You may like to give them an example of your own to get them started. Listen to a few of their ideas in open class.

a Read the question and brainstorm ideas with the class.

b Check that students understand the instructions. Students read the article quickly and find the answers. You could set a two-minute time limit, encouraging a quick reading to focus on finding the information.

Answers

1 They used the word 'expensive' instead of 'dear'.
2 English and Welsh

c ▶ CD2 T22 Read through the sentences with students. Play the recording while students read. You could pause as necessary to check understanding and clarify any difficulties. Students answer the questions and compare answers with a partner before feedback in open class.

TAPESCRIPT

See the reading text on page 68 of the Student's Book.

Answers

1 Students' own answer.
2 You can choose the wrong translation.
3 By translating a sentence from your own language into another language, then translating it back into your own language.
4 They didn't speak Welsh and thought the reply was a translation of the English sign.

Discussion box

In pairs or small groups, students discuss the questions. Monitor and help as necessary, encouraging them to express themselves in English and to use any vocabulary they have learned from the text. Ask pairs or groups to feedback to the class and discuss any interesting points further.

OPTIONAL ACTIVITY

If you have a monolingual class, choose a text in their native language and translate it badly into English. Ask students to work in pairs and decide what the original text was. Show them the original text and ask them to translate it. Allow them to use dictionaries and remind them not to make the same mistakes as in your badly translated version.

2 Grammar

Phrasal verbs review

a Remind the class that phrasal verbs have two or more parts and give a few familiar examples. Ask students to look at the text in Exercise 1 again and underline all the phrasal verbs they can find. Ask them to look at the verbs in their context and to match eight of them with definitions 1–8. Check answers.

Answers
1 bring about 2 looked up 3 went for
4 get away with 5 find out 6 taken off
7 come up with 8 came across

LOOK!

Read through the information with the class, looking carefully at the examples. Point out that there is no rule to help us decide whether a phrasal verb is separable or not. It is up to students to make a note of whether a phrasal verb is separable or inseparable every time they learn a new one. If they aren't sure about this, a good dictionary will tell them if a verb is separable or not.

b Students decide whether the verbs are separable or not. Tell them to look back at the text for help and to use dictionaries where necessary. Check answers.

Answers
1 bring about B 2 looked up B 3 went for A
4 get away with C 5 find out B
6 taken off A 7 come up with C
8 came across A

Language note

The verb *take off* is inseparable if it means 'to rise' (e.g. *sales took off, the plane took off*). However, it is separable when it means 'to remove clothes' (e.g. *I took off my jacket / I took my jacket off*). Other meanings of *take off* are covered in Exercise 3.

c Students put the words in order to make sentences. Go through the example and point out the alternative answer in sentence 5. Ask students whether *give back* is separable or inseparable (separable). Check answers.

Answers
2 He always gets away with not studying.
3 She came up with a great plan.
4 They have brought about many changes.
5 Her career as a translator is taking off / Her career is taking off as a translator.

Grammar notebook

Remind students to note down the rules for phrasal verbs and to write a few examples of their own.

OPTIONAL ACTIVITY

For further practice of the phrasal verbs in this exercise, divide the class into pairs and ask them to write a story using as many of the phrasal verbs as possible. Encourage them to use other phrasal verbs that they know. Give students time to write their stories, but do not offer any help at this stage. Ask them to leave a space between each line of their story for corrections. When the stories are complete, display them around the classroom and ask students to circulate and read the stories. Tell students to correct any errors they find. Monitor and help with any queries. Give stories back to students and invite some of them to read their stories to the group.

3 Vocabulary

Meanings of phrasal verbs

Remind students that some phrasal verbs (e.g. *take off*) can have more than one meaning and that, depending on the meaning, the verb may be separable or inseparable. Read through the sentences with the class. Elicit the meaning of *take off* in each sentence and ask whether the verb is separable or inseparable.

Possible answers
1 started going well (inseparable)
2 imitating (someone) to make fun of them (separable)
3 leaving the ground (inseparable)

4 Pronunciation

See notes on page 123.

5 Listen

If you set the background information as a homework research task, ask the students to tell the class what they found out.

BACKGROUND INFORMATION

Birmingham (population c. one million) is a city in the West Midlands area of England. It is famous for industry and manufacturing, and is the birthplace of heavy metal music and bands like Black Sabbath and Led Zeppelin.

Liverpool (population 444,500) in northwest England became the largest British port, after London, in the 18th and 19th centuries. It is well known as the home of The Beatles and Liverpool Football Club. The word *Scouse* is believed to come from a German sailors' dish called *Labskaus*.

Newcastle (population 269,500) is in the northeast of England, once famous for its shipbuilding industry. Geordie dialect words have origins in Norse and Old English and the Geordie accent is one of the strongest in Britain – many people find it difficult to understand.

Manchester (population 437,000) is a centre of the arts, the media, higher education and big business. The city is world-famous for its sport, being home to Manchester United and Manchester City football clubs.

Glasgow (population 629,500) is the largest Scottish city and the commercial, business and industrial centre of Scotland. Standard Scottish sounds very different from standard English, and in addition there are local dialects spoken in different parts of the country, including Glaswegian.

Estuary English is a term first used in 1984 to describe an accent used in London and southeast England. This style of speech is spreading across southern England and many other local accents are slowly disappearing.

Warm up

Ask students if they think there is a strong local accent in their part of their country. Does their accent sound different from those of TV news presenters or political leaders? Do they know of any local words and expressions that are used only in their own area/region or only by certain groups of people? Discuss these questions with the class and elicit examples if possible.

a **CD2 T25** Look at the map of the UK, say the names of the cities and ask students to repeat them. Tell them they are going to listen to the beginning of a TV programme about local accents. Play the recording. Students listen and draw lines to match the accents with the cities.

TAPESCRIPT

Presenter: Hello, and welcome to the show. The first thing we're going to talk about this week is accents. Regional accents are still very much a part of British life. From Estuary English in parts of London to Brummie in Birmingham, people around the country pronounce words in different ways. Just ask people to say a word like *bath*, and in most places in the south you'll hear it said with a long 'a' – *bath*, like *car* – while in the north, it's generally pronounced with a short 'a' – *bath*, like *cat*.

Sometimes, of course, people use quite different words altogether. Up in Newcastle, where people speak with a Geordie accent, you'll hear people talk about a *canny ganzy* instead of a *nice pullover*, while in places around Manchester and Liverpool, *shorts* become *keks*. And talking of Liverpool, who hasn't heard the Scouse accent that The Beatles made famous around the world in the 1960s? In Scouse, some vowel sounds that you'll hear down south hardly exist, so that *fairy* and *furry* are pronounced almost identically.

Accents are a really important part of people's lives and their personal identities, and many people are very proud of the way they speak. That's certainly true of people in Manchester who speak Mancunian English, and in Glasgow where they speak Glaswegian. But accents can cause some problems too. We asked John Cooper, our favourite Brummie, to talk to some teenagers about their accents. This is what they had to say ...

Answers

1 Brummie: Birmingham
2 Scouse: Liverpool
3 Geordie: Newcastle
4 Mancunian: Manchester
5 Estuary English: London
6 Glaswegian: Glasgow

Language note

Students may have heard the word *cockney* and think this refers to the dialect or accent used throughout London. In reality, *cockney* is a term for a working-class person in the East End of London and the cockney accent is quite different from Estuary English spoken by many Londoners. Students may be interested to hear about cockney rhyming slang, in which words are replaced by rhyming words. Examples include *Can I have a butcher's*? (butcher's hook = look) and *I haven't got any bread* (bread and honey = money).

b **▶ CD2 T25** Make sure students are clear about the difference between *accent* and *dialect*. Play the recording again while students listen and find examples. Students discuss their answers with a partner before feedback. Play the recording again, pausing for clarification if necessary. Check answers.

Answers

1 *Bath* is pronounced /bɑːθ/ in the south and /bæθ/ in the north. *Fairy* and *furry* sound the same in Liverpool.
2 They say *a canny ganzy* in Newcastle to mean *a nice pullover* and they say *keks* in Liverpool to mean *shorts*.

LOOK!

Draw students' attention to the adjectives commonly used to describe accents. Go through them with the class and elicit the meanings. Note that *a heavy accent* and *a strong accent* mean the same.

c **▶ CD2 T26** Draw attention to the names and photos of the four speakers. Explain that these people will be using different UK accents on the recording – it may not be easy to understand them because of variations in their pronunciation. Play the recording. Students read, listen and write the name of the city for each speaker. During feedback, ask where the presenter comes from (*Birmingham*).

TAPESCRIPT

Presenter: Hi there! Well, as Andy said, this week's topic is regional accents. I've got a slight accent myself of course – everyone has. Mine's from Birmingham. And what's interesting is that maybe 30 years ago I wouldn't have got the job on this show because of my accent! So, attitudes have changed. But how much? We've invited a few people in to talk to us about their accents and what they feel about them. First of all, here's Marie from Dundee in Scotland.

Marie: Hi.

Presenter: Marie, tell us how you feel about your accent.

Marie: Well, I'm really proud of it! It's absolutely part of who I am. I'm Scottish and I'm happy about that. And of course I don't notice it, I mean everyone where I live speaks like me of course, so, you know, it's just me.

Presenter: Have you ever had any problems?

Marie: You mean people not understanding me?

Presenter: Yeah, that kind of thing.

Marie: Not really. Except a few years ago when I was in London and once or twice people didn't get what I said. But these days everyone's got a different accent and I think people in Britain accept that. You hear all kinds of different accents now on TV, like you said, so I don't think accents matter any more in Britain, really.

Presenter: OK, thank you, Marie. Now, let's bring in Patrick, he's from Dublin. Patrick, do you feel the same way as Marie?

Patrick: Oh yeah, a hundred per cent. I mean, as far as being proud is concerned. Well, I'm not sure if 'proud' is the right word, but certainly my accent is part of me and I never want to change it. Erm, I have had a little problem, though, nothing much.

Presenter: Oh?

Patrick: Yeah, I grew up in Ireland, but about three years ago our family moved to London and so I started in a new school and one or two of the other kids, I mean not many, they gave me a bit of a hard time at first, but it didn't last. You know, they just laughed a bit when I spoke – they said I was incomprehensible! It didn't last too long, though.

Presenter: Didn't hurt you?

Patrick: Sorry, I didn't catch that.

Presenter: I mean, you didn't get upset at all, they didn't hurt you?

Patrick: Oh, no! No, it was no big deal really.

Presenter: OK, thank you. Now, next we've got Tina – she's from London, and Tina, you've got a slightly different story, right?

Tina: A little, yeah. Erm, well, as you can tell I'm from the East End of London, that's where I'm from, and erm, I left school actually about two years ago when I was 16 and I wanted to get a job and I'm pretty sure that at least one job I didn't get because of my accent.

Presenter: Oh, and why's that?

Tina: Well, I don't know for sure – but I wanted to work as a shop assistant in a West End store, and it was quite a posh place, you know, selling really expensive clothes in an expensive part of London, and I wrote and they invited me for an interview, and as soon as I said hello I could see, you know, they didn't like the way I spoke, and the interview lasted about five minutes and they wrote a week later saying 'No thanks'.

Presenter: Did they say why?

Tina: Yeah, they said I didn't have experience. Well, of course I didn't have experience, I was only 16 and I'd just left school. So why did they interview me? I just think they were lying.

Presenter: So are you going to change how you speak?

Tina: No way, no!

Presenter: Good for you. And now from Liverpool we've got John. What's your view about all this, John?

John: Well, I think what everyone's said is very interesting. Erm, I think in Liverpool when I leave school, if I want to get a job I won't have any problems because almost everyone's got the same accent. Err, maybe I'd have a problem if I went somewhere else, London or somewhere, I don't know.

Presenter: Is your accent important to you?

John: Not especially. I mean, it's OK, I'm not ashamed of my accent. But it could change. You know, if I went and lived somewhere else, it'd probably change a bit. You have to fit in, don't you? I mean, if I went to live in Australia or something, I might lose my accent. I mean, after a few years I'm sure I'd be speaking differently, maybe a kind of mixture of Liverpool and Australia!

Presenter: Well, that would be different! OK. Now, can I ask you all ...

Answers
1 Marie: Dundee (Scotland) 2 Patrick: Dublin
3 Tina: London 4 John: Liverpool

d ▶ CD2 T26 Read through the sentences with the class. Ask students if they can remember any of the answers without listening again. Play the recording again. Students listen, complete the sentences and compare answers with a partner. Play the recording once again to check, pausing at the answers.

Answers
1 Patrick 2 John 3 Tina 4 Tina
5 Presenter 6 Marie 7 John 8 Marie

Discussion box

In pairs or small groups, students discuss the questions. Monitor and help as necessary, encouraging them to express themselves in English and to use any vocabulary they have learned from the text. Ask pairs or groups to feedback to the class and discuss any interesting points further.

6 Vocabulary

✱ Understanding language

a ▶ CD2 T27 Tell students that all the expressions in this exercise are to do with understanding or not understanding what somebody has said. Ask them to read the sentences and choose the correct words to complete them. If they aren't sure of some answers, ask them to guess and to check any new words in a dictionary if they have time. You could tell them to cover the table in Exercise 6b while they complete the sentences. Play the recording for students to check their answers.

TAPESCRIPT/ANSWERS

1 They don't speak English, so of course they didn't understand a word of what I said.
2 He spoke so fast, we just couldn't understand anything. It was totally incomprehensible!
3 Sorry, could you repeat what you just said? I didn't catch it.
4 He's speaking so quietly that I can't make out anything at all.
5 I caught the drift of what she said, but I certainly didn't understand everything.
6 My German is so poor now that I managed to pick a few words out but that was all.
7 I got the gist of it – you know, the general meaning – but no details at all.
8 I don't understand computers, so he lost me completely after about two sentences!

b Check that students understand the words in the table. Ask them to complete the table, using the words in the box. Check answers.

Answers
1 drift 2 pick 3 catch 4 word 5 lost

c In pairs, students complete the dialogues. Point out that there is more than one possible answer for each sentence. Ask students to practise saying the dialogues in pairs.

Possible answers
1 understood
2 can't make out
3 understood/got a lot of what
4 get / catch / pick out a few words
5 understood/got/caught the gist
6 lost me / was totally incomprehensible

Vocabulary bank

Refer students to the vocabulary bank. Read through the words and phrases in open class and check understanding.

Vocabulary notebook

Encourage students to start a new section called *Understanding language* in their notebook and to add these expressions. They may find it useful to note down translations, too.

7 Listen and speak

a ▶ CD2 T28 Write *Australia, Canada, India* and *Jamaica* on the board, and ask students if they can think of something that the countries have in common. Establish that they are all English-speaking, and ask students if they can say why this is so (They all used to belong to the British Empire). Explain that in this listening they will hear four people speaking about their countries in their national accents. Play the recording. Students discuss which country speakers are from.

TAPESCRIPT

Speaker 1: Hi, I'm Meg. I don't know if you know much about my country – you've probably never been there, I guess, it's a long way from most other places! I'll tell you what I really like about living there – I live down in Sydney, down in the south – and that's the climate. I mean, we just have really, really nice weather almost all year round and it means you can get outside a lot and go to the beach and just do lots of things without being stuck inside, know what I mean? I mean, there are other good things about Australia too, of course there are, but that's what I like best, the weather. I just love the fact that you can have barbecues all year round.

Speaker 2: I hope you can understand everything I'm saying OK, because English isn't my first language. My first language is Hindi – it's the language of Delhi, the city where I live – but I speak English quite a lot too. We used to speak English a lot when I was at school and it's a language we use quite a lot here in India because it's such a big country and there are so many different languages here – Urdu, Tamil, Gujarati, Punjabi and so on. There are so many languages it's impossible for anyone to understand anyone else, so some newspapers and things are in English but it isn't the first language here in India by any means. If you look at the films, for example, they're never in English, they're always in one of the Indian languages.

Speaker 3: I live in Vancouver, BC. It's a pretty cosmopolitan place, Vancouver – there are people there from all parts of the world, so you see all kinds of different faces and hear all kinds of different languages too. Mostly that's because of immigration, of course. There are lots of immigrants here from Vietnam and Hong Kong and places like that. A lot of people think that because Vancouver's in Canada, the second language must be French, but it isn't – the second language here is Chinese. That's because there are so many people here from Hong Kong. Everything here is written in English and French because that's the law in Canada, but you'll only hear French spoken over on the east coast, in Quebec and Montreal.

Speaker 4: I live in the land of sun and great music! But that's not all – here in Jamaica we love cricket too. You can see people playing cricket all over the place – on the beaches, in the streets, in yards – they don't need a special place, anywhere is good enough, especially for the small boys who want to play when they're not in school. And of course in Kingston there's a stadium, it's called Sabina Park, where they play the Test matches – that's the international matches if you don't know much about cricket – and me, I just love going there to watch and to listen to the people playing the steel drums and shouting and things, it's just the best atmosphere in the world, man!

Answers
1 Australia 2 India 3 Canada 4 Jamaica

b ▶ **CD2 T28** Play the recording again. You could pause after each speaker to give students time to make a brief note of the topic. Emphasise that they should listen for the main points, without including details. If necessary, play the recording a third time.

Possible answers
1 The weather/climate is very good in Sydney.
2 In India there are lots of languages. English is spoken by most people, but not as a first language.
3 Vancouver is very cosmopolitan. Chinese (not French) is the second language.
4 In Jamaica they love playing and watching cricket.

c Give students time to compare answers with a partner or in a small group before pooling information in open class. Students discuss the four speakers' accents. Encourage them to use expressions from Exercise 6b to help them describe how much they understood.

Culture in mind

8 Read

If you set the background information as a homework research task, ask the students to tell the class what they found out.

BACKGROUND INFORMATION

Ludovic Lazarus (Ludwik Lejzer Zamenhof, 1859–1917) was a Jewish Polish eye doctor and scholar who created the international language Esperanto. He grew up in a multilingual family and he spoke seven languages fluently (Russian, Hebrew, German, French, Latin, Greek and English).

Steven Spielberg (born 1946) is a famous film director. His most famous films are *ET, Jaws, Close Encounters of the Third Kind* and the *Indiana Jones* films. In *Close Encounters of the Third Kind,* aliens visit the Earth and communicate using Solresol.

Marc Okrand (born 1948) is an American linguist who invented the Klingon language for the *Star Trek* series of films. He has written an opera using Klingon and plans to stage Shakespeare in Klingon!

Star Trek III is the third of eleven *Star Trek* films based on the adventures of the crew of the Starship Enterprise, who sail around outer space having fantastic adventures. *Star Trek* was originally a TV series in the 1960s.

Warm up

Ask students if there are any words which they often translate wrongly, for example by adapting a word from their own language and hoping it will be the same in English. Give some examples of your own if possible. Invite them to tell the class about any particularly good or funny examples.

a Look at the title of the text and ask students what they think an artificial language is. Listen to some of their ideas. Ask students to read through the text quickly and find out what happened on the four dates. Encourage them not to worry about every difficult word, but to concentrate on the task. Allow students to compare answers with a partner before feedback.

Answers

1 The first Esperanto journal was published.
2 Solresol was invented.
3 Solresol was used in the film *Close Encounters of the Third Kind.*
4 Klingon was invented.

b **▶ CD2 T29** Read through the questions with students. Play the recording while students read, pausing where necessary to check comprehension and deal with difficult vocabulary: *barrier, overcome, estimates, vary.* Students answer the questions and compare answers with a partner before open class feedback.

Answers

1 It can be a source of miscommunication.
2 Esperanto and Klingon
3 Estimates vary between 1 million and 15 million.
4 Eastern Europe
5 Sosomi
6 Because it was difficult to learn
7 A small number of people
8 Its vocabulary is centred on Klingon concepts and it doesn't have some simple everyday words.

Discussion box

In pairs or small groups, students discuss the questions. Monitor and help as necessary, encouraging them to express themselves in English and to use any vocabulary they have learned from the text. Ask pairs or groups to feedback to the class and discuss any interesting points further.

9 Write

The planning for this exercise can be done in class and the story can be set as homework.

a Ask students to look at the title and picture and describe what they see. Can they guess what the story is going to be about? Students read the text to find out which two words or expressions were misunderstood. Tell them not to worry about the gaps in the text, but just to follow the basic events of the story. Check answers.

Answers

keks (= shorts),
Black Vanilla (= cola and ice cream)

b Check that students understand the words in the box. Point out that they are adverbs or adverbial phrases and that they are used to describe how actions take place. Students complete the text. During feedback, point out that adverbs / adverbial phrases are especially useful in a narrative, as they help to make the actions more lively and dramatic.

Answers

1 suddenly 2 immediately / unfortunately
3 desperately / in a panic 4 Unfortunately
5 In a panic / Desperately 6 easily / immediately 7 Fortunately 8 exactly

d Tell students that they are going to write their own story with the title *Misunderstandings.* Ask students to take some time to think of an incident (real or fictional), then to make notes of the main events of the story and to plan three or four paragraphs. Encourage them to use adverbs / adverbial phrases. Give them as much time as possible for planning in class. Monitor and check their progress. In a subsequent lesson, ask students to read each other's stories and give each other feedback.

Memo from Mario

Language

1 Find another meaning

- You will need an advanced learner's dictionary for each pair of students. Give each pair two sentences including phrasal verbs. If you have more than 10 students, divide up into groups.
- Ask each pair to look up the phrasal verb in the dictionary to find another meaning. They should then write a sentence using the phrasal verb with the new meaning. (If they find more than one alternative meaning, they could write more than one sentence.)
- Now get the students to pass their new sentence to another pair who should try to work out the meaning without using the dictionary.

  Here are some possible starting sentences:

  Can I put up with you next weekend?

  She never gets away with copying off the internet.

  Come round to my house after class.

  The car pulled up at the garage.

  She made up her face before going out.

  How well do you get on with your parents?

  Go through his computer and see if you can find any evidence.

  Take out your books and turn to page 5.

  This thing is dangerous, it could go off at any minute.

  The day cleared up after the rain.

RATIONALE

This activity provides practice in dictionary use and raises awareness of the range of possible meanings and uses of phrasal verbs.

2 Translating ambiguity

- If you have an OHP available, you could write all these sentences on a transparency and show them one at a time for about five seconds, masking the other sentences. If not, write the first sentence on the board. Ask the students to translate it. Write as quickly as you can and tell the students they have only 15 seconds to write their translation. Clean it off the board before writing the next sentence. Then continue with the other sentences, cleaning the board after each one.
- You should not warn the students that the sentences can have more than one meaning. It is important to write the sentences because when spoken intonation can give one meaning or the other.

  The cat feels cold.

  He has no ties at all.

  Visiting relatives can be boring.

  Her mother made her dress.

  Angela likes music more than her brother.

  We didn't go to the museum because it was raining.

  There will be a meeting on bicycles in Room 42 at 3 p.m.

  He was looking at the girl with the binoculars.

  He gave her a ring last night.

  He was questioned by the officers in a state of undress.

  POLICE FOUND DRUNK IN SHOP WINDOW

- Ask the students, in groups of four, to compare their translations. After the group work, bring the class together and run through the ambiguities, so all the students can see the different ways of understanding the sentences.

RATIONALE

This activity gives students the opportunity to make judgements about meaning, which helps to increase their confidence. These sentences were collected by Cynthia Beresford.

Acknowledgement

This is an activity from *Dictation: New Methods, New Possibilities*, Davis & Rinvolucri, Cambridge University Press, 1988.

10 Using fame to help

Unit overview

TOPIC: Fame

TEXTS

Reading and listening: an article about celebrity ambassadors; photostory: *Isn't she that model?*

Reading: a text about the pianist Lang Lang

Listening: opinions on politics and famous people

Writing: a 'for and against' composition

SPEAKING AND FUNCTIONS

Talking about UN Goodwill Ambassadors

Discussing and presenting ideas to promote a charitable organisation

Talking about fame

LANGUAGE

Grammar: reduced relative clauses; question tags review

Vocabulary: fame; expressing opinions

Pronunciation: intonation in question tags

1 Read and listen

If you set the background information as a homework research task, ask the students to tell the class what they found out.

BACKGROUND INFORMATION

The United Nations (UN) is an international organisation that promotes cooperation and peace between countries. It was founded in 1945 after the end of World War II with the hope that it would prevent conflicts between nations. Goodwill ambassadors are famous people who promote the work of the UN around the world.

The United Nations High Commission for Refugees (UNHCR) was set up in 1950 to help refugees (people who have to leave their country for political reasons or because of war).

The United Nations Children's Fund (UNICEF) aims to help and protect children in the areas of health and nutrition, education and protection against abuse, exploitation and discrimination.

Lionel Messi (born 1987) is an Argentine footballer who plays for Barcelona in Spain. He was voted FIFA world player of the year in 2009. In the 2009–10 season he played 53 times and scored 47 goals!

Whoopi Goldberg (born 1955) is an American comedian and actor. Her first film was *The Color Purple* (1985) for which she won a Golden Globe. She also appeared in *Ghost* and *Sister Act*, and as a voice in cartoons *Lion King* and *Toy Story 3*.

Susan Sarandon (born 1946) is an American actor. She has appeared in many films since 1969 and won the best actress Oscar in 1995 for *Dead Man Walking*. She is married to the actor Tim Robbins.

Robbie Williams (born 1974) is an English singer. He was a member of Take That between 1990 and 1995 before going solo. He has sold more than 57 million albums as a solo artist. He rejoined Take That in 2010.

Angelique Kidjo is a singer from Benin, West Africa. In 2008 her album *Djin Djin* won a Grammy for best world music album.

Shakira (Shakira Mebarak Ripoll, born 1977), is a Colombian pop singer-songwriter. She released her first album in 1991 at the age of 13 and went on to massive success with her albums *Laundry Service* and *Oral Fixation*.

David Beckham (born 1975) is an English footballer who plays for LA Galaxy in America. He previously played for Real Madrid and Manchester United and was the captain of the English national team. He advertises many well-known brands and regularly appears in tabloid newspapers.

Ronaldo (Ronaldo Luís Nazário de Lima, born 1976) is a Brazilian footballer who has contributed to two World Cup wins by the Brazilian national team (1994 and 2002). Ronaldo has also set a record of three FIFA World Player of the Year awards (1996, 1997 and 2002). He is regarded as one of the best players in the history of football.

Angelina Jolie (born 1975) is an American actor and former model. She has received three Golden Globes as well as an Oscar for best supporting actress for her performance in the film *Girl, Interrupted*.

Warm up

Write *United Nations* on the board and ask the class what they know about this organisation. Write notes on the board as students suggest ideas. Establish that the UN has a role in negotiations and peacekeeping between nations, but that it also does important humanitarian work. Introduce the terms *UNHCR* and *UNICEF* and elicit or provide some basic information about what these offices do (see Background information).

a Students look at the photos. Ask them to say what they know about the people and to guess what they have in common. Students read the text quickly to check their answers.

Answers
The photos show Ronaldo, Angélique Kidjo and Angelina Jolie. They all work with the UN and use their fame to help other people.

b Read through the list of paragraph headings with the class. Ask students to match the headings with the paragraphs in the text.

Answers
1 C 2 B 3 A 4 D

c ▶ CD3 T02 Read through the questions with the class. Students listen, read the text again and answer the questions. Ask them to compare answers in pairs before feedback. Play the recording again, pausing as necessary to check comprehension and clarify vocabulary.

TAPESCRIPT

See the reading text on page 74 of the Student's Book.

Answers
1 They decided to use celebrities to help promote children's rights.
2 She is famous for her humanitarian work and her acting.
3 The UN looks for people who are well known all over the world and will remain famous for a long time. They must also really care about helping children.

Discussion box

In pairs or small groups, students discuss the questions. Monitor and help as necessary, encouraging them to express themselves in English and to use any vocabulary they have learned from the text. Ask pairs or groups to feedback to the class and discuss any interesting points further. Students could vote on the most suitable person in their country to become a UN Goodwill Ambassador.

2 Grammar

✱ Reduced relative clauses

a Write the examples on the board. Ask students to work out where we can add *that is* and *who are*, and add these words to the sentences on the board. Point out that the clauses formed with the added words are normal relative clauses in the passive. Ask who the pronoun *who* refers to in the first example *(celebrities)* and what *that* refers to in the second *(the agency)*. Ask students to identify the part of speech for *used* and *represented* (past participle). Explain that it is possible to leave out the relative pronoun and the verb *be* when the clause is in the passive. The meaning is carried by the past participle alone.

Answers
There are also celebrities who are used ...
But perhaps the agency that is most represented ...

b Read through the rule with students and ask them to complete it.

Answers
passive, verb *be*

Language notes

1 Emphasise that we can reduce the relative clause like this only when it is in the passive. We can't say **There are a lot of stars represent UNICEF* – here the pronoun *who* must be used because the clause is active, not passive.

2 You may want to mention that when the clause is active, we can sometimes use the present participle instead of a full relative clause, e.g. *There are a lot of stars representing UNICEF.*

c Tell students that they are going to read a text about another UNICEF Goodwill Ambassador. Look through the text with them, and check any difficult vocabulary. Students complete the text with the words in the box. When checking the answers, ask if the full relative clauses with *who* and *which* can be reduced, leaving out the pronoun and the verb *be* (yes, they can).

Answers
1 who is regarded 2 who was born 3 won
4 which was held 5 accompanied
6 which was given 7 attended 8 written

d Draw students' attention to the words in italics in the sentences. Ask them to cross out those which are not needed. Emphasise that the extra words in sentence 1 are not incorrect – they just aren't necessary. Ask why ***whose*** is needed in sentence 2 (because it's a non-defining relative clause).

Answers
These words should be crossed out: 1 that was

Grammar notebook

Remind students to note down the rules for reduced relative clauses and to write a few examples of their own.

3 Vocabulary

Fame

a Ask students to read the sentences and try to choose the correct answer before looking back at the text for help. Encourage them to think of these expressions as single pieces of vocabulary even though they are made up of several words. Check answers.

Answers
1 is famous for
2 made a name
3 made it big
4 household name
5 enjoyed
6 sensation

b Students work in pairs to think of names of people that fit the descriptions. Ask different pairs for their ideas and invite others to say if they agree or disagree.

OPTIONAL ACTIVITY

For further practice of this vocabulary, play a guessing game. Ask students to write sentences about a famous person, using some of the target language. They should not mention the person's name and should avoid saying *he* or *she* – tell them to use *X* instead. For example: *X made it big in 2001 and is a household name all over the world. X is famous for acting in the Harry Potter films. (Daniel Radcliffe).* In small groups, students read out their sentences, while the others guess.

Vocabulary notebook

Encourage students to start a new section called *Fame* in their notebook and to add these expressions. They may find it useful to note down translations, too.

4 Listen

Warm up

Ask students to think of famous people who are involved in politics, either in their country or in other countries. Write a few examples on the board.

a ▶ CD3 T03 Write the names *Paul* and *Maria* on the board. Tell students they are going to listen to these two people talking about famous people getting involved in politics. Play the recording while students answer the questions. Check answers and, if necessary, play the recording again, pausing to check comprehension.

TAPESCRIPT

Paul: Look at this, Maria. Again! I'm fed up with these people.

Maria: What people? What are you talking about?

Paul: Look – these pop stars talking to presidents and getting their photos on the front page of the papers.

Maria: What's the problem? They're just famous people trying to help.

Paul: Yeah, help themselves. Help their careers. That's what it's all about.

Maria: Wow, that's pretty cynical, Paul. Just because they're pop stars or film stars, it doesn't mean they're completely inhuman, you know. I think it's fine – especially if they help to get things done for poorer people.

Paul: Well, OK – I just think it's wrong, that's all. I mean, entertainment is entertainment, politics is politics – you shouldn't mix 'em.

Maria: Oh I don't agree. Everyone should get involved in politics – even people like you and me.

Paul: Yeah, but that's different isn't it? I mean ...

Answers
1 Maria is in favour because she thinks everyone should get involved in politics.
2 Paul is against because he thinks famous people aren't involved for the right reasons.

b ▶ CD3 T04 Explain to students that they are going to hear six more people answering the question *Should famous people get involved in politics?* Play the recording twice. Students listen to the speakers' opinions and tick the correct box for each one. During the first listening, pause after each speaker to give students time to consider their answers.

TAPESCRIPT

Radio presenter: Today we're out on the streets asking people 'Should celebrities get involved in politics?' Let's hear what ordinary people have to say about this.

Speaker 1: No, they shouldn't. I mean, I couldn't care less what these famous people think. The ones I hear on the radio or TV, they don't really know what they're talking about anyway, do they? So I don't pay any attention to them, I'm not influenced by them at all. To be honest, I think they should keep out of the way and leave politics to professionals, people who know what they're talking about, shouldn't they?

Speaker 2: It doesn't really matter either way. The way I see it, if there are people who are influenced by pop stars and so on, well, they aren't going to listen to politicians anyway, are they? And people who think seriously about politics won't be influenced by a rock star – they've formed their opinion already, haven't they? So it just doesn't matter.

Speaker 3: I'm against it. I'd have thought that politics is for politicians, just like music is for musicians and films are for actors. I mean, we wouldn't expect to see the prime minister getting involved in music, would we? If you ask me, these people should stick to what they know and keep out of politics altogether.

Speaker 4: I'm all for it, myself. It gets lots of people interested, doesn't it? Especially young people. I mean, it can't be a bad thing, can it, if people listen more because it's a famous person speaking, someone they look up to. They don't have to agree with the famous person, after all. But it's good because they listen and think.

Speaker 5: Well, I think it's a really good thing. There's a lot of people in this country who think it's boring to listen to these politicians on TV, and let's face it, they're right! You know, most of them look and sound really old and boring, yeah? So what's the problem if a famous person stands up and says 'Look, this is an important issue' and so on. Then more people get involved. It's good, yeah. I'm all for it!

Speaker 6: Frankly, I really don't care. It's getting harder and harder to tell the difference between them, isn't it? The politicians and the celebrities, I mean. They're all the same. The politicians want to get elected again, and the pop stars want to have their face in the papers and sell more records. I guess that's cynical of me, well, it is, I know, but on the whole I just couldn't care less.

Answers
Speaker 1 Same as Paul **Speaker 2** Neither
Speaker 3 Same as Paul **Speaker 4** Same as Maria
Speaker 5 Same as Maria **Speaker 6** Neither

c CD3 T04 Read through the sentences with the class and then play the recording again. Students listen to identify the speakers, and then decide who the underlined pronouns refer to. Play the recording again for them to check their answers.

Answers
b 2 c 4 d 3 e 6 f 5

d Invite different students to state their opinions and to give reasons. Encourage class discussion.

5 Vocabulary

✱ Expressing opinions

a Ask students to complete the phrases, using the words in the box. Then say the phrases and ask students to repeat. Point out that they should place a stress on *I*, *me* or *my* for emphasis.

Answers
1 mind 2 thought 3 concerned 4 ask
5 opinion 6 see

b Read through the expressions with students and ask them to decide if they are used to agree, disagree or neither. Check answers.

Answers
1 ✗ 2 ✓ 3 ∅ 4 ✓ 5 ✗ 6 ∅

c Read the topics in the box and elicit some initial responses – positive or negative. In groups, students discuss their opinions more fully. Encourage them to use the expressions in Exercises 5a and 5b, and to give reasons for their opinions.

✱ OPTIONAL ACTIVITY

If students enjoy this activity, you might like to expand it into an open class debate. Ask students to decide on one of the topics that interests them. Divide the class into two groups, one in favour of the topic and the other against. Give each group a set amount of time to organise their arguments, then ask them to debate the topic. Encourage as many people as possible to give their opinions.

Vocabulary bank

Refer students to the vocabulary bank. Read through the words and phrases in open class and check understanding.

Vocabulary notebook

Encourage students to start a new section called *Expressing opinions* in their notebook and to add these expressions. They may find it useful to note down translations, too.

6 Grammar

✱ Question tags review

a Books closed. Write these simple sentences on the board:

You've got a cat.
She can speak French.
They didn't finish their homework.

Ask students to turn the sentences into questions using question tags. Elicit the correct tags *(haven't you? can't she? did they?)* and write them on the board. Remind students that question tags are formed with a positive or negative auxiliary or modal. Show how the tense and subject of the tag depend on the first part of the sentence. Ask students why we use question tags. Establish that we use them when we want to check information or when we are inviting someone to agree with us.

Students open their books, read the sentences and choose the correct question tags.

Answers
1 doesn't it? 2 can it? 3 haven't they? 4 do they? 5 are they? 6 isn't it? 7 shouldn't they? 8 would we?

b Read the rule with the class and ask students to complete it. Refer them back to Exercise 6a for examples of the different types of question tags.

Answers
negative; positive

Language notes

1 Point out that in conversation we often don't expect answers to questions with tags – they may be simply a way of encouraging someone to follow what we are saying.

2 Question tags usually follow the positive–negative or negative–positive patterns described in the rule. However, in some circumstances we may use a positive tag after a positive statement e.g. *An octopus has got three hearts, has it?* We use this form when expressing surprise or disbelief at something somebody has said. The tag suggests: 'I find that hard to believe – is it really true?'

c Ask students to read through the sentences and look for modal verbs before completing them with the appropriate question tags. You may want to look at sentence 5 with the class as an example, showing that we use the modal *would* in the tag (not the auxiliary *have*). Ask students to compare answers with a partner before feedback.

Answers
1 wasn't 2 did 3 was 4 didn't 5 wouldn't 6 shouldn't 7 won't 8 do

Grammar notebook

Remind students to note down the rules for question tags and to write a few examples of their own.

7 Pronunciation

See notes on page 123.

8 Speak

Warm up

Ask students if they have ever done anything for charity. Brainstorm the names of some different charities and write them on the board. What do the charities raise money for? How do they raise money?

a Tell students they are going to imagine they run a charitable organisation. Read through the instructions and check understanding. Divide the class into small groups and ask them to decide which organisation they are going to represent and what they will raise money for. It could be real (refer students to the logos on page 77 for inspiration) or imaginary. Try to ensure that each group is representing a different organisation and working with different celebrities. Give them sufficient time to decide what they will do to raise money and encourage them to make a note of their ideas. Circulate and help with any difficult vocabulary.

b Ask each group to present their ideas to the class. Encourage them to go into detail about how they will raise money and allow time for questions after each presentation. You may like to finish with a vote to decide on the best presentation.

✱ OPTIONAL ACTIVITY

As an extension to this activity, you could give each group a sum of money, say £1,000. When they have heard each of the presentations, students decide which organisation(s) they want to give their money to. Add up the donations on the board and see which group has raised the most money!

Photostory: Isn't she that model?

9 Read and listen

Warm up

Write these questions on the board: *Have you ever seen a famous person? If you saw a famous person, would you speak to him/her?* Students ask and answer the questions in pairs. Ask some pairs to report back to the class.

a ▶ CD3 T06 Students look at the photos, identify the people and describe what they are doing. Ask them to guess the answers to the questions, but don't comment on their answers at this stage. Play the recording. Students read and listen to check their answers.

TAPESCRIPT

See the dialogue on page 78 of the Student's Book.

Answers
First photo: Lily thinks she has seen a famous model.
Second photo: The model has disappeared.

b Students read the text again and find the answers to the questions.

Weaker classes: Before students look at the questions, you may want to play the recording again, pausing as necessary to clarify any problems. Then read through the questions with the class and check that the meaning is clear.

Answers
1 To buy a present for Lily's mum
2 He thinks a famous model wouldn't be shopping in their town.
3 He is disappointed that she is excited at seeing a celebrity.
4 She doesn't care and she thinks that Jack would act the same way with a famous sportsman or actor.

Discussion box

In pairs or small groups, students discuss the questions. Monitor and help as necessary, encouraging them to express themselves in English and to use any vocabulary they have learned from the text. Ask pairs or groups to feedback to the class and discuss any interesting points further.

10 Everyday English

a Ask students to locate the expressions 1 to 6 in the story on page 78 and decide who says them.

Weaker classes: Check answers at this stage.

Answers
1 Lily 2 Lily 3 Jack and Lily 4 Lily 5 Lily 6 Lily

Students then match the expressions with the meanings. Go through the first item with them as an example, if necessary. Check answers.

Answers
1 c 2 a 3 d 4 b 5 e 6 f

b Ask students to read through the sentences and complete the answers. Go through the first sentence with them as an example if necessary.

Answers
1 leave it out 2 might as well 3 What do you reckon? 4 I thought as much 5 I bet 6 I couldn't care less

OPTIONAL ACTIVITY

See Unit 2, Exercise 9 Everyday English, Optional Activities.

11 Improvisation

Books closed. Divide the class into pairs. Ask them to write down as many expressions from Exercise 10a as they can remember. Circulate and check they are writing expressions correctly. Read through the instructions with students. Give them two minutes (or more if necessary) to prepare a short role play. Invite some of the groups to act out their role play for the rest of the class and hold a vote on which was the most entertaining and which included the most expressions from Exercise 10a.

12 Making Waves DVD Episode 3

a Look at the photo with students and ask them to describe what is happening and to guess the answers to the questions. Listen to some of their ideas in open class.

b Divide the class into pairs. Students read the sentences and discuss what the underlined words might refer to. Listen to some of their ideas but do not comment at this stage.

Answers
1 celebrities 2 Jason, the footballer and former pupil 3 the interview 4 Fairbank college

c Play Episode 3 of the DVD while students answer the questions and check their answers to Exercise 12b.

> **Answer**
> She says it was a success. 'A celebrity with the right attitude can do a lot of good.'

13 Write

The planning for this exercise can be done in class and the composition can be set as homework.

a Tell students that they are going to read a composition about politicians becoming media stars. Students read the text and make a note of the different arguments for and against politicians becoming media stars. Draw attention to the organisation of the composition and the content of each paragraph. Let students discuss their findings with a partner before feedback.

> **Answers**
> For: Entertainment is part of our daily lives, so politicians need to adapt to this and appear on TV chat shows. The more we see politicians, the more we get to know them. Good politicians can get more support if they appear a lot on TV.
> Against: Politics shouldn't be about fun. Politicians shouldn't be distracted from important work by seeking celebrity status. Politicians spoil enjoyable TV shows. Politics should be about truth and reality, not entertainment.

b Ask students to read the composition again and complete it with the words in the box. Check their answers.

> **Answers**
> 1 past 2 days 3 course 4 addition
> 5 hand 6 same 7 but 8 things

c Read through expressions a–h and check that students understand them all. Students look again at expressions 1–8 in the text and match them with a–h. Check answers, and point out the usefulness of all these expressions in signalling to the reader how ideas are linked together.

> **Answers**
> a On the other hand
> b All things considered
> c In the past
> d Of course
> e these days
> f In addition
> g In the same way
> h last but not least

d In pairs, students discuss the writer's opinions and conclusion. Ask students to decide which of the opinions they agree or disagree with. Ask for feedback from a few pairs and discuss any interesting points in open class.

e Tell students they are going to write their own composition entitled *Should pop stars become political?* Read through the writing guide with them and encourage them to follow this procedure for their composition. Give them as much time as possible for the planning and organisation stages in class. Monitor and check their progress. In a subsequent lesson, ask students to read each other's compositions and give each other feedback.

Check your progress

1 Grammar

a The words can be crossed out in sentences 2 and 5.

b 2 can't you 3 did she 4 wouldn't you
5 is he 6 will you

2 Vocabulary

a 2 word 3 lost 4 catch 5 gist 6 pick

b 2 name 3 big 4 household 5 enjoyed

c 2 I'm all for it.
3 I couldn't care less.
4 It really doesn't matter.
5 It can't be a bad thing.
6 I'm completely against it.
7 It's not a good idea.

How did you do?

Students work out their scores. Check how they have done and follow up any problem areas with revision work.

Memo from Mario

Using fame to help

1 Would I lie to you?

- Start by demonstrating the activity yourself. Write six statements about yourself and your family on the board. Include three affirmative and three negative sentences. Only one affirmative and one negative sentence should be true, but the false statements should be plausible. Make them as interesting as you can. For example: *I have never been to a bullfight, even though I have visited Spain. / Last year my sister went to India to learn to meditate. / I didn't watch the Harry Potter films because I loved the books. / Before I was sixteen, I had lived in six different houses. / I don't like Japanese food because I hate fish, especially raw. / My father lives in New York because he works for the United Nations.*
- Tell the students that only two of the statements are true and give them a couple of minutes in pairs to decide which they believe. Then ask them to check their ideas, using tag questions.
- Now ask the students to write similar sentences about themselves and/or their families. Ask them to make the statements as interesting as possible.
- Put the students in pairs to exchange lists and check the statements they believe, using tag questions to check the information. When they have discovered the true sentences, they should ask more questions to find out more about the subject.

RATIONALE

Using tag questions to check information that you believe to be correct is very common. The uncertainty adds an element of challenge and a bit of fun to a grammar practice activity.

2 A panel discussion

- Write the five points of view below on slips of paper – enough for one set for each group of students. Put the students in groups of three. Explain that they have been asked to give a panel discussion in front of an audience of students. The topic of the discussion is

People well-known to the public, whether in sport, entertainment or politics, have an obligation to lead exemplary lives to set an example to the public.

- Remind the students about the phrases for giving opinions in section 5.
- They should choose one point of view and prepare to defend it to their colleagues. They should take it in turns to defend their chosen point of view before the other members of the group can question them.

Public figures are free agents. What they do in their private life is their own business.

As public figures, they are role models for many people. Therefore, they should act ethically and morally at all times.

In their public life, celebrities should behave morally and ethically; but privately, they can behave as they wish as long as they keep it out of the public eye.

Naturally, public figures should behave with propriety in every way possible. However, celebrities are not famous for being automatons and we should accept that they are human and have imperfections like everybody else.

The public have the right to know everything about celebrities, who cannot therefore expect to have a private life.

- When the discussion is finished, ask if anyone changed their minds.

RATIONALE

This activity gives students the opportunity to practise expressing and defending their opinions and helps to raise awareness of issues connected with celebrity.

11 Music is everywhere

Unit overview

TOPIC: Music and talent

TEXTS
Reading and listening: an article about TV music talent shows; an extract from *High Fidelity* by Nick Hornby
Listening: an interview about music and musical instruments
Writing: a mini saga, a limerick and a haiku

SPEAKING AND FUNCTIONS
Discussing the merits of talent shows
Talking about music

LANGUAGE
Grammar: indirect questions review; verbs and *wh*-clauses
Vocabulary: qualifying comparisons; listening to music
Pronunciation: *record* (noun) and *record* (verb)

1 Read

If you set the background information as a homework research task, ask the students to tell the class what they found out.

BACKGROUND INFORMATION
Joe McElderry (born 1991) is an English singer who won the TV talent show, *The X Factor*, in 2009. His single 'The Climb' reached no. 1 the week after Christmas 2009. His debut album *Wide Awake* reached no. 6 in the UK album chart in October 2010.

Rage Against the Machine is a rap-metal band formed in 1983 in Los Angeles, USA. As well as recording best-selling albums such as *Evil Empire* and *Renegades*, the band are well-known for their political activism.

Jon Morter is an English DJ, known for motivating 750,000 Facebook users to support the campaign to stop *The X Factor* winner reaching no. 1. The campaign raised over £70,000 for the homeless charity Shelter.

Peter Serafinowicz (born 1972) is an English comedian and actor. He has appeared in various comedy shows on British TV such as *Spaced* and his own *Peter Serafinowicz Show*. He provided the voice for Darth Maul in *Star Wars Episode 1: The Phantom Menace*.

Paul McCartney (born 1942) was a member of the Beatles and Wings before starting a solo career in 1981. He has received more than 60 UK gold discs. His hits include 'Jet', 'Mull of Kintyre' and 'Wonderful Christmas Time'.

Steve Brookstein (born 1968) is an English soul singer. He won *The X Factor* in 2004. His first album *Heart and Soul* reached no. 1 in the UK charts in May 2005.

Warm up

Books closed. Ask students to discuss these questions in small groups, and then to give feedback to the class:

What type of music do you most enjoy?
What type of music do you least enjoy?
Have you seen any talent shows on television?

a Students look at the photographs and answer the questions. Ask different students for their ideas and encourage discussion in open class.

b Tell students that they are going to read an article about the two artists in the photographs. Students read the article quickly to see how the artists became involved in a battle and who won. Tell them not to worry about unknown vocabulary. Discuss answers in open class.

Answers
The artists were competing for the 2009 UK number one single. After an online campaign, the Rage Against the Machine single was bought in protest against the blandness of *The X Factor*-style music, typified by Joe McElderry. Rage Against the Machine won.

c ▶ CD3 T07 Play the recording while students read the text again and answer the questions. Allow students to compare answers with a partner. Play the recording again, pausing as necessary to check comprehension and help with difficult vocabulary. Check answers.

TAPESCRIPT
See the reading text on page 82 of the Student's Book.

Answers

1 Because *The X Factor* winner had been number one for the last four years.
2 They had not been aware of the internet campaign.
3 It was downloaded 50,000 more times than the number two record.
4 They wanted to protest against manufactured pop stars.
5 He was supported firstly by Peter Serafinowicz, then by other celebrities.
6 He wondered whether he was dreaming.
7 He offered his congratulations.
8 They promised to give the profits from the single to charity and to perform a free concert.

OPTIONAL ACTIVITY

Write these words on the board:

1 *nearly* (almost)
2 *easy to remember* (catchy)
3 *strange* (unusual)
4 *invented* (dreamed up)
5 *tried* (attempted)
6 *very happy* (delighted)
7 *concert* (gig)

Ask students to read the text and find words with a similar meaning.

Discussion box

In pairs or small groups, students discuss the questions. Monitor and help as necessary, encouraging them to express themselves in English and to use any vocabulary they have learned from the text. Ask pairs or groups to feedback to the class and discuss any interesting points further.

2 Grammar

Indirect questions

a **Weaker classes:** Write this question on the board: *Where is Timbuktu?*

Elicit some suggested answers, and then write this sentence opening on the board:

I don't know ...

Tell students that we do not say *I don't know where is Timbuktu.* If possible, elicit the correct form and write it on the board, i.e. *I don't know where Timbuktu is.*

Point out that the question is now a statement (there is no question mark at the end) and draw attention to the difference in word order. Then follow the procedure for stronger classes.

Stronger classes: Read through the examples from the text. Then elicit the direct questions. Point out that in the examples, these questions are now embedded inside statements. We still use the question word, but the words following it are no longer in question form. As in any other statement, the subject comes before the verb, and we do not use the auxiliary *do*.

Answers

1 Was he dreaming?
2 Who were the band?

b Ask students to complete the rule and use the previous examples to show how indirect questions are formed.

Answers

invert, sometimes; don't invert, never

c Look at the example with the class. Ask students to join each pair of sentences in a similar way. They should start with the words in the second sentence. Students compare answers with a partner before feedback.

Answers

2 I don't know how much it costs.
3 It's easy to find out where people buy CDs.
4 We don't always know when people need to listen to music to relax.
5 I wonder how easy it is to beat the status quo.
6 I'd like to know how Joe McElderry felt.

Grammar notebook

Remind students to note down the rules for indirect questions and to write a few examples of their own.

OPTIONAL ACTIVITY

Write these sentence openings on the board:

1 *I don't know ...*
2 *I'd like to find out ...*
3 *I'm not sure ...*
4 *Maybe you can tell me ...*
5 *I wonder ...*

Ask students to think of ways of completing them, using the question words *who, what, when, where* and *why.* They should use each question word only once. Ask different students to read out their sentences. Invite others to respond, either by giving the information if they know it or by saying *I don't know* if they don't.

3 Vocabulary

✱ Qualifying comparisons

Warm up

Briefly revise comparisons using comparative adjectives and *(not) as ... as*. Write *pop music – classical music* on the board and elicit some example sentences comparing the two.

a Explain that the words in the box can be added to comparisons to make them stronger. Students complete the sentences, then look back at the text to check. Check answers, and write them on the board:

> **Answers**
> 1 just 2 almost 3 nowhere near 4 even
> 5 far

b Look at the answers to Exercise 3a with students and ask them to decide which can be replaced with *much / a lot* and which with *not nearly*. Make it clear that the expressions in each group are interchangeable – the meaning is the same.

> **Answers**
> 1 far, even 2 nowhere near

c Students add words to make the comparisons stronger. Ask them to use all the words/phrases from Exercise 3a in their answers. Students compare answers with a partner before feedback in open class. Explain that the words added to make comparisons stronger are often stressed for extra emphasis when we say them. Encourage students to do this when giving feedback.

> **Possible answers**
> 2 Rock music is far more interesting than classical music.
> 3 Sara plays the guitar almost as well as she plays the piano.
> 4 The Charity Rock concert is just as expensive as the Rock In London concert.
> 5 It's nowhere near as difficult to get tickets for Saturday's gig as for the one on Sunday.

✱ OPTIONAL ACTIVITY

Record a selection of types of music (about six different types, each about 20 seconds long). Write these adjectives on the board: *catchy, noisy, exciting, boring, irritating, relaxing*. Play the music and ask students to give each extract a score from 1 to 10 for each of the six adjectives. They then make sentences comparing the music, using the target language from Exercise 3, e.g. *I thought number 1 was far more relaxing than the others.* Monitor and check that they are using the language correctly. Ask students to work in small groups and discuss their reactions to the songs. Ask the class to vote on the best song.

Vocabulary notebook

Encourage students to start a new section called *Making comparisons stronger* in their notebook and to add these words in example sentences.

4 Speak

Give students a few minutes to complete the sentences by themselves. You may like to give them some example sentences of your own to get them started. C rculate and help with vocabulary as necessary. In pairs, students compare sentences. Ask some students to report back on their partner's answers.

5 Listen

Warm up

Books closed. Ask students to name all the musical instruments they know, and write the words on the board. You could group them under the headings *Strings, Wind,* and *Percussion*. Ask different students to say which instruments they can, or have tried to, play. Encourage students to add any new words to their vocabulary notebook under the heading *Music*.

a Look at the pictures and ask students if they recognise any of the instruments. If not, can they imagine what the instruments sound like?

b Students match the instruments with the countries, making guesses if they are not sure. Ask for their answers, but don't comment at this stage. The instruments are top row; (left to right) ukulele, dizi, middle row; bodhran, wobble board and bottom row; hosho and babendil.

c ▶ CD3 T08 Tell students they are going to listen to a radio programme in which a music expert talks about the instruments. Students listen and check their answers to Exercise 5b.

TAPESCRIPT

Jeremy: Well, our next guest is a lady who knows just about everything there is to know about music and musical instruments from all around the world. Please welcome Hope Staunton.

Hope: Hi, Jeremy.

Jeremy: So, Hope, I believe you've just brought out a book about music all around the world.

Hope: That's right. I spent about a year and a half travelling round the world doing my research and the book's out next week.

Jeremy: Hard life, eh?

Hope: That's right.

Jeremy: Can I ask you where you went?

Hope: Oh, it would take me a long time to tell you! All over the place, basically. But I learned lots about musical instruments, some that perhaps you've heard of and maybe some that aren't so familiar.

Jeremy: And you've brought one or two along to the studio today too!

Hope: That's right – and I've brought a couple of people with me who can play on each of them for us.

Jeremy: Well, that's great. Now, this first one, this one I recognise. This is a wobble board.

Hope: That's right. Of course, this Australian instrument was made famous here in the UK by the Australian entertainer, Rolf Harris.

Jeremy: But I've always wondered how you play it.

Hope: Well, you sort of put it between your hands and bounce it about.

Jeremy: So can we hear a bit?

Hope: Sure.

Jeremy: That's a great sound, isn't it. ... Right, what's next?

Hope: Well, this one should be quite familiar, it's a ukulele.

Jeremy: Of course it is. And can you tell us where it's from?

Hope: The ukulele is actually originally from Hawaii but not many people realise that. But you'll find many similar instruments all over the world.

Jeremy: Is it hard to play?

Hope: Not especially. It's a lot easier than a guitar, for example.

Jeremy: So let's hear it. ... Sounds quite like a banjo. Now I don't really recognize any of the other instruments. Well, I mean this must be some kind of drum but I've no idea where it's from.

Hope: It's actually not from too far from here. It's called a bodhran and it comes from Ireland. Some people believe that it was originally a weapon of war. Soldiers would play it as they marched into war. But these days it's very popular in traditional Irish music. Would you like to hear it?

Jeremy: Absolutely! ... Right now, what's this. I'm guessing it's something you blow into?

Hope: Exactly. This is a dizi.

Jeremy: What a great name. And where is it from?

Hope: From China. It's a kind of Chinese flute and it's very popular in all sorts of music from traditional Chinese folk to opera.

Jeremy: And do you know what it's made of?

Hope: Yes, it's made from bamboo.

Jeremy: So what does it sound like?

Hope: Ok, let's listen. Here we go.

Jeremy: That's beautiful ..... Now what's this? It looks like something you shake.

Hope: It's called a hosho, and it's from Zimbabwe. It's a percussion instrument and it's made from the shell of a dried fruit known as a gourd.

Jeremy: And what's inside?

Hope: Inside you'll find lots of dried seeds. That's what makes the noise when you shake it.

Jeremy: OK – let's hear it. ... Very nice. Now I guess we're saving the loudest to last.

Hope: Well, it depends how hard you hit it but yes, this can be very loud. It's called a babendil and it comes from the Philippines.

Jeremy: Right ...

Hope: And as you can see, it's basically a big metal dish which you hit with this.

Jeremy: A bit like the man at the cinema.

Hope: I'm sorry.

Jeremy: You know, that man who plays the gong before the film starts.

Hope: Of course. Now I understand. So let's have a bash. You have to stand up to play this one.

Jeremy: That's a lovely sound.

Hope: Yes it is.

Answers
1 d 2 a 3 f 4 b 5 c 6 e

d **▶ CD3 T08** Read through the sentences with students and check understanding. Then play the recording. Students listen and answer the questions. Play the recording again, pausing if necessary for clarification.

Answers
1 dizi 2 bodhran 3 wobble board
4 ukulele 5 hosho 6 babenbil

e Ask students to discuss which instrument they like the most/least and encourage them to use language from Exercise 3. Listen to some of their answers in open class.

6 Vocabulary

✱ Listening to music

a Read through the sentences with the class. Students match the underlined words to the definitions. If they are unsure about some of the vocabulary, encourage them to guess the meaning from its context. During feedback, say the underlined words and ask students to repeat them.

Answers
1 d 2 h 3 c 4 f, e 5 a, g 6 j 7 b 8 i

b Students read the sentences in Exercise 6a again and decide if they are true for them. Ask them to change the sentences if they disagree.

Answers
Students' own answers

c In pairs, students discuss their opinions. Monitor and help with vocabulary if necessary. Listen to some of their answers in open class.

Vocabulary bank

Refer students to the vocabulary bank. Read through the words and phrases in open class and check understanding.

Vocabulary notebook

Encourage students to start a new section called *Music* in their notebook and to add these words. They may find it useful to note down translations, too.

7 Pronunciation

See notes on page 123/4.

8 Grammar

✱ verbs + *wh-* clauses

a **Weaker classes:** Write this question on the board: *How much did you pay for those shoes?*

Point out that it might seem a bit impolite to ask this question. However, we can add words at the beginning so that the question is less direct. Write the sentence openings *Can I ask you* and *Could you tell me* and help students to form the following:

Can I ask you how much you paid for those shoes?
Could you tell me how much you paid for those shoes?

Now follow the procedure for stronger classes.

Stronger classes: Look at the examples and ask students to choose the correct words.

Answers
1 you went? 2 it's from? 3 it is made of?

b Students underline the *Wh-* question words in the examples in Exercise 8a. Point out that they now appear in the middle of the sentences.

Answers
1 where 2 where 3 what

c Read through the rule with students and ask them to complete it. Point out the similarity to the indirect questions studied in Exercise 2: the subject comes before the verb and we don't use the auxiliary *do*. However, we must use a question mark at the end, because the whole sentence is in the form of a question: *Can I ask you (something)?*

Answer
statement

d Students read the interview and change the direct questions to indirect questions. Ask them to compare answers with a partner before feedback. Point out that the interview is a formal situation and the interviewer is using the indirect form in order to be polite.

Answers
2 when hip-hop music started?
3 how many CDs you've got?
4 where you keep them?
5 how much money you've spent on them?
6 which was the first record you bought?
7 which band you like the most?
8 how often you listen to their stuff?

e Students work in pairs and ask each other the questions. They might like to insert their favourite type of music to replace *hip-hop*. Encourage them to use vocabulary from Exercise 6 in their answers.

Grammar notebook

Remind students to note down the rules for indirect questions and to write a few examples of their own.

9 Speak

If you set the background information as a homework research task, ask the students to tell the class what they found out.

BACKGROUND INFORMATION

Hip-hop is made up of rapping (speaking very quickly in rhyme) and mixing or DJing (mixing different types of music and sounds). There is usually quite a simple rhythm with a heavy drumbeat and a strong melodic background, over which the singer speaks. Lyrics are often aggressive comments on politics and relationships. It is currently the most popular style of pop music in many parts of the world. Famous hip-hop artists include Tupac Shakur (2Pac), Jay-Z and Fifty Cent.

Dance music usually has a strong repetitive beat and is either instrumental or has very simple lyrics. There are many different styles of dance music including techno, house, trance, electro and breakbeat.

Disco music refers to the dance music played in discos in the 1970s. It became very popular after the film *Saturday Night Fever* in 1977 and has come back into fashion in recent years. Popular disco artists include The Bee Gees, Michael Jackson, Village People and Kool and the Gang.

Check that students understand the meaning of the words in the box by asking for one or two examples. Students work in pairs or small groups and discuss the questions. Encourage them to speak in full sentences and to use comparisons. Monitor and help with vocabulary if necessary. In feedback discuss the questions further and find out what the most popular type of music is in the class.

OPTIONAL ACTIVITY

If students are interested in music, ask them to prepare presentations on their favourite type of music. This could be given as a homework task and students could bring in pieces of music to illustrate their presentations.

Literature in mind

10 Read

If you set the background information as a homework research task, ask students to tell the class what they found out.

BACKGROUND INFORMATION

Nick Hornby (born 1957) is a British novelist and screenwriter. He is best known for his novels *High Fidelity, About a Boy* and *Fever Pitch*, all three of which have been made into successful films. His work frequently focuses on music, sport, and the aimless and obsessive natures of his protagonists.

High Fidelity was published in 1995. The film of the book was released in 2000 and shifted the action from North London to Chicago. It starred John Cusack, Iben Hjejle and Jack Black. The plot concerns the owner of a record shop and his difficulties in committing to his girlfriend. The film took $47 million at the box office.

Warm up

Books closed. Write the following on the board:
CD MP3 LP cassette.

Divide the class into pairs and ask students to discuss the advantages and disadvantages of each of the formats. Do they (or their parents) have any LPs (vinyl albums) or cassettes at home? Listen to some of their ideas in open class and encourage debate.

a Books open. Ask students to look at the cover of the book and read the summary. In open class discuss whether or not they would like to read the book.

b Students read the text quickly and answer the question. Remind them that they don't need to understand every word at this stage. Check answer.

Answer
3

c **▶ CD3 T10** Read through the questions with students and check understanding. Ask students to read the text again and listen. You may want to play the recording again, pausing where necessary to check comprehension. Students answer the questions and check answers with a partner before feedback.

Answers
1 They reduce the price to 10p or throw them away.
2 Just in case someone borrows one and forgets to return it.
3 He is amazed and immediately rushes to the counter and buys the record.
4 Because they can't believe somebody has bought the record and the fact that somebody has gives them hope that good things will always happen.
5 They feel very disappointed.

d Students find words in the text to match the definitions and compare answers with a partner. Check answers and pay attention to the pronunciation of the words.

Answers
1 browsing 2 flog 3 flicking through 4 haggle 5 shift 6 grow on 7 clutching 8 aghast

Discussion box

In pairs or small groups, students discuss the questions in the box. Monitor and help as necessary, encouraging students to express themselves in English and to use any vocabulary they have learned from the text. Ask pairs or groups to feedback to the class and discuss any interesting points further.

11 Write

a Pre-teach *saga* and *humorous,* and make sure students know the meaning of *poem/poetry, rhythm* and *rhyme.* Ask them to read the descriptions (1–3) and match them with the texts

(A–C). You may choose to read the texts aloud yourself, creating a sense of drama and tension until the last moment in text B and bringing out the regular rhythm and rhyming pattern of text C. As you check the answers, discuss the poems briefly. Ask students what is being described in the haiku and ask what they thought was happening in the mini-saga before they read the last sentence. Ask them to pick out the stressed words and the rhyming words in the limerick (note that *Crewe* is pronounced /kruː/).

Answers
1 B 2 C 3 A

b In pairs, students discuss which of the texts they like best and why. Listen to some pairs' opinions in open class.

c Read through the types of writing with the class.

Students choose one of the types and start planning their own piece of writing. You could ask them to choose one of the types as a class exercise and set another as homework.

Mini-saga: A good way to approach this is to use a well-known story (e.g. a legend or fairy story). Elicit some ideas and point out to students that they will have to be very selective about the events they include, and that the effect of doing this is often funny.

Limerick: It is important that students hear the rhythm, so practise by repeating the example, then simply the rhythm (*da DUM da da DUM*, etc.).

Point out that the first line of a limerick often gives the name of a person or place. You could write an example on the board (e.g. *There was a young lady called Jane* or *There once was a boy from Japan*) and get the class to help you form a second rhyming line (e.g. *Who went round the world in a train / Who lived in the back of a van*). Elicit other rhyming words that they could use for their last line (e.g. *rain, brain, Spain, insane / man, can, began*, etc.).

Haiku: Haikus are short, but this does not make them easy to write. Look back at text A and ask students to check the number of syllables in each line. You could take one of the example topics and gather suggestions from the class to form a first line of five syllables on the board.

d If you set the writing as a homework task, ask students to read each other's work in a subsequent lesson. Invite some students to read out their work to the class.

Memo from Mario

Music is everywhere

1 Prove it!

- Write the following sentences on the board. (You can adapt the statements and/or the numbers depending on the your class.)

  Only two people in this class like classical music.

  At least six people listen to hip-hop.

  Almost everybody has bought some music on the internet.

  More than five people like folk music.

  Most people in this class own more than 20 music CDs.

  Nobody owns a country music CD.

  Most people in this class prefer female singers.

- Ask the students which sentences they think are true and which false. Then challenge them to prove it by asking people in the class. Tell them to be polite when they ask the questions, reminding them about the phrases in section 8C.
- Put the students in groups of three to work together to collect information from the class to prove which statements are true or false. Have a whole-class feedback to check results.
- You can adapt the statements and/or the numbers depending on the class.

> RATIONALE
> This activity gives the students an opportunity to practise both grammar and vocabulary in a situation where the main focus is the challenge.

2 Song translation

- This will only work if you have a monolingual group.

  Take a popular song in the students' L1 and translate it into English or translate an English song into the students' L1. Write the words as continuous text and put them on an OHT or photocopy. Don't tell the students that it is a song, let them work it out on the way through. When they finish, play the original to let them check.

> RATIONALE
> Students often want to work with songs, and the translation adds an extra dimension to the activity, as well as raising awareness of language differences.

3 A quickie

- Ask the students to think of a singer or group that they like and write the name vertically down a page. Make sure the names have at least six letters. They should then think of a word for each letter of the name. The words must have a connection to the singer or group or their music. This could be done in pairs. There is an example below. A variation is also shown.

Beat	**B**and
Energy	L**E**nnon
Artistes	P**A**ul
Tunes	Ringo S**T**arr
Lyrics	**L**iverpool
Electric	G**E**orge
Song	clas**S**ics

> RATIONALE
> This type of activity revises a lot more vocabulary than goes on the page, as words run through the mind and are sorted, accepted or rejected.

12 Nature's best

Unit overview

TOPIC: The natural world

TEXTS

Reading and listening: extracts from a travel guide, a travel blog and a work of fiction

Listening: a holiday story; Song 'Somewhere over the rainbow'

Writing: a description of your favourite place in the world

SPEAKING AND FUNCTIONS

Discussing your own seven wonders of the world

Talking about trips

LANGUAGE

Grammar: participle clauses; *didn't need to* vs. *needn't have*

Vocabulary: geographical features; travel verbs

Pronunciation: /ɪ/ *sit* and /iː/ *seat*

1 Read and listen

If you set the background information as a homework research task, ask the students to tell the class what they found out

BACKGROUND INFORMATION

Muir Woods is a 559-acre forest situated 20 km north of San Francisco. 240 acres of the forest are made up of Giant Redwood trees. As the woods are close to the Pacific Ocean, they are often covered by fog, which is the perfect environment for the Redwoods to grow so tall.

Ayers Rock (*Uluru*) is a sandstone rock formation in the southern part of the northern territory, central Australia. It is a 450-km drive from the nearest large town, Alice Springs. Humans first settled in the area more than 10,000 years ago. The rock is sacred to local Aborigine tribes and many waterholes, rock caves and ancient paintings can be found there. Ayers Rock is listed as a World Heritage Site.

The Amazon River is the largest river in the world and has more water than the next ten largest rivers combined. The width of the Amazon varies between 1.6 km and 10 km at a low stage but expands to 48 km in the wet season. At the point where the Amazon meets the Atlantic Ocean, the river enters an estuary which is 240 km wide.

Warm up

Books closed. Write the title of the unit on the board: *Nature's best.* Ask students what they understand by the title and which things they would call nature's best. Are there any natural wonders in their country? Elicit ideas and write examples on the board.

a Books open. Students look at the photos and match them with the names. Ask students to say what they know about each of these places.

Answers

A Meeting of the waters **B** Muir Woods
C Ayers Rock/(*Uluru*)

b Tell students they are going to read three texts about the places in the photos. Ask them to read quickly to decide what types of text they are. Tell them to ignore unknown words and the gaps in the first paragraph at this stage. During feedback, ask them how they decided on their answers.

Answers

1 Ayers Rock text 2 Muir Woods text
3 The Meeting of the Waters text

c Look at the questions with students and ask them to read the texts again themselves, using a dictionary for new words if they can't guess the meaning. Alternatively, read the texts with the class, checking comprehension and helping with difficult vocabulary. Students answer the questions and compare answers with a partner before feedback.

Possible answers

1 Muir Woods are in California; the trees are over 70 m tall; some of the trees are over 1,000 years old.
2 Its aboriginal name is Uluru; it is 9 km in circumference; there is a 1.6 km climb to the top.
3 1 muddy 2 little 3 ahead 4 painted

d ▶ CD3 T11 Students listen to the recording to check their answers to Exercise 1c, number 3.

TAPESCRIPT

See the reading text on page 88 of the Student's Book.

OPTIONAL ACTIVITY

Write these sentences on the board:

1 *The people in the boat were feeling comfortable.* (False. The heat and mosquitoes were very uncomfortable.)
2 *They were sailing at sea.* (False. They were on the Amazon.)
3 *A lot of people live on Ayers Rock.* (Don't know)
4 *It is easy to climb Ayers Rock.* (False. It is a tricky 1.6 km climb.)
5 *Muir Wood is in California.* (True)
6 *Muir Wood has the tallest trees in the world.* (False. The tallest trees are further south in California.)

Students decide if the sentences are true or false or if the answer is not in the text. During feedback, ask students to give evidence supporting the true statements and to correct the false ones.

2 Grammar

Participle clauses

a **Weaker classes:** Write these sentences on the board:

1 *While I was sitting on my bed, I called Lisa.*
2 *When I had called her, I went downstairs.*

Ask students how many actions there are in each sentence (two) and if they happened at the same time or one after the other (1 at the same time, 2 one after the other). Now write the same sentences with participle clauses:

1 *Sitting on my bed, I called Lisa.*
2 *Having called her, I went downstairs.*

Point out that the meaning is the same, but here we are using an *-ing* verb form to replace the subject and the full verb. Follow the procedure for stronger classes.

Stronger classes: Ask students to look at the two examples and to identify the subject in the underlined part of each sentence. Check answers. Make it clear that there are two clauses in each sentence, and that both have the same subject.

Answers
A you (the reader) B we (the writers)

b Ask students to work with a partner to match the sentences with the meanings. Make sure they recognise that in sentence 2 the first action happened before the second. Then read through the rule with the class and elicit the words to complete them. Refer back to the example sentences in Exercise 2a to clarify the rule.

Answers
1 b 2 a
Rule: present, past

Language note

Students may make the mistake of using participle clauses when the subject is different, making sentences like: **Riding my bicycle, a dog ran into the road* or **Having switched on the computer, it suddenly stopped working.* You may like to give students some incorrect examples like these and show how they don't make sense.

c Look at the example with the class. Point out that we use the present participle *Swimming* here because this action was happening at the same time as the action *I saw.* You might want to go through the whole exercise with the class before students write their answers.

Answers
2 Waving her hands, she tried to keep the flies from her face.
3 Walking between the trees, you can see the sun coming through the branches.
4 Having watched the sunset on the rock, the visitors walked back to their hotel.
5 Having travelled 1,000 km, the Amazon River meets the Rio Negro.
6 Standing in the forest, the trees seem to be indestructible.
7 Listening to the sounds of nature, the man felt very alone.

LOOK!

Read through the examples in the Look! box to emphasise that the subject must be the same in both clauses.

OPTIONAL ACTIVITY

Write these sentence openings on the board, referring to the Ayers Rock trip:

Having always wanted to see Ayers Rock, ...
Arriving at my hotel, ...
Watching the sun set on Ayers Rock, ...
Climbing the rock, ...

Ask students to think of some possible endings for the sentences, using their own ideas.

Grammar notebook

Remind students to note down the rules for participle clauses and to write a few examples of their own.

3 Vocabulary

✱ Geographical features

a Students match the words with the pictures and compare answers with a partner.

b ▶ CD3 T12 Play the recording for them to check their answers. Then play the recording again and ask them to repeat the words.

TAPESCRIPT/ANSWERS

1 c a coral reef 2 a a bay 3 j a lake
4 f a canyon 5 g a waterfall
6 b a mountain range 7 e a cliff 8 d a plain
9 h a glacier 10 i a desert

c In pairs, students think of as many examples of the features as possible in three minutes. Ask them to go right through the list first, writing one item for each feature if possible. They can then go back and add more if they have time. Ask different students to give their answers. Ask a few questions about where the places are and what they are like.

4 Speak

If you set the background information as a homework research task, ask the students to tell the class what they found out.

BACKGROUND INFORMATION

The Seven Wonders of the World: The original list of the Seven Wonders of the World was written in the second century and included works located around the Mediterranean. Only one still exists – the Great Pyramid of Giza. The following is an example list of the top seven wonders existing today: the Great Pyramid of Giza, the Great Wall of China, the Taj Mahal, the Serengeti migration, the Galapagos Islands, the Grand Canyon, Machu Picchu.

In pairs, students make lists of natural and man-made wonders. In open class, ask some pairs for their ideas and write them on the board. Try to create a list of seven wonders (natural and man-made) which the whole class agrees on.

5 Listen

If you set the background information as a homework research task, ask the students to tell the class what they found out.

BACKGROUND INFORMATION

Machu Picchu means 'Old Mountain'. It is an Inca site located 2,430 m above sea level on a mountain ridge in the Urubamba Valley in Peru. It is often called the Lost City of the Incas as it was unknown to the outside world until 1911. It became a World Heritage Site in 1983, but there is now concern that it is visited by too many tourists (400,000 in 2003), and that this may damage the site.

a Students look at the picture. Read the instructions and discuss ideas with the class.

b ▶ CD3 T13 Tell students that they are going to listen to the first part of a story about a boy and his dad who went on holiday to Peru. Read through the sentences. Explain the meaning of *trail* and *rails,* and check pronunciation of the place names. Play the recording twice. Students listen and mark the sentences true or false. Check answers and ask students to correct the false statements.

TAPESCRIPT

Girl: So, I hear you had quite an exciting adventure while you were on holiday.

Michael: Well, sort of. I mean I don't know if you can really call it 'exciting', but it was different.

Girl: You went to Peru, didn't you?

Michael: Yes. Well, we went to Ecuador too but the 'adventure' happened while we were in Peru.

Girl: So – tell me!

Michael: Well, you know that I went on holiday with my dad. And we were in Peru and of course we wanted to go and see Machu Picchu, the ancient Inca city up in the Andes mountains.

Girl: Yeah, I've heard of that.

Michael: Well the thing is, we wanted to do the famous walk to get there, a thing called the Inca Trail, but we didn't have enough time, so we flew up to a place called Cuzco and stayed in a hotel for a night, and the next morning we got the train to go to Machu Picchu. The train leaves really early, about six o'clock in the morning.

Girl: Ouch!

Michael: Yeah! Anyway, we got up early and got on this little train. It was packed – there were tourists from all over the world, lots of them had suitcases with them 'cos they were going to stay up in the mountains, but we didn't need to take suitcases, because we were going back the same day. We just took a backpack each – which was a good thing, as it turned out.

Girl: Oh? Why?

Michael: Hang on – let me tell you the story! The train set off and after about an hour we were right up in the mountains, the sun was out, it was really gorgeous. And the train was going along beside this mountain river with perfect clear blue water. But – it had rained quite heavily the night before and further along, some mud had come down the mountain and on to the railway line.

Girl: Uh, oh!

Michael: Right! So the driver saw the mud and tried to stop, but he couldn't stop in time and the two front wheels of the first carriage came off the rails.

Girl: Big problem.

Michael: BIG problem!! There we are, in the middle of nowhere almost, and the train can't go any further. Dad and I got off the train with everyone and looked at the wheels. And at first we thought 'Oh no! We've only got today, we won't get to see Machu Picchu!'. But we needn't have worried, because we got there OK in the end.

Girl: Oh? How?

Answers
1 F (they also went to Ecuador)
2 F (they took a train)
3 T
4 T
5 F (only backpacks)
6 F (it had rained the night before)
7 F (the two front wheels came off)

c ▶ CD3 T14 Ask students to predict what happens in the next part of the story. Play the recording twice while students listen and make notes. Then give them time to think about how to reconstruct the story from their notes. In pairs, students take turns to retell the story. For feedback, retell the story in open class, with different students contributing one sentence each.

TAPESCRIPT

Michael: But we needn't have worried, because we got there OK in the end.

Girl: Oh? How?

Michael: Well, my dad speaks some Spanish and he heard the driver say that the station for Machu Picchu was only about five kilometres away. So dad and I looked at each other, picked up our backpacks, and off we went.

Girl: To Machu Picchu? You walked there?

Michael: Yes.

Girl: But how did you know how to get there?

Michael: We just followed the railway track! It was easy. It took us about an hour, that was all. It was just wonderful, walking alongside the river!

Girl: Were you the only ones who walked?

Michael: No, there were a few other backpackers like us. But not a lot. And the best thing was that of course, when we got to Machu Picchu, we were almost the only ones there.

Girl: Why?

Michael: Because the train hadn't arrived with all the other tourists! The old city was almost empty so we walked around and took photographs without other people getting in the way.

Girl: Cool! And what did you think of the place?

Michael: Oh, fantastic! I mean, ...

6 Grammar

★ *didn't need to / needn't have*

a Read through the example sentences and elicit answers to the concept questions.

Answers
1 No, they were going back the same day.
2 Yes. No.

b Ask students to complete the rule. To clarify, you might like to write these sentences on the board:

I didn't take my phone because I didn't need to take it.
I took my phone, but I needn't have taken it.

Talk through the sentences with students and check that they understand the difference in meaning.

In the second example, draw attention to the structure: *needn't* + *have* + past participle. Emphasise that *needn't* is not followed by *to*.

Answers
didn't do; did

Language notes

1 Note that when *need* or *don't need* is followed by another verb, we always use *to*, e.g. *We didn't need to use our map.* We can't say **We didn't need have used our map.* The structure with *have* + past participle is used only with *needn't,* which is a special case.

2 You may like to take this opportunity to remind students that when we use modal verbs to talk about the past, they are also followed by *have* + past participle, e.g. *I think I might have made a mistake. They're not here – they must have gone home. You shouldn't have bought that car.*

c Students complete the sentences with the correct phrases. Ask them to check their answers in pairs before feedback.

Answers
1 didn't need to take
2 needn't have taken
3 needn't have bought
4 didn't need to phone
5 needn't have phoned
6 didn't need to buy

d Ask students to complete the sentences with the correct form of the verb in brackets. Do the first two sentences as examples with the class. Students write their answers and compare answers with a partner before feedback in open class.

Answers
1 needn't have worried
2 didn't need to get up
3 needn't have taken
4 needn't have bought
5 didn't need to use
6 didn't need to wait

Grammar notebook

Remind students to note down the rules for these structures and to write a few examples of their own.

7 Vocabulary

* Travel verbs

a Ask students to briefly tell you what they remember from the listening text in Exercise 5. Students complete the three sentences from the listening text.

Answers
1 on 2 off 3 off

b Read through the table of travel verbs with students. Individually or in pairs, they complete the table using the words in the box.

Answers
1 cruise 2 home 3 taxi 4 bicycle 5 flight 6 car

c Students complete the sentences, referring back to the table as necessary. You could ask stronger students to complete the sentences without looking at the table and then to check their answers at the end.

Answers
1 drove 2 went, set, got 3 went, took 4 got, rode 5 going, go 6 got/went, go 7 going away 8 gets, rides 9 're leaving / setting off

OPTIONAL ACTIVITY

In pairs or small groups, students work through the table of verbs, making sentences based on their own experience, e.g. *I went for a walk last Saturday. I've never been on a cruise.* Encourage students to ask their partners for further information and to expand on their sentences. Listen to some examples in open class.

Vocabulary bank

Refer students to the vocabulary bank. Read through the words and phrases in open class and check understanding.

Vocabulary notebook

Encourage students to start a new section called *Travel verbs* in their notebook and to add these words. They may find it useful to note down translations too.

8 Pronunciation

See notes on page 124.

9 Speak

a **Weaker classes:** To help students with ideas, make a very basic sentence about a trip you have made, e.g. *Two years ago I went on holiday to Prague.* Elicit a list of questions that students could ask you about the trip and write them on the board in note form, e.g. *When / set off? How / get there?* Invite students to ask you about your trip, and give answers. Then ask them to report back some of the things you told them. Follow the procedure for stronger classes.

Stronger classes: Students think of an interesting trip they have made. Encourage them to remember particular facts and interesting details. In pairs, students take it in turns to ask questions about their partner's trip, making notes of the answers. Tell them to follow up information with further questions and to ask for explanations if they need them.

b Students take it in turns to tell the story of their partner's trip. Their partner listens and makes any necessary corrections. Monitor and give help with vocabulary if needed.

c Regroup the students into new pairs. Students retell the story of their previous partner's trip to their new partner. As feedback, ask different students to report a few interesting things that they have heard from either of their partners.

10 Speak and listen

a Tell students they are going to listen to a song called 'Somewhere over the Rainbow'. Look at the three sentences with students and check understanding.

Ask students to read through the lyrics and decide which sentence best describes how the singer is feeling. Ask individual students to explain their choices.

Answers
Students' own ideas

b ▶ CD3 T17 Ask students to read through the lyrics and try to guess what the correct words are. Listen to some of their ideas but do not comment. Students listen to the song and correct the underlined words. Let them compare their answers with a partner before playing the recording again. Check answers in open class.

TAPESCRIPT

See the song on page 92 of the Student's Book.

Answers
1 land 2 dreamed 3 skies 4 dreams
5 a star 6 clouds are 7 troubles 8 find
9 blue 10 birds

c Ask students to read through the lyrics and find the phrases to complete the sentences. Check answers.

Answers
1 high above 2 way up high 3 far behind

d Tell students that the singer is dreaming of a paradise. Ask them to work individually and write a short description of their idea of paradise. Circulate and help students with vocabulary. As feedback, ask individual students to read their paragraphs out and have a class vote to decide which is the best.

> **Did you know?**
> Read the information in the box with students. Ask students if they have watched *Glee* and if so whether they like it or not. Do they know any other songs from old musicals that have had a revival?

11 More speaking

a Give students time to look carefully at the pictures and ask them to think of at least two adjectives to describe each one. Let them compare their adjectives with a partner before listening to some of their ideas. Write any interesting words on the board.

b Read through the sentences with students and ask them to decide which of the pictures each speaker might be talking about. Tell them there is no right answer. Divide the class into small groups and ask them to discuss their answers. Circulate and encourage them to expand on their answers.

c In small groups, students discuss the photos and make a list. Get feedback from some of the groups. Write the most interesting ideas on the board and invite comments.

12 Write

The planning for this exercise can be done in class and the writing can be set as homework.

a Tell students that they are going to read a composition describing somebody's favourite place. Ask them to read the text quickly and identify the place.

Answer
The writer's bedroom

b Students read the composition again and answer the questions. They could work on this in pairs.

Possible answers
1 The unusual colour (he/she seems to be an imaginative person with a strong personality); the objects in the room (he/she seems to be quite untidy, he/she seems to like pop music and he/she enjoys watching the world on his/her own).
2 The questions make you feel that the writer is talking to you personally. They make you want to continue reading to find the answers.

c Read through the instructions with students. Point out that grouping ideas in longer sentences often produces a richer description than writing a series of short sentences. Ask students to look at each group of ideas and to combine them to make a sentence. They could think about this on their own for a few minutes, then work with a partner to decide on the best way to combine the ideas. When they have reached a decision, ask students to look back at the text and compare their answers. Ask students if they think they have created descriptions that are as good as or better than the original and listen to some ideas in open class.

Answers
Students' own answers

d Ask students to think of three objects that have some importance to them. Tell them to brainstorm ideas about each object and to make brief notes. They then combine their ideas into one or two sentences. Encourage students to show their sentences to a partner.

e Tell students they are going to write a composition about their favourite place or object. Encourage them to:

- brainstorm ideas and take notes.

- experiment with different ways of putting together their ideas to make interesting sentences.
- ask questions in the text to make the reader want to read on.
- use interesting adjectives.

In a subsequent lesson, ask students to read each other's compositions. If you take in the work to mark, you could make a list of particularly interesting descriptive sentences from different compositions. Hand them out to the class and discuss why they work well.

OPTIONAL ACTIVITY

Stronger classes: Ask students to read the composition again quickly and then close their books. Write these words on the board: *tiny, wild, Switzerland, juicy, pop stars, overlooks, joke.* Ask students to work in pairs and discuss how the words were used in the composition. Encourage them to try to reconstruct the passage of description where they appeared. Students look back at the text to compare their answers with the original.

Check your progress

1 Grammar

a
2 Do you know how many people there were at the party?
3 Could you tell me where the post office is?
4 Let's find out when the concert starts.
5 I don't know who the teacher said was responsible.

b
3 Looking out of the window, she thought about her father.
4 Having climbed the mountain, they sat down to look at the view.
5 Having swum across the lake, he collapsed on the shore.
6 Seeing the *Aurora Borealis,* we gasped in amazement.

c
2 It wasn't raining, so we didn't need to take our raincoats.
3 I needn't have studied all weekend because the test on Monday was cancelled.
4 There was no test, so I didn't need to study at the weekend.
5 We didn't need to cook any food because there was a restaurant.

2 Vocabulary

a 2 F (you don't sing the words) 3 T 4 T

b 1 bay 2 lake 3 glacier 4 coral reef 5 range 6 plain 7 canyon

How did you do?

Students work out their scores. Check how they have done and follow up any problem areas with revision work.

Memo from Mario

Nature's best

1 Choosing your holiday

- Ask the students to write their name on a slip of paper.
- Ask the students to think of a good place for a holiday and prepare to 'sell' the idea to other people. They should describe the place, what the surrounding area is like, what people can do there, what it's famous for, what the weather is like, etc. and speak about all the advantages of holidaying there.
- Tell the students they are going to talk to as many people as possible in a limited time (five to ten minutes, depending on your group) and try to persuade them to go to the place they have chosen. At the same time, they need to listen to other students' ideas because they have to decide where they are going on holiday.
- Let the students mingle and try to persuade each other. About one minute before the end of the time limit, tell them to give their name slip to the person whose sales pitch they found the most convincing. Tell them that they must give their name to somebody or they won't have a holiday at all!
- When everyone is sitting down again, see who has the most names and where the most popular place is.

RATIONALE

To exercise travel vocabulary persuasively and efficiently in an enjoyable way.

2 The empty chair

- Put an empty chair at the front of the room. Tell the students there is somebody sitting in the chair and that they should ask questions to discover as much about the person as possible. They can ask any questions they like and you will answer for the person in the chair. Stand behind the chair. Think of somebody you know very well and answer the students' questions honestly, using the first person, so that it seems that the person in the chair is speaking. (If you do this after the section on 'Somewhere over the Rainbow', they may think of asking about hopes and dreams or special places.) Don't stop the activity too soon, as later questions tend to be more interesting. At the end of the activity, you could ask the students for suggestions of a holiday destination for the person.
- Now put the students in groups of at least three and tell them to repeat with one of the group answering for the person in the empty chair. Make sure these students realise the person they put in the chair must be someone they know well and they must answer honestly. If the students are enjoying the activity, you could repeat with another student answering.

RATIONALE

This activity gives the students total control. They can take it seriously or light-heartedly. It is unpredictable and this, in itself, makes it exciting.

13 Natural health

Unit overview

TOPIC: Health and medicine

TEXTS
Reading and listening: article about animal behaviour; article on great breakthroughs in medicine
Reading: an advert for alternative medicine
Listening: friends discussing flower remedies
Writing: article for your school magazine

SPEAKING AND FUNCTIONS
Talking about animal behaviour
Talking about flower remedies
Discussing the most significant medical breakthroughs

LANGUAGE
Grammar: passive report structures
Vocabulary: health and medicine; feelings
Pronunciation: /n/ *thin* and /ŋ/ *thing*

1 Read and listen

If you set the background information as a homework research task, ask the students to tell the class what they found out.

BACKGROUND INFORMATION

Tanzania (population c. 43 million) is a country in East Africa. It is believed that humans have lived in the area for more than two million years. The main commercial city and seaport is Dar Es Salaam.

Gombe National Park is a 52 km^2 national park on the shore of Lake Tanganyika in Western Tanzania. The park's chimpanzees were made famous by primatologist Jane Goodall in the 1960s. The park is home to a number of other large primates as well as more than 200 bird species.

Warm up

As an introduction to the topic of illness and medicine, ask students what they do when they have a cold. What do they do to feel better? Who looks after them? Do they take medicine? Do they stay in bed? Give students a short time to discuss in pairs before open class discussion.

In pairs, students make a list of different illnesses and imagine what they would do to get better. Circulate and help with vocabulary if required. When students have a list of illnesses, listen to some of their ideas as feedback and come to some agreement as to the best ways to cure illnesses.

a Look at the photos with students and ask them to describe what they can see. Discuss the question with students in open class. Can any students tell the class about what happened when their pet was ill? You may like to give them some ideas of your own to get the conversation started.

b Students read the text quickly to find the answers. Encourage students not to look up every word, but just to read and get the general idea of the text.

Answers
1 Tanzania, the University of Oxford, the University of Kyoto, Gombe National Park, Kenya, Mount Elgon
2 Hugo picked the leaf carefully, rubbed the leaves before putting them in his mouth and kept them in his mouth for a little while before swallowing them. He chose a plant that local people use as a medicine, and he also took the medicine in the morning.

c ▶ CD3 T18 Read through the questions with the students. Check any problems. Play the recording while students listen and read to answer the questions. After the first listening, let students compare their answers with a partner. Check answers. If necessary, play the recording again, pausing to clarify any problems.

TAPESCRIPT
See the reading text on page 96 of the Student's Book.

Answers
1 c 2 b 3 b 4 b 5 a

Discussion box
In pairs or small groups, students discuss the questions. Monitor and help as necessary, encouraging them to express themselves in English and to use any vocabulary they have learned from the text. Ask pairs or groups to feedback to the class and discuss any interesting points further.

2 Grammar

* Passive report structures

a Read through the sentences with the class. Students look back at the text to find and underline sentences with the same meaning.

Answers
1 ... chimpanzees in the wild are thought to choose certain herbs ...
2 ... is known to be used by local people
3 Elephants in western Kenya, for example, are said to go regularly ...

b Ask students to describe the difference in verb form between the sentences in Exercise 2a and those in the text. Point out that the word *Experts* does not appear in the passive structure. The source of the belief or knowledge is not identified; however, the implication is that the belief is generally shared.

Answer
The verbs in the text are passive, while sentences 1–3 are active.

c In pairs, students complete the eight sentences, using passive report structures.

Answers
2 are said to be able to do
3 are said to eat
4 are believed to be able to make
5 are said to be
6 are known to behave
7 are believed to have
8 are said to be dying

Language notes

1 Note that continuous forms of the infinitive can also be used with this structure, e.g.
Temperatures around the world are known to be rising. Humans are believed to have been living here for thousands of years.
2 The passive form of the verb is also often used with the dummy *it* and followed by *that* + a clause, e.g. *It is thought that the name Canary Islands has a Latin origin.*

Grammar notebook

Remind students to note down the rules for passive report structures and to write a few examples of their own.

OPTIONAL ACTIVITY

Brainstorm the names of some famous people and write them on the board. In pairs, students write a mixture of true and false sentences about these people, using passive report structures, e.g. *Brad Pitt is said to have 16 cats. Mariah Carey is known to have bought a house in Spain.* Monitor to make sure that students are using the structures in the correct way, and encourage them to use their imagination. Then put pairs together to form small groups and ask them to tell each other their sentences. They should try to convince the other pair that their information is likely to be true, adding extra detail if possible. The others say whether or not they believe the information they hear. Ask a few different students to say one of their sentences to the class and invite the others to comment.

3 Read

a Look at the title of the text and the photo, and ask students to guess what the text is about. Listen to some of their ideas in open class. Ask students to skim the text quickly and decide where it is taken from.

Answer
b

b Read through the questions with students and check understanding. Ask them to read the text in more detail and answer the questions. Let students compare answers with a partner before feedback.

Answers
1 all over the globe
2 acupuncture, massage therapy, herbal medicine
3 Because patients are becoming interested in them and asking for them.

OPTIONAL ACTIVITY

For further work on the vocabulary in the text, write these words on the board, and ask students to find words or expressions with the same meaning in the text:

1 a different way
2 simple
3 medical examination
4 methods
5 Because of this
6 contact

Answers
1 an alternative 2 basic 3 check-up
4 techniques 5 As a result 6 get in touch

4 Vocabulary

✱ Health and medicine

Warm up

Draw a sick-looking man on the left-hand side of the board and a well man on the right. Elicit from students some of the steps the man may have to take to be cured. Try to elicit as much of the vocabulary for the matching exercise as possible and write notes on the board.

a ▶ CD3 T19 Ask students to match the definitions with the expressions. Play the recording for students to listen and check their answers.

TAPESCRIPT/ANSWERS

1 c to operate on (someone)
2 h a painkiller
3 j to recover (from)
4 g an anaesthetic
5 b an operating theatre
6 f a diagnosis
7 i to suffer (from)
8 a a surgeon
9 e a symptom
10 d a check-up

b Students complete the sentences, using expressions a–j from Exercise 4a. Remind them that they should write the correct form of the words. Students compare answers with a partner before feedback. As you check answers, draw attention to the useful medical expressions in the sentences: *a thorough check-up, in great shape, bad flu, seriously ill, terrible headaches.*

Answers
1 check-up 2 operated on 3 surgeon
4 an anaesthetic; a painkiller 5 recover from
6 diagnosis 7 is suffering

Language note

Students may be surprised at the term *operating theatre.* Explain that in the 19th century, operations took place in auditoriums and were watched by large groups of medical students, making the room resemble a theatre.

Vocabulary notebook

Encourage students to start a new section called *Health and medicine* in their notebook and to add these words. They may find it useful to note down translations, too.

✱ OPTIONAL ACTIVITY

For more medical vocabulary, write these sentences on the board and ask students to put the verbs in the correct places:

took took wrote saw felt got

1 *Barbara .... the medicine.* (took)
2 *The doctor .... her a prescription.* (wrote)
3 *Barbara .... better.* (got/felt)
4 *Barbara .... ill.* (felt)
5 *She .... a doctor.* (saw)
6 *The doctor .... her temperature and blood pressure.* (took)

Check answers. Then ask students to put the six sentences into the order in which the events happened (4, 5, 6, 2, 1, 3).

5 Pronunciation

See notes on page 124.

6 Listen

If you set the background information as a homework research task, ask students to tell the class what they have found out.

BACKGROUND INFORMATION

Flower remedies: The most popular flower remedies in the UK are Bach flower remedies – dilutions of flower essences discovered and developed by Dr Edward Bach in the 1930s. Practitioners claim that the energy of the flower is transmitted to the user, but some researchers say that any success is an example of the placebo effect. There are 38 original Bach remedies, each prescribed for certain mental and emotional problems, including depression, anxiety, insomnia and stress. Remedies can be used alone or in conjunction with other remedies, and some say each flower gives specific qualities to the remedy. Up to six or seven remedies are typically mixed together by a naturopath or other healer for each patient to meet his/her individual needs. The best-known Bach flower remedy is Rescue Remedy™, which is believed to relieve acute stress, anxiety and panic attacks, especially in emergencies. It has been claimed that this remedy has been effective in calming domestic animals and in the treatment of diseased plants.

a ▶ CD3 T22 Tell students they are going to listen to Dan and Joanna talking about flower remedies. Look at the six pictures and ask them to identify the plants in L1. Read out the plant names in English and ask students to repeat. Look at the list of problems (a–f) and check understanding of the vocabulary. You can also pre-teach *nostalgic* and *proud.* Play the recording. Students listen and match the remedies with the problems. Ask them to compare answers with a partner before feedback.

TAPESCRIPT

Joanna: What's the matter, Dan? You really don't seem your usual self these days.

Dan: Me? Oh, I'm OK. I guess. I mean ... oh, I don't know. I'm just really, really tired. I think it's because of those exams. You know, I worked and studied so hard for weeks and weeks, and now the exams are over but I'm still just exhausted.

Joanna: And what are you doing about it?

Dan: Sorry?

Joanna: I mean, are you taking anything?

Dan: Medicine, you mean?

Joanna: Uh huh.

Dan: Well, no. I haven't fallen ill. I'm just tired. I'm not going to see a doctor for that.

Joanna: Sure. But do you know what you should do? You should get some olive flower remedy and take that.

Dan: Flower remedy? Oh please!

Joanna: What?

Dan: Come on, Joanna! That stuff doesn't work. Olive flower remedy!

Joanna: It certainly does! I took it when I was very tired and I felt so much better. Flower remedies are excellent!

Dan: Right. Show me a flower remedy that can heal a broken leg.

Joanna: Well, of course not. There isn't one. That's just silly. And anyway, flower remedies are much more about curing the mind, not just the body.

Dan: Oh, I see. So if I'm feeling nostalgic or something, there's a flower remedy that will get me out of it and bring me back to the present!

Joanna: Well, in actual fact – yes. It's honeysuckle. And before you laugh, my granny spent a long time feeling like she was living in the past, and she took honeysuckle and it helped a lot.

Dan: So what is this stuff? I mean, do you eat it?

Joanna: No, it's drops of liquid extracted from flowers. You put the drops in water and drink it, and after a few days, you start getting over the problem.

Dan: The problem.

Joanna: Yes – a psychological problem, usually. Like, sometimes people feel really scared all the time, frightened, it's a horrible feeling – but there's a flower remedy for that. It's rock rose.

Dan: So these flower remedies can cure just about anything.

Joanna: Well, I don't know about that. But there are all kinds of psychological problems that people have, and flower remedies can help. I heard of someone who was always very proud of himself, and he took the violet remedy, and it helped.

Dan: So they work even for things like pride?

Joanna: Yes. There are almost 40 remedies. If you're feeling really selfish, self-centred – take heather. If you feel kind of hopeless, like there's no future and there's no point in doing anything, you can get over it with gorse. It's all good stuff!

Dan: Well, I'm still not so sure. But I guess I could take something. It can't do me any harm – can it?

Answers
1 d 2 c 3 b 4 f 5 a 6 e

b ▶ CD3 T22 Read through the statements with the class. Students listen to the recording again to decide if the statements are true or false. Remind them to correct the false statements.

Answers
1 F (He doesn't think he needs medicine.) 2 T
3 T 4 T 5 F (almost 40)

7 Vocabulary

★ Feelings

Warm up

Books closed. Write the words *feeling sorry for yourself, depressed, guilty, having no confidence, exhausted, jealous* on the board. Ask students if they can think of any other words for negative feelings.

a Books open. Write these sentences on the board and ask students how they feel in these situations. Elicit or explain the six adjectives from the list 1–6.

1 *You are going to a concert and you can't find your ticket.* (panicky)
2 *You are on a school trip and want to go home and see your friends and family.* (homesick)
3 *You aren't listening to what people are saying to you.* (inattentive)
4 *You always forget where you put your keys.* (absent-minded)
5 *You have two exams tomorrow that you must pass. You can't sleep.* (over-anxious)
6 *You are looking at photographs of happy times five years ago.* (nostalgic)

Students match the adjectives with the definitions.

Answers
1 c 2 d 3 a 4 e 5 f 6 b

b Ask students to read through the sentences and check any difficult vocabulary. Students complete the sentences. Ask them to compare answers with a partner before getting feedback from the whole class.

Answers
1 absent-minded 2 homesick 3 inattentive
4 nostalgic

OPTIONAL ACTIVITY

Ask students to think of a situation when they have had negative feelings. In pairs, they describe the situation to their partner, without mentioning their feelings. The other person guesses how their partner felt, using one or more of the adjectives in Exercises 6 and 7.

Vocabulary bank

Refer students to the vocabulary bank. Read through the words and phrases in open class and check understanding.

Vocabulary notebook

Encourage students to start a new section called *Feelings* in their notebook and to add these words. They may find it useful to note down translations, too.

8 Speak

a In pairs, students discuss the questions.

b Pairs join up to form groups of four and discuss again. Then ask some students to give examples of problems and possible remedies to the class.

Culture in mind

9 Read and listen

If you set the background information as a homework research task, ask students to tell the class what they have found out.

BACKGROUND INFORMATION

William Harvey (1578–1657) was an English physician. He became a doctor at the University of Cambridge in 1602 and was physician to King James I.

William Jenner (1815–98) was an English physician primarily known for having discovered the distinction between typhus and typhoid. He was physician to Queen Victoria.

René Laennec (1781–1826) was a French physician, chiefly remembered for inventing the stethoscope.

Louis Pasteur (1822–95) was a French chemist and microbiologist. He was one of the first scientists to encourage doctors to wash their hands before treating patients.

Wilhelm Rontgen (1845–1923) was a German physicist whose invention of the X-ray won him the first Nobel Prize for Physics in 1901.

Francis Crick (1916–2004) and James Watson (born 1928) co-discovered the structure of the DNA molecule in 1953. They won the Nobel Prize for Physiology or Medicine in 1962.

Joseph Murray (born 1919) is a retired American plastic surgeon. He won the Nobel Prize for Physiology or Medicine in 1990 for his work on organ transplantation.

Warm up

Books closed. Ask students to think of typical things found in a hospital or a doctor's surgery. You may need to help with any difficult vocabulary. Write some of their ideas on the board. In pairs, students discuss which are the most important objects and think of reasons why. Ask them to imagine what we would do if the objects didn't exist. Listen to a few ideas in open class.

a Ask students to look at the pictures and invite individuals to describe what they can see. Write any interesting vocabulary on the board.

b Ask students to read the text quickly and check their ideas. Tell them not to try and understand every word but to look for the specific information to help them match the pictures with the paragraphs. Students check their answers with a partner before feedback.

Answers
A3 Stethoscope B1 Blood pumped around body C5 X-rays D2 Vaccinations E7 Discovery of DNA F8 First kidney transplant G4 Pasteurization H6 Blood transfusions

c ▶ CD3 T23 Read through the sentences and help with any new vocabulary. Play the recording while students read and listen to answer the questions. If necessary, play the recording again, pausing to help with vocabulary and comprehension. Students answer the questions and check their answers with a partner before feedback. Encourage students to correct the false sentences.

TAPESCRIPT

See the reading text on page 100 of the Student's Book.

Answers
1 True 2 True 3 False (We now use metal or electronic stethoscopes.) 4 True 5 False (They use radiation.) 6 True 7 False (They discovered DNA.) 8 False (He carried out the transplant.)

Discussion box
In pairs or small groups, students discuss the questions. Monitor and help as necessary, encouraging them to express themselves in English and to use any vocabulary they have learned from the text. Ask pairs or groups to feedback to the class and discuss any interesting points further.

10 Write

The planning for this exercise can be done in class and the writing can be set as homework.

a Read through the poster and the list with students. Ask students what else they would do to improve the quality of their life. Elicit ideas and write them up on the board.

b Students read the paragraphs quickly and identify the topic from the list in Exercise 10a.

Answer
think positively about yourself

c Explain that the text contains two topic sentences that introduce the ideas in each paragraph. Ask students to read the text again to find the two topic sentences.

Answers
People often don't do what they really want to because of a fear of failure.
The secret to overcoming this problem is learning to believe in yourself.

OPTIONAL ACTIVITY

Write these sentences on the board:

1 *People these days have too much to do and not enough time to do it.* (learn how to use your time well)
2 *A happy mind needs a healthy body.* (watch what you eat)
3 *They say that a problem shared is a problem halved.* (talk about your problems)

Tell students that these are topic sentences and ask them to decide which of the ideas in Exercise 10a they correspond to. Students check their answers with a partner before feedback.

d Point out that a paragraph should go on to develop the idea expressed in the topic sentence. One way to do this is to give examples. Ask students to look back at the text and find the examples used.

Answers
You don't apply for a job in case you don't get it. You don't perform at the school concert because others might laugh at you.
Talk about your problem with a friend. Look for advice on the internet. Visualise yourself being successful. Practise breathing techniques.

OPTIONAL ACTIVITY

Write these sentences on the board:

1 *Watch what you eat.*
2 *Learn how to do something well.*
3 *Laugh a lot.*

Read through the three ideas and ask students to write some examples for each one. Students compare ideas with a partner before class feedback.

e Students write two more paragraphs. This may be an opportunity for them to create a poster with drawings to illustrate their writing. These can be displayed around the room and students can vote on the best one.

Memo from Mario

Natural health

1 When? What?

- Dictate these words to your students.

panicky

homesick

worried

nostalgic

lonely

bored

tired

annoyed

- Put the students in pairs to compare ideas on these questions.

(a) *Do you ever feel ...?*

(b) *What kind of situation makes you feel...? / would make you feel...?*

(c) *What do you do when you feel...? / would you do if you felt...?*

(d) *What could you do to avoid feeling...?*

- Put pairs together to pool ideas on what can be done to avoid or counteract negative feelings, and make lists of suggestions.
- If your group likes chants or raps, they could make up a better chant than this very simple one.

I'm tired.	*Take a nap!*
	Go for a walk!
	Put your feet up!
I'm bored.	*Read a book!*
	Watch a film!
	Phone a friend! etc.

- They could perform their chant or rap with a rhythmic accompaniment of clapping, stamping, etc.

RATIONALE
This activity gives students the opportunity to talk about their own feelings and share ways to avoid negative feelings. Making up a rap or chant is just for fun!

2 How could this be?

- Write the following prompts onto slips of paper. You will need enough copies to give one to every student.

man – son – driving – home – school sports

dangerous – road – truck – fast

man – avoid – collision – lost control

turned over – kill man – injure boy

ambulance – boy – hospital

operating theatre – prepared – surgery

surgeon – boy – cannot operate – my son

- Tell the students you are going to give them prompts, not complete sentences, which form a story. They should read their prompt, but must not show the slip to other members of the group. They should 'flesh out' the prompts into continuous text – one or two sentences – and tell their part of the story. The group should put the story in order and then discuss possible reasons for the apparently impossible situation.
- Put the students into groups of seven and give out the slips in random order. If the numbers don't work out, you can give some students two slips, or use the first prompt as a demonstration of 'fleshing out'.
- The traditional explanation is that the surgeon is a woman, the boy's mother, but your students may have other ideas.

RATIONALE
Asking the students to work from prompts is more challenging than just reading something out. The students need to cooperate to put the story in order and to agree an explanation.

3 A quickie

- Put the students in groups of four or five. Give them a topic – a subject or even a grammatical form, noun, verb, etc. The first student says a word and the next tries to think of a related word that begins with the last letter of the first word. They continue round the group to see how many times they can circle the group, either in a given time or until they can't think of any more words.

14 Movie magic

Unit overview

TOPIC: Films

TEXTS

Reading and listening: article about movie therapy; photostory: *What's so funny?*

Listening: talking about the effect a film can have on a person

Writing: synopsis of a film

SPEAKING AND FUNCTIONS

Talking about films and movie therapy

LANGUAGE

Grammar: clauses of purpose: *to / in order to / so as to*; result clauses with *so / such (that)*

Vocabulary: reacting to films;

Pronunciation: word stress in multi-syllabic words

1 Read and listen

If you set the background information as a homework research task, ask the students to tell the class what they found out.

BACKGROUND INFORMATION

Rocky is a 1976 American film about boxing, written by and starring Sylvester Stallone. It tells the story of a poor man from Philadelphia who becomes a champion boxer. The film won three Oscars in 1976 including Best Film.

Ghost is a romantic film made in 1990 and stars Patrick Swayze and Demi Moore. It tells the story of a woman whose dead husband comes back as a ghost to help her. *Ghost* made $505 million at the box office.

Alfred Hitchcock (1899–1980) was an English filmmaker and producer, famous for making thrillers and suspense movies. His films include *Rope, Psycho, Vertigo* and *The Birds.*

Rebecca is a 1940 thriller directed by Alfred Hitchcock. It tells the story of a young woman who is haunted by the memory of her husband's ex-wife.

Warm up

Ask students how often they watch films. Ask them to name any films that are particularly important to them, or which they like watching again and again. Can they say why?

a In pairs, students discuss the question. Ask some pairs for their ideas and invite the rest of the class to comment or add their own ideas.

b Pre-teach *unlock emotions.* Students read the text quickly to decide on the best title. You could set a two-minute time limit, encouraging a quick reading to get the general idea of the text. Tell them to ignore the gaps in the text at this stage.

Answer

2 Films help unlock emotions

c ▶ CD3 T24 Read through the phrases with students and help with difficult vocabulary: *high-powered, argument, surface, magnet.* Students put the phrases into the correct places in the text. Play the recording while students read and listen to check their answers. Play the recording again, pausing as necessary for clarification.

TAPESCRIPT

See the reading text on page 102 of the Student's Book.

Answers

1 f 2 b 3 a 4 d 5 e 6 c

d Ask students to read the questions and help with any difficulties. Students read the text again and answer the questions. Ask them to compare answers with a partner before feedback.

Answers

1 It involves finding a film which relates to someone's problem, then discussing the feelings it causes.
2 *Rocky*: to help a man overcome insecurity. *Ghost*: to come to terms with death
3 *Rebecca.* It made Bette realise she felt second best.
4 Because they conjure up nostalgia and innocence.

Discussion box

In pairs or small groups, students discuss the questions. Monitor and help as necessary, encouraging them to express themselves in English and to use any vocabulary they have learned from the text. Ask pairs or groups to feedback to the class and discuss any interesting points further.

2 Grammar

* Clauses of purpose: *to / in order to / so as to*

a **Weaker classes:** Books closed. Write the following on the board:

Why do you come to school?
Because I want ...
Why do you go to the cinema?
Because I want ...

Elicit answers from students, e.g. *Because I want to learn English. Because I want to watch a film.* Tell students that it is possible to remove *Because I want* from the sentences without losing meaning. The word *to* on its own carries the idea of purpose. Ask further questions (*Why do you go to the bank / the clothes shop?* etc.) and encourage students to answer beginning with *To*. Then follow the procedure for stronger classes.

Stronger classes: Ask students to read the examples. Point out that *to* on its own means the same as *so as to* and *in order to* – they are all used to express purpose. Students complete the rule. Draw attention to example 3 and clarify the point about the use of *not*. Explain that when the purpose is negative, we must use *so as not to* or *in order not to*. We can't say **I came in quietly not to wake the baby.*

Answer
so as to, in order to; to

b Students match the questions with answers a–d. Check answers. They then make sentences as in the example. Ask them to compare answers with a partner before feedback.

Answers
2 d She cried a lot in order to release her emotions.
3 c They went to the supermarket so as not to run out of food over the weekend.
4 a She arrived early so as not to miss the beginning of the show.

*** OPTIONAL ACTIVITY**

Ask students to think of several things they did last weekend and why they did them. In pairs, students tell their partner about each action and their partner has to guess why they did it, using *to, so as (not) to* or *in order (not) to.*

Grammar notebook

Remind students to note down the rules for this structure and to write a few examples of their own.

3 Grammar

Result clauses with *so / such (that)*

a Books closed. Write on the board:

The book was really exciting. I read it in one day.

Tell students that we can make this into one sentence, using either *so* or *such*. Write up the two alternatives:

*The book was **so** exciting that I read it in one day.*
*It was **such** an exciting book that I read it in one day.*

Give students a few moments to consider the differences between the two sentences, but do not analyse at this stage. Students open their books at page 103. Ask them to complete the sentences, using the phrases in the box. They can find the sentences in the text in Exercise 1 to check their answers.

Answers
1 such strong feelings 2 so passionate

b Students complete the rule. Emphasise the point that *such* is followed by adjective + noun.

Answers
so, such

Language note

You may want to tell students that it is possible to use *so* and *such* without a *that* clause, e.g. *It was so boring! It was such a boring film!* This usage is very common in conversation.

c Students join the sentences using *so* or *such ... that.* As you check the answer to number 2, ask students to change the word order and make an alternative sentence with *so.* (*The film was so moving that I almost cried.*) Do the same with sentences 3 and 4. (*It was such a boring film that ... This actor is so bad that ...*)

Answers

2 It was such a moving film that I almost cried.
3 They were so bored by the film that they fell asleep.
4 He's such a bad actor that you feel like laughing when you watch him.
5 Film therapy is so effective that many people overcome their problems.

d Students think of their own sentences using the phrases in the box. Give them one or two examples of your own to get them started. In pairs, students compare sentences. Monitor and check that they are using the correct structures. Ask a few pairs to tell you some of their partner's sentences.

OPTIONAL ACTIVITY

Write this on the board:

1 *hot – have a cold shower to cool down* (It was so hot that I had a cold shower to cool down.)
2 *expensive – borrow £500 to buy it* (It was so expensive that I had to borrow £500 to buy it.)
3 *silly film – walk out* (It was such a silly film that we walked out.)
4 *heavy box – not carry it* (It was such a heavy box that they couldn't carry it.)
5 *worried – not sleep* (I was so worried that I couldn't sleep.)

Ask students to work together and make sentences using *so* or *such*. Do the first one with them as an example. The answers given above are suggestions – other answers using different subjects and tenses are possible.

Grammar notebook

Remind students to note down the rules for this structure and to write a few examples of their own.

4 Pronunciation

See notes on page 124.

5 Speak

If you set the background information as a homework research task, ask the students to tell the class what they found out.

BACKGROUND INFORMATION

Avatar is a 2009 epic science-fiction film directed by James Cameron. Its incredible special effects show a planet in the Alpha Centauri star system in 2154. The film cost $237 million to make and has so far taken $2.8 billion.

Up is a computer-animated comedy-adventure film made by Pixar Studios. It was the first Pixar film to be shown in 3D and the second animated film ever to be nominated for a Best Film Oscar. The film made over $730 million at the box office, making it the third most popular Pixar film after *Finding Nemo* and *Toy Story 3*.

The Box is a 2009 American science-fiction psychological thriller. It stars Cameron Diaz and James Marsden as a couple who receive a box from a mysterious man who offers them one million dollars if they press the button sealed within the dome on top of the box.

Where the Wild Things Are is a 2009 American fantasy film, based on a 1963 children's book, and directed by Spike Jonze. It combines live action, performers in costumes, animatronics, and computer-generated imagery (CGI). The film is about Max, a lonely eight-year-old boy, who sails away to an island inhabited by creatures known as the 'Wild Things', who declare Max their king.

Warm up

On the board, make a list of the words for film types in Exercise 5a. Ask students to give examples for each type of film.

a Look at the photos with the class and ask students if they recognise any of the actors. Focus on the film titles and ask if anyone has seen any of these films. If so, invite students to say a little about them. Students read the descriptions and decide which type of film they are. Check answers in open class.

Answers

Avatar – science fiction
Up – cartoon
The Box – thriller
Where the Wild Things Are – fantasy

b Ask students how they feel when they go to the cinema. What type of films make them feel happy/sad/scared? Tell them that they are going to read about some people who want to try film therapy. Students read the descriptions of the people and work with a partner to decide which of the films would be most suitable as therapy for each person and why. Ask students to make brief notes about their decisions. Note that there are no 'correct' answers to this question – students will have different opinions. During feedback, try to come to a class decision about the best film for each person.

Answers

Students' own answers

c In small groups, students discuss which other films they have seen that they think might be suitable as therapy for the people. Listen to some ideas in open class.

OPTIONAL ACTIVITY

Write the names of these Pixar films on the board: *Finding Nemo, Monsters Inc., Toy Story, Toy Story 2, Toy Story 3, Ratatouille, Up, A Bug's Life, The Incredibles, Wall-E.* Divide the class into small groups and ask students to discuss which of the films they have seen and which ones they liked the best. Ask each group to agree on the three best films and hold a class vote to decide the favourite Pixar film in the class.

6 Listen

If you set the background information as a homework research task, ask the students to tell the class what they found out.

BACKGROUND INFORMATION

The Beach is a 2000 film directed by Danny Boyle and starring Leonardo Di Caprio. It is based on the novel by Alex Garland. The film tells the story of a young American backpacker who travels to Thailand to find adventure. He meets a strange man in a hostel who gives him a map with directions to a secret paradise beach. He meets a young couple and the three of them go to find the paradise beach. They find it and join the hippy community that lives there. As time passes, disagreements begin within the community and the backpacker begins to go mad. The beach community has a dispute with a group of local criminals. Eventually the community breaks up and the backpacker returns to his normal life.

a Ask students if they have seen *The Beach*. If any students have seen the film, ask them to describe what happens. If not, ask students to imagine what the film might be about and explain the plot to them (see Background information). Ask students to look at the scene from the film and describe how they feel.

b ▶ CD3 T26 Tell students they are going to listen to two friends discussing a podcast interview with Bernie Wooder (the film therapist from Exercise 1). Ask students to read through the sentences and check understanding of difficult vocabulary; *dissatisfied, straight from*. Play the recording while students listen and decide if the sentences are true or false. Encourage students to concentrate on the task and not to worry if they don't understand every word. Check answers.

TAPESCRIPT

Speaker 1: I was listening to this podcast the other day. It was an interview with Bernie Wooder.

Speaker 2: Who's he?

Speaker 1: He's a film therapist and he wrote a book called *Film Therapy – How it Changes Lives*.

Speaker 2: That sounds interesting. Did he give any examples?

Speaker 1: Yeah, lots. The most interesting was about this woman in her twenties who had a pretty good job, a boyfriend, a house and everything. So it was like, everything was perfect and then suddenly, one day, by chance she saw this film called *The Beach* and it changed her life.

Speaker 2: So, what's the film about?

Speaker 1: It's about this boy called Richard who goes to Thailand and finds himself in possession of a strange map. He hears that the map leads to a tropical paradise and he decides to go and look for it.

Speaker 2: Wow, that sounds good! So what happened to this woman who had everything?

Speaker 1: Well, there's this one scene where he's swimming from one island to another and when she saw it she just felt that she wanted to be as free as he was. So she decided, there and then, to leave her job and go to Thailand.

Speaker 2: What about her boyfriend?

Speaker 1: She asked him to go with her but he said that he couldn't leave his job. But she was still determined to go.

Speaker 2: So, did she go?

Speaker 1: Well, first she went to see this Bernie Wooder because she couldn't work out why she felt so strongly about it all and he said to her, 'What's so powerful about the film?' And she couldn't really work it out and then she said, 'You know, when I walk to work every day I never see a thing of beauty in London.' And when she said it, she started crying.

Speaker 2: Wow, yeah, that is powerful!

Speaker 1: The thing is, she hadn't taken a gap year and everyone she knew had – so she felt she'd missed out and needed that time to discover new things. In the end she left everything and went to Thailand to teach.

Speaker 2: How amazing, seeing what films can do to you. Has anything like that ever happened to you?

Answers

1 F (She's in her twenties.) 2 F (She'd watched it before she saw him.) 3 T 4 T 5 F (She wanted her boyfriend to come too.) 6 T 7 T 8 F (The girl went to Thailand to work.)

c Divide the class into small groups and ask them to discuss which films have had a really powerful effect on them. Encourage them to focus on the effect the film had on them and the particular parts of the film that affected them, rather than describing the plots of the films. Circulate and help with vocabulary as necessary. You may like to give an example of your own to get them started. Listen to some of the most interesting ideas in open class as feedback.

7 Vocabulary

★ Reacting to films

a Tell students they are going to read a quiz about four different types of film. Students read and complete the gaps with the words in the box. To check the answers, go through all three alternatives for each question in the questionnaire and elicit the meanings. Ask students what type of film each question is asking about (1 comedy, 2 drama, 3 horror, 4 science fiction).

Answers
1 funny 2 sad 3 scary 4 exciting

b Students do the quiz, then turn to page 126 to find out their score. Encourage them to discuss their answers in pairs or small groups. Then listen to some of their responses in open class.

c Students match the definitions with the expressions in the questionnaire.

Answers
1 yawning 2 fall about laughing 3 scream 4 cry your eyes out 5 chuckle 6 bite your lip 7 be on the edge of your seat 8 jump out of your seat

d Students complete the sentences with six of the expressions from the quiz.

Answers
1 yawning 2 jumped out of my 3 my eyes 4 bit my lip 5 fell about 6 the edge of my

Vocabulary bank

Refer students to the vocabulary bank. Read through the words and phrases in open class and check understanding.

Vocabulary notebook

Encourage students to start a new section called *Reacting to films* in their notebook and to add these expressions. They may find it useful to note down translations, too.

★ OPTIONAL ACTIVITY

Ask students to think of two films of different kinds that they have seen. Tell them to make notes about each one, focusing on:

- who starred in the film.
- what happened in it.
- what they especially liked about it.

Encourage them to use some of the expressions from Exercise 7 in their descriptions. You may like to give them an example of your own to show the type of description you are looking for. Monitor and help with vocabulary if necessary. When students have made notes and thought carefully how to describe the films, put them in small groups to explain their choices. Listen to some of the descriptions in open class.

Photostory: What's so funny?

8 Read and listen

Warm up

Write these questions on the board: *Have you ever seen a scary film? Did you watch it from start to finish? Were there some parts you couldn't watch? Were there some parts you watched more than once?* Students ask and answer the questions in pairs. Ask some pairs to report back to the class.

a ▶ CD3 T27 Students look at the photos, identify the people and describe what they are doing. Ask them to guess the answers to the questions, but don't comment on their answers at this stage. Play the recording. Students read and listen to check their answers.

TAPESCRIPT

See the dialogue on page 106 of the Student's Book.

Answers
They laugh because they were talking about two weird-looking guys appearing when Jack and Nick walked in.

b Students read the text again and find the answers to the questions.

Weaker classes: Before students look at the questions, you may want to play the recording again, pausing as necessary to clarify any problems. Then read through the questions with the class and check that the meaning is clear.

Answers
1 They have been revising too much.
2 Anything. As long as it's good.

3 It's about four guys who get lost in the woods.
4 Because she says the film will be too scary for him.

Discussion box

In pairs or small groups, students discuss the questions. Monitor and help as necessary, encouraging them to express themselves in English and to use any vocabulary they have learned from the text. Ask pairs or groups to feedback to the class and discuss any interesting points further.

9 Everyday English

a Ask students to find the expressions 1 to 6 in the story on page 106 and decide who says them.

Weaker classes: Check answers at this stage.

Answers
1 Lily 2 Amy 3 Lily 4 Lily 5 Jack 6 Nick

Students then match the expressions with the situations. Go through the first item with them as an example, if necessary. Check answers.

Answers
a 3 b 6 c 5 d 1 e 2 f 4

b Ask students to read through the sentences and complete the answers. Go through the first sentence with them as an example if necessary.

Answers
1 rings a bell 2 Got anything in mind? 3 this and that 4 I'm easy 5 all the way through 6 it's on the tip of my tongue

OPTIONAL ACTIVITY

See Unit 2, Exercise 9 Everyday English, Optional Activities.

10 Improvisation

Divide the class into pairs. Ask them to write down as many expressions from Exercise 9a as they can remember. Circulate and check they are writing expressions correctly. Read through the instructions with students. Give them two minutes (or more if necessary) to prepare a short role play. Invite some of the groups to act out their role play for the rest of the class and hold a vote on which was the most entertaining and which included the most expressions from Exercise 9a.

11 Making Waves (DVD Episode 4)

a In small groups, students discuss creative work. Do they do anything creative? When is the best time of day to be creative? Ask them to look at the photo and discuss why Melanie doesn't want to be interviewed by Nick.

b This exercise introduces some of the language from the DVD. Read through the sentences with students. Ask students to work in pairs and discuss which of the options they think the person will say in the DVD. Listen to some of their ideas but do not comment at this stage.

Answers
1 touch 2 up 3 stress 4 Teamwork

c Play Episode 4 of the DVD and ask students to answer the questions and check their ideas from Exercise 11b.

Answer
The film makes Melanie feel more positive and determined about her painting. Likewise it also makes Nick feel more positive about his work on the radio show.

12 Write

If you set the background information as a homework research task, ask the students to tell the class what they found out.

BACKGROUND INFORMATION
School of Rock is a 2003 comedy directed by Richard Linklater. The child actors in the film really play all the music and the star, Jack Black, is a musician as well as an actor – he records and tours in the pop group Tenacious D.

The planning for this exercise can be done in class and the synopsis can be set for homework.

a Ask students to imagine that they can learn anything they want at school. Which subjects would they like to include in the school timetable? Listen to a few of their ideas. Then tell them they are going to read about a film in which students learn to play rock music at school. Students read the synopsis and answer the questions. Tell them not to worry about the words in bold at this stage.

Answers
1 Yes, the writer likes the film.
2 Student's own answers

b Ask students to read the text again and to answer the questions.

Possible answers
1 It is all factual information about the film.
2 The story is told in the present simple as this makes it more immediate.
3 There is a lot of information about the main events in the first part of the film.
4 He stops at an important point so that the reader wants to know what happens next.

Language notes

1 We use the present simple as the main tense to tell the story of films and books. In a sense, the action is not finished as it still exists in the film/book and is therefore permanent. We also often use the present simple when telling jokes.

2 On film websites, writers use the word *spoiler* for a synopsis which tells the ending of a film. Any such review should begin with the expression *spoiler warning*.

c Draw students' attention to the pronouns in bold in the text, and remind them that pronouns refer back to someone/something previously mentioned. Students read the text again and identify who/what each pronoun refers to. Ask them why the pronouns are used (to avoid unnecessary repetition of nouns).

Answers
It stars Jack Black: the film
his dream: Dewey's
it's becoming almost impossible: his dream of living a rock 'n' roll lifestyle
his band: Dewey's
his on-stage clowning: Dewey's
they have a better chance: the other band members
him: Dewey
his flatmate: Dewey's
his services: Ned's
their teacher: the ten-year-olds'
He puts *them:* the kids
their weekly music lesson: the children's
There: in the music room
his kids: Dewey's

d Tell students they are going to write a synopsis which tells part of the story of a film they have seen recently. Tell them to plan what information they are going to include and to think about where they will end the story. Encourage them to:

- give a few basic facts about the film at the beginning.
- focus on the story.
- use the present simple for telling the story.
- use pronouns to avoid repetition and make sure it is clear who/what they refer to.
- end at a suitable point, without giving away the ending.

In a subsequent lesson, encourage students to read and discuss each other's synopses.

Check your progress

1 Grammar

a 2 are thought 3 is said 4 are expected 5 to derive

b 2 I studied hard so as to get better marks than last time.
3 He wore his best clothes in order to impress her.
4 We kept very quiet so as not to disturb him.

c 2 such a 3 so 4 such 5 such

2 Vocabulary

a 2 diagnosed with 3 painkiller 4 symptom 5 operating theatre 6 anaesthetic

b 2 edge 3 fell 4 cried 5 bite 6 chuckled

How did you do?

Students work out their scores. Check how they have done and follow up any problem areas with revision work.

Memo from Mario

Movie magic

1 Why did they do that?

- After doing section 2, tell the students this story:

  One evening I was on a bus (train/tube) and there were two men sitting near me. One was wearing white socks and the other was wearing black socks. Suddenly, they each took off one shoe and sock and exchanged socks so that when they got off, they were each wearing one black sock and one white sock.

- Put the students in pairs to write as many explanations of this as they can, using *They could / might / must have done that / in order (not) to / so as (not) to* etc. Then group the pairs into fours or sixes to pool their ideas and choose their two favourite explanations to report to the class.

> **RATIONALE**
> Creating hypotheses for unlikely situations challenges the students' creativity.

Acknowledgement

This activity comes from *Grammar Games*, Rinvolucri, Cambridge University Press, 1985.

2 Make a movie

- Choose one student to act as secretary and brainstorm different types of films onto one half of the board. Change the secretary, and brainstorm types of film roles onto the other half; try to get them to think of more than the obvious hero / heroine / villain. If necessary, ask them to remember films they have seen and think of the other characters.
- Divide the class into two groups, A and B. Subdivide group A into pairs and group B into groups of three or four. Tell those in group A that they are going to be film producers, the group B are actors' agents.
- Tell the producers (group A students) to work in their pairs to decide on the type of film they are going to produce, the three or four main characters needed and the type of actors these parts will require.
- The agents (group B students) receive the actor descriptions below. They should choose one actor for each agent. They can invent more details if they wish. They should invent names for the actors they have 'on their books'.
- When they are ready, tell the agents to circulate and try to 'sell' their actor to a pair of producers. The producers can ask questions about the actors and the agents should try to convince the producers that their actor is perfect for the part.
- You could ask the producers to describe their film and its cast to the class at the end of the activity and check how many of the agents managed to find a part for their actor.

  OR

  You could group the producers together with the agents of their cast to design publicity flyers, press releases, etc. for the film.

Actor descriptions

Men

1 *mid-30s; pale skinned with reddish hair; quite strong features; tall and a little fat round the middle; a deep confident voice; looks like someone used to making decisions and taking charge.*

2 *elderly (perhaps 60–70) but still handsome, with a head of white hair; a face with many laughter lines; a light, musical voice; slim and athletic-looking.*

3 *young adult; short, prematurely a bit fat, but strong-looking; a narrow face with alert eyes that dart about nervously; thinning dark brown hair.*

4 *about 30; tall, slim and very fit-looking; handsome, firm features with dark eyes and a ready smile; plenty of dark brown hair; an easy confident walk, almost (but not quite) arrogant-looking.*

5 *mature (50-ish); quite slender but slightly stooping, with thinning grey hair; a warm, confident voice with clear diction and well modulated speech; an expressive face and hand gestures.*

Women

1 *elderly, a commanding presence; quite heavily built; a handsome and deeply lined face with stern grey eyes; a strong deep voice; a lot of elegantly styled grey hair.*

2 *mid-20s; a round face with a small nose and mischievous-looking green eyes; blonde hair with a hint of red in a ponytail; quite petite, slim with a shapely but not voluptuous figure; a soft sweet voice.*

3 *about 35; quite tall, with a curvaceous full figure; bright, dark brown eyes and full lips; a luxuriant mass of glossy black hair; smooth-speaking, with a deep strong voice.*

4 *mature, nearing middle age, getting a bit plump; a round friendly face with warm brown eyes surrounded by laughter lines; a gentle melodious voice; dark brown hair cut in a short functional style.*

5 *mid-40s; tall and slender, with light brown hair pulled back into a single long plait; a narrow triangular face with grey eyes; a strong, musical voice; a quick, firm walk and hand gestures.*

> **RATIONALE**
> Once the activity has been set up, the students have a large amount of control. Creative thinking is involved on both sides, producers and agents.

Pronunciation

Unit 1 Exercise 6

* Intonation in questions

a ▶ CD1 T09 Students read the sentences on page 110. Play the recording several times and ask students to decide whether the intonation rises or falls at the end of each question.

Answers

1 ↓ 2 ↑ 3 ↓ 4 ↑ 5 ↓

b Ask students to look at the sentences and help them to work out this rule: Intonation usually falls in questions that begin with a question word. Intonation usually rises in questions that have no question word and require a yes/no answer. However, warn students that this rule is not invariable. The intonation can vary, depending on the context and the speaker's feelings.

c ▶ CD1 T09 Play the recording again, pausing after each sentence for students to repeat. Encourage them to produce the same intonation patterns as on the recording.

TAPESCRIPT

1 Where are you going on holiday?

2 Are you going somewhere nice?

3 When did you go to Italy?

4 Did you enjoy your holiday?

5 What did you see there?

Unit 2 Exercise 4

* Sentence stress and rhythm

▶ CD1 T13 Students read the sentences on page 110. Play the recording and ask students to focus on the rhythm of the sentences. Ask them to underline the stressed syllables. Check answers, then play the recording again, pausing for students to repeat each sentence.

TAPESCRIPT/ANSWERS

1 I always <u>forget</u> what to <u>do</u>.

2 I don't know <u>who</u> he <u>is</u>.

3 I don't <u>remember</u> what she <u>said</u>.

4 What I <u>like</u> about her is that she's <u>polite</u>.

Unit 3 Exercise 4

* Schwa /ə/

a ▶ CD1 T18 Tell students that the schwa is the most common vowel sound in the English language. Students read the sentences on page 110. Play the recording, pausing after each sentence. Point out that the /ə/ sound is often used to shorten longer vowel sounds in natural speech (*was* /wɒz/ becomes /wəz/, *can* /kæn/ becomes /kən/, etc.) and is not stressed. Encourage students to concentrate on how the underlined words are pronounced. Draw attention to the same /ə/ sound for the unstressed syllable in *lesson*.

TAPESCRIPT/ANSWERS

1 A: Who are you talking <u>to</u>? /tuː/
B: To Katie. /tə/

2 A: What are you waiting <u>for</u>? /fɔː/
B: For the bus. /fə/

3 A: What are you looking <u>at</u>? /æt/
B: At that bird. /ət/

b ▶ CD1 T19 Play the recording, pausing after each sentence for students to repeat. Make sure they are following the intonation patterns on the recording and that they are not stressing the schwa.

TAPESCRIPT

1 We need to finish but we're running out of time.

2 I was just too late to see the thing I wanted to watch.

3 Look at the clock – we're not at all late for the lesson.

Unit 4 Exercise 8

* /æ/ *accident* and /e/ *excitement*

a ▶ CD1 T23 Say the words *accident* and *excitement*, exaggerating the difference between the two vowel sounds. Students turn to page 110 and read quickly through the words. Play the recording twice. Students tick the words they hear and then listen again to check. Play the recording once again and ask students to repeat.

TAPESCRIPT/ANSWERS

1 set 2 pet 3 bat 4 tan 5 pan 6 band
7 men 8 said

OPTIONAL ACTIVITY

For further practice of the difference between these sounds, put students in pairs and ask them to say the words to each other. Their partner has to tell them which of the words they are saying.

b ▶ CD1 T24 Ask students to read through the sentences on page 110. Play the recording while students listen and then repeat.

TAPESCRIPT

1 What the man said was sad.
2 If this bat bends, then it's a pretty bad bat.
3 I bet ten pounds that it isn't a real tan.

Unit 5 Exercise 5

Contractions in third conditionals

a ▶ CD2 T04 Students turn to page 110 and read through the sentences. Play the recording while students listen and complete the sentences.

Answers
1 a 'd (had) b would c have
2 a 'd (had) b been c 'd (would) d 've (have)

b ▶ CD2 T05 Students read the sentences on page 111. Play the recording and ask students to listen carefully to the underlined words. Draw their attention to the way the words are contracted and linked together. Give special attention to the unstressed sound in the contracted form of *have* /əv/ and the sound link with the word before: /təv/ Ask students how *wouldn't have* and *couldn't have* are pronounced and elicit the correct pronunciation: /cʊdn't əv/,/wʊdnt əv/.

TAPESCRIPT

1 If she'd asked me, I'd have told her.
2 I'd have bought it for you if I'd had enough money.
3 If we'd left any later, we'd have missed the train.
4 We'd have won the game if he'd scored that penalty.

Unit 6 Exercise 5

/ð/ the and /θ/ thing

a ▶ CD2 T09 Students turn to page 110 and read through the words. Play the recording, pausing after each word for students to repeat. Ask them to write the words on the correct line according to the pronunciation of *th*. Go through the first few with them if necessary.

Answers
1 ð the, these, that, them, this
2 θ thing, three, think, thanks, thirty, thief

b ▶ CD2 T10 Before playing the recording, ask students to read the sentences on page 110 and think about how to pronounce them. Play the recording, pausing after each sentence for students to check and repeat. Encourage them to pronounce the *th* sounds correctly and to use correct intonation.

TAPESCRIPT

1 I think it's over there.
2 I'd like these three things, thanks.
3 I think that's the thief in there.
4 There are thirty things in those three bags.

Unit 7 Exercise 6

Linking sounds

a ▶ CD2 T16 Students read the sentences on pages 110–11. Play the recording and ask students to note how the underlined sounds are pronounced. Draw attention to the way a consonant sound at the end of a word links up with a vowel sound at the beginning of the next word: /faində/, /sɔːtəʊt/.

b Ask students if they can think of a rule about when final consonants are pronounced. If they have difficulty with this, refer to the examples in Exercise 6a. Pay attention to the difference between sentences 4/5.

Answer
The consonant is pronounced when followed by a vowel and not pronounced when followed by a consonant. Point out to students that the final consonant is pronounced when the word ends the sentence. e.g. *It's hot.* and *That's good.*

c ▶ CD2 T16 Play the recording again, pausing after each sentence for students to repeat.

TAPESCRIPT

1 I'm getting stuck with my maths homework.
2 I'm sure we can sort out an answer.
3 She's really good at sorting them out.
4 Let's try to find a solution.
5 I've tried hard but I can't find the answer..

Unit 8 Exercise 4

* Linking sounds (intrusive /w/ and /j/)

a ▶ CD2 T19 Write this sentence on the board: *Hello, I am* ... (your name). Explain to students that when we speak, words are often joined together and different sounds are sometimes created as our mouths move to form the next word. This is especially true when a vowel sound at the end of one word is followed by another at the beginning of the next. Say the words *hello, I, am* separately and then join them together in natural speech, showing students that a /w/ is created between *Hello* and *I* and a /j/ between *I* and *am*. Students read the sentences on page 111. Play the recording. Ask students to note down which sound they hear between the underlined words. Go through the first one with them if necessary.

Answers
1 /w/ 2 /j/ 3 /w/ 4 /w/

b ▶ CD2 T19 Play the recording again, pausing after each sentence for students to repeat. Encourage them to link the sounds as on the recording.

TAPESCRIPT

1 It's too easy to start a war.

2 Come with me and we'll find a solution.

3 So I decided to become an expert.

4 Can I give you any help?

Unit 9 Exercise 4

* Words ending in *-ough*

a ▶ CD2 T23 Students turn to page 111 and read through the words. Ask students to say the words out loud and to match the words that rhyme. Play the recording, pausing after each one for students to repeat. Draw attention to the different vowel sounds.

Answers
1 d 2 c 3 a 4 b

b ▶ CD2 T24 Students read the sentences on page 111. Play the recording, pausing after each sentence for students to repeat.

TAPESCRIPT

1 He coughed all through the night.

2 Don't go through there, though.

3 The new material wasn't tough enough.

Unit 10 Exercise 7

* Intonation in question tags

a ▶ CD3 T05 Write these two sentences on the board: *It's cold, isn't it? A mosquito is an insect, isn't it?*

Point out the difference between these two sentences. In the first, the speaker knows it's cold and is just expecting the other person to agree – he/she doesn't need to know the answer to the question. In questions like this, the intonation falls at the end. In the second sentence, the person isn't sure of the information and really wants an answer. In this case, the intonation rises.

Students read the sentences on page 111. Point out that in all these sentences the intonation could go either up or down at the end, depending on whether or not the speaker really wants to know the answer. Play the recording. Students mark the sentences with arrows to show the intonation they hear.

Answers
1 ↑ 2 ↓ 3 ↓ 4 ↑

b ▶ CD3 T05 Ask the question and play the recording again, pausing after each sentence. Ask students to repeat and to answer the question for each sentence.

Answers
Looking for information: 1, 4
Making conversation: 2, 3

c With the whole class, say the sentences with rising and falling intonation and ask students to repeat. In pairs, students practise saying the sentences in the two different ways. Their partner tells them which type of question they have used.

Unit 11 Exercise 7

* *record* (noun) and *record* (verb)

a ▶ CD3 T09 Explain that certain words in English look identical, but are pronounced differently depending on what part of speech they are. Students read the sentences on page 111. Play the recording. Ask students to underline the stressed syllable in each of the words in italics and to say if the word is a noun or a verb. Play the recording again, pausing after each sentence for students to repeat.

Answers
1 record (noun) 2 recorded (verb)
3 extracted (verb) 4 extract (noun)
5 contract (noun) 6 contracted (verb)

b ▶ CD3 T09 Play the recording again. Students listen and repeat.

Unit 12 Exercise 8

* /ɪ/ (sit) and /iː/ (seat)

a ▶ CD3 T15 Say the words *sit* and *seat*, exaggerating the difference between the two vowel sounds. Students read quickly through the words on page 111. Play the recording twice. Students tick the words they hear and then listen again to check. Play the recording again and ask students to repeat.

TAPESCRIPT/ANSWERS

1 seat 2 beat 3 fit 4 hit 5 sheep 6 tin

*** OPTIONAL ACTIVITY**

For further practice of the difference between these sounds, put students in pairs and ask them to say the words to each other. Their partner has to decide which of the words they are saying.

b ▶ CD3 T16 Ask students to read through the sentences. Play the recording, pausing after each sentence for students to repeat, first all together and then individually.

TAPESCRIPT

1 Don't sit on my feet.

2 You win – you beat me!

3 We need a bit of heat in here.

Unit 13 Exercise 5

* /n/ *thin* and /ŋ/ *thing*

a ▶ CD3 T20 Students look at the pairs of words on page 111. Play the recording. Students listen, and decide which word they hear. Check answers. Play the recording again, paying attention to the differences in pronunciation.

TAPESCRIPT/ANSWERS

1 thing 2 sung 3 ran 4 sing 5 ban 6 run

b ▶ CD3 T21 Read through the sentences with students. Play the recording, pausing after each sentence for students to repeat. Play the recording again, pausing after each sentence for students to repeat the words with /n/ and /ŋ/.

TAPESCRIPT

1 He ran in when the phone rang.

2 Don't bang on the table – it's banned in here.

3 Sorry, Ron – you're wrong!

Unit 14 Exercise 4

* Word stress in multi-syllabic words

a Students read through the words on page 111. Ask them how many syllables the words in each group have.

Answers
1 two 2 three 3 four

b ▶ CD3 T25 Students underline the words with a different stress pattern from the others in their group. Play the recording for students to check their answers. Play the recording again, pausing after each word for students to repeat.

Answers
1 delay 2 departure 3 reservation

Get it right! key

Unit 1 *win* or *beat*?

2 won 3 winning 4 beat 5 win 6 beat

Unit 2 *like* and *would like*

2 ✓
3 ✗ but I don't like running
4 ✗ I'd like to invite you to stay ...
5 ✓

Unit 3 Collocations: verb + *time*

2 wasted 3 took 4 spent 5 save

Reporting verbs: *recommend* and *suggest*

2 snowboarding 3 a hotel 4 I stay 5 going
6 looking

Unit 5 Talking about age

2 the age of 14
3 six years old
4 two-year-old
5 aged 12 to 18

Unit 6 The environment

2 wildlife
3 wild
4 environmental
5 environment

Unit 8 *may be* or *maybe*?

2 may be 3 may be 4 maybe 5 may be
6 maybe

Unit 9 Language

2 e 3 f 4 a 5 c 6 d

Unit 10 *In my opinion ...*

2 ✓
3 ✗ As far as I'm concerned ...
4 ✗ (Personally), I disagree ...
5 ✗ in my opinion
6 ✓

Unit 11 Comparisons

2 more comfortable
3 happier
4 faster
5 more experienced
6 better

Unit 12 *get* and *arrive* + preposition

2 to 3 in 4 in 5 to 6 –

Unit 14 Purpose

2 for 3 for 4 to collect 5 to

Project 1

A class presentation: a special person

1 Do your research

a Divide the class into pairs. Ask pairs to brainstorm to make a list of 'special people'. You could give an example of your own from each category to get them started. Encourage students to go into detail about why they think the people are special.

b Ask pairs to choose one of the people who they are interested in and want to know more about. Monitor to make sure that pairs have all chosen different people.

c Students do some preliminary research, either at home or in the library, on the person they have selected. They could take a 'timeline' approach and organise information chronologically. Students compare notes on their special person. Encourage them to work through the questions in the book and to make sure they have an answer for each question. If not, they should go back and do further research. Stress the importance of quotations, other people's opinions and anecdotes, as these points make presentations interesting.

2 Prepare the presentation

a Look at the mind map on page 122. Show students that they should choose four or more main areas to focus on and build up the mind map using your own example.

b In pairs, students decide which points each of them is going to focus on. Students may choose to do this in different ways, either one after the other, doing half each, or alternating several times during the presentation. If they have found pictures, maps, etc. that they can use in their presentation, one person can hold these up at relevant points while the other speaks. They may want to use the board to write key names or places.

c Students rehearse the presentation in pairs and give each other suggestions if it needs improving.

3 The presentation

a In pairs, students come to the front and give their presentations to the class. Encourage them to use their notes as little as possible and to keep their heads up and look around the classroom. Their classmates should write questions to ask later. If you have a large class, you may like to have students giving presentations over a series of lessons, rather than one after the other.

b After the presentation, invite questions from the rest of the class. The speakers should answer as if they were the person in the presentation. Encourage them to guess the answers if they do not know them.

4 Closing up

In open class, elicit the most important points when giving a presentation. Write some of the best ideas on the board and discuss which students gave the best presentation and why.

Project 2

A group presentation: design a social initiative or a charity

1 Do your research

a Divide the class into groups of three or four. Look at the photos and ask students to describe what they can see. What are the charity workers doing and what are they aiming to achieve? Give students time to decide which type of charity they want to set up and whether they want to work locally, nationally or internationally.

b In their groups, students discuss the aims of their charity. Encourage them to think carefully about what results they want to achieve.

c Brainstorm the names of a few charities and elicit some examples of slogans. Students then decide on the name and slogan for their charity and design an eye-catching logo.

d Students discuss the questions and work together to plan the activities of their charity. Encourage them to be as practical and specific in their planning as possible.

2 Prepare the presentation

a Students work together to decide what information they are going to include on their poster or website and make a rough sketch of the design. Ask them to draw or find suitable pictures. Give each group a large piece of paper to make a final version of their poster. If possible, they should also create a leaflet which describes their charity in more detail. You could photocopy each group's leaflet, or students may be able to design it on a computer and print out copies themselves. The leaflets can then be handed out to other students before the group's presentation.

b Ask students to plan what they are going to say. They should divide different parts of the presentation amongst themselves and make notes of what they are going to say. Remind them not to read from their notes, but just to use them to refer to where necessary. Give students time to practise their presentations and give each other feedback.

3 The presentation

a Ask each group to come to the front, stick their poster to the board or the front wall and present their charity. Encourage them to speak clearly and project their voices. Stand at the back of the class yourself to make sure they are audible. Give time at the end of each presentation for other students to ask questions.

b You may like to end with a discussion of whether they could use their ideas in any way in the school or in their community.

4 Closing up

Ask students to work in pairs or small groups and decide which charity idea they liked best. You could give each pair £100 and ask them to divide it among the charities according to which was the best presentation. The charity that gets the most money is the winner!

Project 3

A multimedia presentation: a foreign country

1 Do your research

a In pairs, students choose a country that they would like to find out and write about. Encourage them to choose a lesser-known country rather than a very familiar one, and try to ensure that pairs are working on a range of different countries.

b Read through the instructions with students and encourage them to think of topics of their own to add to the presentation. In their own time outside class, students research the information. You might like to give them a word limit, so they know how much information they need to find. In a subsequent lesson, students share their findings with their partner and decide what information they will use in their presentation.

2 Design your multimedia presentation

a–e If possible, students create a computer presentation. Read through instructions and hints with students to ensure that their presentations look as professional as possible.

f Encourage students to rehearse their presentation to check on timings and suitability of slides and information.

3 The presentation

Ask each pair to prepare to present their country. Encourage them to take a few notes about each area so they do not need to read from the screen and can face the audience. Give time at the end of each presentation for students to ask the presenters questions about their country.

4 Closing up

In open class, discuss the presentations and decide which ones were the most effective and why. Point out the positive aspects of using multimedia in the class.

Project 4

A class survey and a report: health

1 Choose the area you want to research

a Divide the class into groups of three or four. Read through the instructions with the class. Look at the sample topics and ask students what questions they could ask on each topic. In their groups, students think of more possible topics they could ask questions about. Listen to some of their ideas in open class and write the best ideas on the board.

b In their groups, students focus on the topics on the board and think about the questions they will ask in their survey. Ask each group to elect one person to take notes.

2 Prepare and carry out the survey

a Students transform their notes into questions for use in the survey. Read through the examples of different question types. Encourage students to choose mostly Yes/No or Ranking questions, to get answers which can be compared and scored. Tell them to work out a scoring system for their survey. Make sure that all students in the group write down the completed survey questions.

b Students in each group agree on who they are each going to interview, so that they cover the whole class. Students circulate, ask their questions and make a note of the answers.

3 Write up the results

a–b Back in their groups, students collate their results, add up the scores from their questionnaires and work out the average score.

c Students work together in their group to summarise the information for each topic and draw conclusions. Encourage them to create graphs as in the example to illustrate the information they have gathered.

4 Present your report

Ask students to decide who will present each part of the report, and give them time to rehearse. Then ask groups to present their report to the rest of the class. At the end of each presentation, invite other students to comment or ask questions. Finally, in open class, discuss whether the groups' results tallied and how great the class's awareness of health issues is. Invite students to suggest ways to make it better if necessary.

5 Closing up

Hold a class vote to decide which survey had the most interesting results.

Workbook key

Welcome section

A

1 2 caught 3 was 4 had heard 5 had never had 6 went 7 had had 8 had all been 9 found 10 took 11 showed

2 2 getting up 3 to ride 4 kissing 5 to tell 6 working 7 to be 8 drinking

3 2 imaginative 3 sensible 4 bossy 5 independent 6 ambitious 7 considerate 8 bad-tempered

B

1 2 should have told 3 should take 4 shouldn't have taken 5 should have brought 6 shouldn't have pushed 7 should be 8 shouldn't watch

2 2 I wish I had more time. 3 I wish it was Saturday 4 I wish I had seen that film when it was on. 5 I wish I didn't worry about everything. 6 I wish I hadn't given that dog my hamburger. / I wish that dog would go away. 7 I wish I had told the truth. / I wish I wasn't in trouble. 8 I wish I knew what she was thinking

3 2 over 3 out 4 up 5 over 6 away 7 on 8 back

4 2 a 3 e 4 f 5 b 6 d

C

1
2 The show will be called *Jail Break*.
3 Ten contestants have been chosen to spend three weeks in a prison.
4 The contestants will be asked to do various tasks.
5 Contestants will be nominated to leave the prison.
6 The last contestant to leave will be crowned 'King of the Prison'.

2 students' own answers

3 2 shoplifting 3 pick-pocketing 4 vandalism 5 joyriding 6 arson

4 2 doing 3 committing 4 caught 5 pay 6 do 7 put 8 sent 9 Breaking

D

1
2 It's a real antique. He must have paid a lot for that.
3 I might have paid. I can't remember.
4 She's not talking to me. I may have said something to upset her.
5 You live next door to the crime scene. You must have heard something.

2 2 am not allowed to 3 make 4 am not allowed to 5 make 6 am allowed to 7 let 8 make

3 2 viewing figures 3 audience 4 viewers 5 serial 6 celebrity 7 an episode 8 contestant

4 2 bit 3 headed 4 bear 5 tantrum 6 temper 7 cool 8 cross

1 Sport with a difference

1

a 2 where 3 whose 4 which 5 that/which 6 that/which 7 whose 8 where 9 that/which

b
2 ~~Those~~ students who have passed their exams don't need to come to the revision course.
3 The man ~~who~~ Tony was speaking to is my boss.
4 Saturday, which is my birthday, is also my day off.
5 The pasta ~~that~~ I had for lunch was delicious.
6 The sauce that came with the pasta was amazing.
7 I got an email from the lady ~~who~~ I contacted about the youth hostel.
8 I have to take a flight that stops in Birmingham.
9 The restaurant where we ate was very expensive.
10 The book ~~that~~ I'm reading is about the human mind.

c 2 whose 3 where 4 who 5 that 6 which 7 whose 8 what

d 2 a 3 a 4 b

e
2 Kate won the tennis match, that/which she played against Akeela.
3 I spoke to the man who works at the information desk.
4 Yesterday I met Jenny, whose sister was in my class in college.
5 They've started training for the match that/which will decide the championship.
6 Suren, who has lived next door for three years, has moved to London.

7 I asked him to post the letter that/which I had written to my cousin.
8 My brother booked a holiday to New York, where he lived for six months.

f 2 his 3 that 4 what 5 ✓ 6 it 7 ✓ 8 it

2 1 d 2 b 3 c 4 a

3 **a** Across: 4 court 6 kick 8 goggles 9 racket
Down: 1 puck 2 surfing 3 pitch 5 gloves 7 helmet 9 rink

b 2 beat 3 scored 4 scored 5 draw 6 sent off 7 scored 8 lost

4 ▶ CD4 T02 TAPESCRIPT/ANSWERS

1 What time does the flight take off? ↓ In about half an hour.
2 Are you going away for the weekend? ↑ No, I'm staying at home.
3 Do you want to go for a drive in my new car? ↑ I'd love to.
4 Where do we get off the bus for the museum? ↓ It's the next stop.
5 Will you send me a postcard when you get there? ↑ Of course I will.
6 Are you leaving for Paris tonight? ↑ Yes, at about ten thirty.

5 **a** 1 d 2 a 3 b 4 c

b 2 T 3 T 4 F 5 T 6 T

c 1 Each team has fifteen players and five substitutions are permitted during the game.
2 The field, goals and the number of players are the same as is a lot of the terminology.
3 By hitting the *sliotar* into the net under the crossbar.
4 They can hit the ball with the *hurley*, kick it or slap it.
5 Because there are a lot of Irish communities in other countries.

6 **a** Students' own answers.

b ▶ CD4 T03 TAPESCRIPT

1 Now Martin has the ball. He's tackled by Jones, but no, Martin dribbles past him, gets the ball past him. Martin still has the ball, and he passes to Fairhouse who heads it forward to MacColl. It's MacColl against Murphy now. They're the fastest men on the pitch. Is it going to be a goal? And … oh no, what a foul! The ref's blown his whistle and it looks as if Murphy's going to be sent off.
2 And it's Williams to serve. Yes, it's just on the line but Smith gets to it and forces Williams to run to the net. Is she going to get it? What a lob! What a hit! But Smith manages to get her racket up and smashes the ball back across the net. But it's not powerful enough and Williams gets her backhand volley in but just outside the line. Love-fifteen.
3 And the flag is down and they're off. Collins is off to a good start in the inside lane. But Fletcher is gaining speed, he's going faster, he's catching up. It looks like he's going to try to overtake on the bend. That's the hardest corner in the race! So many drivers have fallen out of the race here … But Collins is accelerating, he's getting faster, and oh no, he's skidding all over the place. Collins' car is on fire, and he's out of the race.
4 And now it's Summers. She takes a deep breath as she focuses her mind. After her disaster in the last part of the competition, on the beam, she'll want to do well on the vault. She's got a good speed up as she hits the board. She jumps higher than anyone else. Yes. What great height, although her balance could be better. But what a perfect landing.
5 Next one up is Jenson, the current champion. He makes his way to the top of the ramp. And he's off. He's looking cool and confident on the board today. Let's see what tricks he has planned for us today. What a jump! And now he's flying through the air. His favourite jump! It's breathtakingly high – and then he flies back down and up to the other side of the ramp … No protective gear, no helmet, nothing, for Jensen. Is he brave or is he just crazy? Let's hope he doesn't fall.

D 1 C 2 E 3 F 4 A 5
B is the extra picture.

c A ramp / board / tricks / jump breathtakingly high / flies back down and up / protective gear /helmet / fall
C serve / on the line / net / lob / hit / racket /smashes / backhand / volley / line / love-fifteen
D ball / tackled / dribbles / passes / heads / pitch / goal / foul / ref / whistle / sent off
E they're off / in side lane / gaining speed / going faster / catching up / overtake on the bend / corner / drivers / accelerating / skidding / car / race
F beam / vault / board / jumps higher / height / balance / landing

Unit check

1 2 whose 3 when 4 where 5 which 6 who 7 that 8 what 9 it 10 why

2 2 a 3 c 4 a 5 c 6 b 7 c 8 b 9 a

3 2 scored 3 helmet 4 drew 5 off 6 beat 7 goggles 8 pitch 9 league

2 People are people

1 **a** ▶ CD4 T04 TAPESCRIPT

A It was my cousin's birthday and my mum suggested that I call him to wish him a happy birthday. I rang the number and as soon as he picked up I started singing 'Happy birthday to you' really loudly. Once I'd finished I shouted: 'and have a really great day'. Imagine my horror when I heard someone saying: 'I think you have the wrong number.'

B We were playing cricket at school and I'm not really the sporty type so, when it was my turn to bat, I just swung and hoped for the best. As usual I missed the ball but I managed to let go of the bat. It went flying through the air and guess what, it hit my teacher right on the head!

C My dad's a teacher at my school. One day in assembly he was using his laptop and a projector to show everyone pictures he had taken at a school event. When he had finished he closed the programme and to my horror the background was a picture of me lying on the sofa in my pyjamas. Everyone burst out laughing, even Dad. I could've killed him.

D The night before sports day I decided to put on some fake tan cream so I wouldn't look so white. The packet said the cream would make my skin go a lovely golden brown colour. It took a really long time to put the cream on, and I thought I was very careful not to put too much on my arms and legs. But the next morning my skin was bright orange. I had to wear shorts and a T-shirt all day. It was so embarrassing. The worst thing was that no one said anything to me, they just giggled and looked away.

1 D 2 A 3 C 4 B

b 2 is 3 ✓ 4 that 5 thing 6 ✓

c 2 What's very frustrating about John is that he always changes his mind.
3 What makes life difficult for her parents is that she argues a lot with her sister.
4 It's essential to do the things that the teachers ask you to do.
5 What makes that restaurant special is that it has a good atmosphere.
6 It's good to know what you should do when people are hurt.

2 **a** ▶ CD4 T05 TAPESCRIPT/ANSWERS

1 What I <u>really</u> want to do is have a <u>rest</u>.
2 I <u>never</u> listen to what he says.
3 What really <u>impressed</u> me was her <u>presentation</u>.
4 I never know what to <u>say</u> in these situations.
5 What I would like to know is where are we all going to <u>stay</u>?
6 This isn't what you were saying last <u>week</u>.

3 **a** 2 c 3 f 4 e 5 b 6 a

b 1 d 2 a 3 b 4 c

c 2 cheeky 3 pushy 4 smug 5 sympathetic 6 shallow

d Across: 2 eccentric 5 selfish 9 approachable 10 unselfish
Down: 1 downbeat 3 calm 4 considerate 6 excitable 7 upbeat 8 bright

4 **a** *Pisces*: to repeat *Aries*: following *Taurus*: to pay *Gemini*: believing *Cancer*: to meet *Leo*: to talk *Virgo*: feeling *Libra*: thinking *Scorpio*: being *Sagittarius*: to think *Capricorn*: to lose

b 2 to get 3 being 4 going out 5 going 6 meeting 7 hanging around 8 to call

5 **a** 2 out 3 No 4 have 5 so 6 at

b 1 don't look at me 2 No chance 3 and so on 4 mind out 5 I can do without 6 I'd have thought

6 2 b 3 a 4 c

7 **a** Yes.

b 1 Text 2 is more detailed.
2 [suggested answers] He is returning to the room after not seeing it for a long time, and he is shocked at how the room has changed. He is also afraid that he won't be able to find his mother's diary.
3 It is dark and in a mess. It hasn't been used for years.
4 Yes, but not for a long time.
5 He want to find about what happened one night in the past.

Unit check

1 2 being 3 excitement 4 loved 5 to be 6 secret 7 whenever 8 tried to 9 pretentious 10 witty

2 2 c 3 b 4 c 5 a 6 c 7 a 8 b 9 b

3 2 sympathetic 3 calm 4 pushy 5 upbeat 6 eccentric 7 scatty 8 approachable 9 cheeky

3 Time travellers

1 **a** 2 c 3 a 4 e 5 f 6 d 7 h 8 i 9 g

b 2 Call 3 Did you take 4 I'll call 5 I saw 6 I'm going out

c 2 No, I haven't, but I'm reading the book.
3 Will you lend me the book when you've finished with it?
4 What do you know about the author?
5 The author, J. K. Rowling, has always wanted to write books.

2 **a** 3

b 1 took 2 gives 3 spends 4 've wasted

c 1 off 2 in 3 on 4 out

d 2 time off 3 take your time 4 ran out of time 5 just in time

e 2 of all 3 from 4 to lose 5 a matter of 6 a lot f 7 at the 8 to kill

3 **a** ▶ CD4 T06 TAPESCRIPT/ANSWERS
2 He wastes a lot of time on the Internet.
3 Michael arrived just in time to have dinner with us.
4 You can take some time off next week when we're not so busy.
5 Have you got time for a cup of tea?

4 **a** 2 a 3 b 4 h 5 d 6 c 7 f 8 e

b ▶ CD4 T07 TAPESCRIPT

Dad: Hello, Pete Richmond speaking.

Cathy: Hello, Dad. It's me, Cathy. I was just ringing to see if you got my letter.

Dad: Hi, Cathy. Yes, I got it last week. Thanks for writing.

Cathy: And ...?

Dad: And what?

Cathy: And what do you think? Did you find it interesting?

Dad: Well, to be honest with you, I just skimmed through it. I didn't have enough time to sit and read it properly.

Cathy: Oh, Dad! That's exactly why I wrote to you. You need to start making time for yourself. You work too hard. You need to take some time off.

Dad: Now, don't tell me what to do, young lady. I'm not going to listen to an eighteen-year-old who wanted to leave school three years ago.

Cathy: That's right, Dad. But you told me to think carefully and you also told me it was your duty to tell me what you thought. Now I'm doing the same thing fcr you. I love you. I can't stop you working and I don't want to. But I do want you to start making some time for yourself.

Dad: OK, OK. I get the message. As soon as I hang up I'll sit down and read your letter properly. Now what was the party like?

2 got 3 didn't read it properly 4 take time off 5 refuses 6 read the letter

c 2 Laura recommended buying / that I buy the latest Coldplay album.
3 Their mum warned them never to do that again.
4 She suggested going / that they go to the cinema at the weekend.
5 Jane advised me not to buy that mobile phone.
6 The instructor claimed that if we joined their gym, we'd be super fit in just a month.
7 She denied breaking / that she had broken the vase.
8 The teacher emphasised that he/she wouldn't accept homework that wasn't done on time.

5 **a** 2 c 3 a 4 c 5 c 6 a 7 b 8 a

b 1 Because there was a small swell.
2 Because there was a sense of repression and he was breathing very fast.
3 Because he was frightened by the scream.
4 A reddish piece of rock.

6 **a** It's about the future. We know because it says that the earth has been destroyed.

b b conversely c misinterpreted d sophisticated e elegant f subtle

c 1 b 2 c 3 a 4 b

Unit check

1 2 on 3 asked 4 that 5 offering 6 warned 7 spent 8 time 9 denied 10 has promised

2 2 a 3 b 4 b 5 c 6 b 7 c 8 b 9 c

3 2 waste 3 off 4 all 5 life 6 give 7 out 8 in 9 take

4 In and out of fashion

1 **a** 2 ✓ 3 ✓ 4 ✓

b (possible answers)
2 use electricity
3 buy toys from shops
4 travel in cars and planes
5 write emails / use the phone
6 wear jeans, T-shirts, short skirts, shorts
7 listen to CDs/MP3 players
8 have only one or two children

c (possible answers)
2 In the past, people used to use candles, but now they use electricity.
3 In the past, children used to make their own toys, but now they buy toys from shops.
4 In the past, people used to travel in carriages, but now they travel in cars and planes.
5 In the past, people used to write letters, but now they write emails / use the phone.
6 In the past, women used to wear long skirts and dresses, but now they wear jeans, T-shirts, short skirts and shorts.
7 In the past, people used to listen to records, but now they listen to CDs or MP3 players.
8 In the past, people used to have lots of children, but now they have only one or two children.

d 2 would spend 3 used to find 4 used to be 5 wouldn't go 6 used to drive

2 2 craze 3 catch on 4 spread 5 overwhelming 6 hooked

3 **a** 2 The dog barked at us in a horrible way.
3 He teaches English in a fun way.
4 They listened to her with enthusiasm.
5 We found the house with difficulty.
6 He said hello to me in a friendly way.
7 We need to do this again in a different way.
8 The children waited with excitement for the clown to arrive.

b 2 with enthusiasm 3 in public 4 in a different way 5 in a fun way

4 2 He reads as slowly as he talks.
3 Frank doesn't work as hard as he plays.
4 She plays the guitar as nicely as she sings.
5 We arrived as soon as we could.
6 I don't speak French as well as I speak Spanish.

5 **a** 2 in private 3 in a hurry 4 in secret 5 in a panic 6 in public 7 on purpose 8 by accident

b 1 public 2 hurry 3 private 4 panic 5 row 6 secret 7 accident 8 purpose

c 2 out 3 wrong 4 back 5 toe 6 down

6 **a** ▶ CD4 T08 TAPESCRIPT/ANSWERS
1 He lost his bat.
2 Have you got my pen?
3 It's Dad!
4 There's a bend in the road.
5 The cat sat by the fire.
6 The man can stay.

7 **a** 2 like 3 broke 4 influence 5 important 6 level 7 clothes 8 attempt 9 time 10 have

b ▶ CD4 T09 TAPESCRIPT

Host: So, good morning everyone. Welcome to the show and today we're inviting you to call us and tell us your favourite song, or songs, about fashion. Songs about fashion. OK? Well I bet I know what some of the answers will be, but let's see ... and wow, that was quick, we have a caller already and it's Janine. Hi Janine, where are you calling from?

Speaker 1: Hi Mike. I'm in Manchester.

Host: OK, Janine and your song is ...?

Speaker 1: Well there's only one choice really, isn't there? It has to be 'Vogue' by Madonna.

Host: Well there's a surprise! I'd never have guessed that anyone would choose a Madonna song!

Speaker 1: Well right, but isn't it a great song?

Host: I'm not going to answer that, Janine! Thanks anyway for your call and next we have Andy from ...?

Speaker 2: From Scotland. Dundee, Scotland.

Host: Morning Andy. So, tell us.

Speaker 2: Well I'm a huge David Bowie fan ...

Host: So you're going to choose 'Fashion' – right?

Speaker 2: That's the one. 'Fashion' by Bowie. Brilliant stuff. It reminds me of my days at university ...

Host: Thanks, Andy. No time for all that kind of stuff! University days – pah! Next please – and it's Phyllis. Hi Phyllis.

Speaker 3: Hi Mike.

Host: Where are you, Phyllis?

Speaker 3: I'm in Brighton.

Host: And what's your song?

Speaker 3: Well, Mike, as you can probably tell I'm a bit older than your other callers so I'm going with a 60s classic. It's The Kinks ...

Host: 'Dedicated Follower of Fashion'?

Speaker 3: Yep! Still love it after all these years.

Host: Well, it's good to know someone still likes it, Phyllis. Thanks for the call and next we have ...

Speaker 4: Mark. Hi Mike. I'm phoning from London and I'm going to choose 'Freedom' by George Michael.

Host: What? That isn't about fashion! We want songs about fashion, Mark!

Speaker 4: I know Mike – but have you seen the video? It's full of fashion models.

Host: That's not the point, Mark. Oh dear. Let's forget that one. Next please! Actually, no, let's have some music and listen to one of those songs now – we're going to play 'Fashion' by Bowie.

1 'Vogue', Madonna 2 'Fashion', David Bowie
3 'Dedicated Follower of Fashion', The Kinks
4 'Freedom', George Michael

8 ▶ CD4 T10 TAPESCRIPT

Presenter: Welcome to *The People Show*. This week we'll be talking to Philippa Chandler. Philippa works as a forecaster for Next Big Thing, a company which predicts what the next big youth trends will be. Philippa acts as eyes and ears for some of the world's top companies. She lets them know what their clients like and dislike and what they listen to. Her job is to keep her clients up-to-date, so she regularly interviews people on the street, goes clubbing and surfs the net. The information she gives could help her clients create the next big thing. How did she find a job like that? Well, Philippa read an article on William Higham, the founder of Next Big Thing, Britain's first trend forecasting agency. She sent Higham an email saying she was perfect for the job as a trend spotter because she was very sociable and she had answered questions such as 'Why we buy things' as part of her Cultural Studies degree. He immediately offered her a part-time job as a trainee and six months later she was part of the staff. So, Philippa tell us about your job ...

Philippa: I love my job. It satisfies my curiosity but it also makes me even more curious.

Presenter: How do you start your research?

Philippa: I often start by surfing the net for new trends and fashions. I can spend an hour looking at a new website. It's work, but it's not really productive or useful if I spend too long on one thing.

Presenter: What's your advice to young people looking for a job?

Philippa: First of all they should choose a course they are going to enjoy as well as something they think will be useful for work. Then they should try to get as much work experience as they can. The more experience you have, the easier it is for you to realise what you are good at and what you really like doing. If you haven't tried something, you'll never know.

a She works as a forecaster for the Next Big Thing, a company which predicts what the next trends for young people will be.

b 1 F 2 D 3 T

c 1 c 2 c 3 a 4 b

d (possible answers)
1 Something new and exciting that a lot of people will want.
2 It tells them what young people are interested in, and what the latest fashions are.
3 When she spends too long looking at one website.
4 Study something you enjoy, and get as much work experience as you can.

Unit check

1 2 popular 3 sharing 4 demand 5 group 6 are concerned 7 For a start 8 potentially 9 fashion 10 warnings

2 2 a 3 c 4 c 5 b 6 a 7 c 8 c 9 a

3 2 in 3 with 4 by 5 in 6 row 7 front 8 upside 9 purpose

5 Do something!

1 **a** 2 f 3 a 4 g 5 b 6 h 7 e 8 c

b 1 a 2 d 3 e 4 f 5 b 6 c

c 2 had 3 goes 4 'd visit 5 didn't have 6 don't go 7 'll throw 8 had made

2 **a** 2 donation 3 voluntary 4 leaflets 5 demonstration 6 help 7 involved 8 petition 9 marathons

b 2 help 3 voluntary 4 leaflets
5 donations 6 demonstration
7 petition 8 involved

c 1 worker 2 backed 3 hand
4 volunteered 5 collaborated 6 aid
7 with 8 voluntary

3 ▶ CD4 T11 TAPESCRIPT/ANSWERS

1 If you'd eaten that, you'd have been ill. /dəv biːn/
2 If you'd asked me, I'd have told you. /dəv/
3 If you hadn't told him, he wouldn't have known! /əv/
4 I'd have been delighted if you'd come. /dəv biːn/
5 It would have been difficult if he'd been there. /əv biːn/
6 Would you have come if we'd invited you? /əv/

4 **a** 2 PO 3 PP 4 PO 5 PP 6 PP

b 1 c 4 a 6 b

c 2 e 3 d 4 h 5 a 6 f 7 b 8 g

d 2 If I swam well, I would have / could have won the race.
3 If she hadn't worked extremely hard, she wouldn't be successful.
4 If my brother didn't love U2, he wouldn't have spent €200 on a ticket for their concert.
5 If I didn't hate action films, I would have gone to see Iron Man 2.

5 **a** c

b 1 It's named after a 'bogle' which is a kind of ghost – which the original organizers saw one night on their way home.
2 a
3 About 50% of those who enter.
4 The Ramble is shorter than the Stroll and participants don't have to walk at night.
5 It's for cyclists.
6 It's run by full-time students with a large team of volunteers.

6 **a** 1 will make all the difference
2 speak with one voice
3 saved ancient forests from logging
4 who want to get involved
5 informs or inspires you
6 Let your imagination run wild

b 2 F 3 T 4 F 5 T 6 F

Unit check

1 2 involved 3 donation 4 volunteers
5 I'd be 6 sponsored 7 I finished 8 support
9 handed 10 I'd finished

2 2 b 3 a 4 c 5 a 6 a 7 c 8 c 9 b

3 2 aid 3 collaborate 4 hand 5 raised
6 volunteer 7 involved 8 demonstration
9 sign

6 Our world

1 **a** 2 ... she'll be discussing the new Paris shop with George
3 ... she'll be having lunch with Alain Dupont
4 ... she'll be interviewing people for the shop manager's job
5 ... she'll be visiting the Le Clerc factory
6 ... she'll be looking at the new designs
7 ... she'll be flying back to Manchester
8 ... she'll be watching the film on TV

b 2 We won't be eating any natural food.
3 Children will be studying at home on computers.
4 We will be driving electric cars.
5 We won't be using telephones.
6 People won't be working more than 25 hours a week.

2 **a** 2 will have found 3 will have increased
4 won't have left 5 will have been
6 will our lives have changed
7 will have sold

b 2 The school will have disappeared.
3 The river will have dried up.
4 The shops will have become a supermarket.
5 They will have closed down the factory.
6 They will have put the car park underground.
7 People will have put solar panels on the roofs of their houses.

c 2 have lived 3 will be doing 4 will have played 5 will be watching 6 will be sitting

3 **a** /θ/: thin, bath, month, theatre, thin, Thursday, thirsty
/ð/: other, brother, clothes, weather

b ▶ CD4 T13 TAPESCRIPT

1 I think their brother is thin.
2 There are three rooms with a bath.
3 I thought I saw them at the theatre last month.
4 My mother bought new clothes on Thursday.

4 **a** 2 temperature 3 atmosphere 4 waste 5 species 6 starvation

b 2 dying out 3 go up 4 fouling up 5 get rid of 6 used up

5 2 turn up 3 sit back 4 turn into 5 turn down 6 take on 7 stand up for 8 look into

6 **a** 2 mind 3 Hang 4 break 5 business 6 face

b 1 Are you out of your mind 2 it's none of your business 3 Give me a break 4 Let's face it 5 Whatever 6 Hang on a minute

8 **a** 1 A plan to build a new supermarket.
2 He hopes there will be a full discussion of the advantages and disadvantages.

b 1 F 2 T 3 F 4 T 5 F 6 T

Unit check

1 2 have become 3 species 4 dying 5 is going 6 will have 7 will need 8 will be 9 bring about 10 starvation

2 2 a 3 b 4 c 5 b 6 a 7 c 8 b 9 a

3 2 up 3 of 4 up 5 up 6 about 7 species 8 starvation 9 resources

7 Peacemakers

1 **a** 2 was 3 were 4 had been 5 had been 6 had been 7 were

b 2 The front window had been left open.
3 The sofa had been torn.
4 The TV had been left on.
5 The books and CDs hadn't been tidied away.
6 The letters hadn't been collected.

c 2 I opened my bag and saw that my wallet had been stolen.
3 The street was very different – the trees had all been cut down.
4 When I got home, the TV had been fixed.
5 I didn't go to the party because I hadn't been invited.
6 We didn't watch the programme because we hadn't been told about it.

2 **a** 2 been fighting 3 been causing 4 been developing 5 played 6 become known 7 not studied 8 spent

b 2 a had/'d read
b had/'d been reading
3 a had/'d saved
b had/'d been saving
4 a had/'d been eating
b had/'d eaten
5 a had/'d been watching
b had/'d watched
6 a had/'d talked
b had/'d been talking
7 a had/'d been cooking
b had/'d cooked
8 a had/'d been writing
b had/'d written

3 **a** 2 a 3 b 4 d 5 a 6 c 7 b 8 a

b 2 on speaking terms 3 quarrel 4 pick a fight 5 come to blows 6 to the bottom 7 misunderstanding 8 negotiate 9 give-and-take 10 by the horns

4 **a** 1 b 2 b 3 a 4 a

5 **a** 1 a 2 b 3 b 4 a 5 c 6 a

b (possible answers)
1 Because he was expecting danger.
2 Do you speak English?
3 He thinks they are playing.
4 Yes. He whistles softly (in surprise).
5 Before things started to go wrong.

6 **a** 2

b who the person is / why they deserve the title / what charity your Samaritan supports / why your Samaritan has chosen this charity

c 1 An English teacher who teaches immigrants to the UK.
2 Because he really cares about his students and spends a lot of extra time helping them.
3 New Home – because this charity helps immigrants to adapt to their new life.

Unit check

1 2 from 3 travelling 4 arrived 5 been 6 had 7 what 8 with 9 about 10 for

2 2 b 3 c 4 c 5 a 6 a 7 b 8 a 9 c

3 2 have fallen out 3 came to blows 4 've made up 5 reached a compromise 6 resolving the conflict 7 aren't on speaking terms 8 picks fights 9 sort out

8 Kindness matters

1 **a** 2 It's wonderful to be kind.
3 It feels good to see people smile.
4 It's important to say you're sorry.
5 It isn't hard to be nice to other people.
6 It doesn't cost anything to help people.
7 It's not unusual to see people who are stressed.
8 It's difficult to understand why people don't talk to each other.

b 1 d 2 a 3 f 4 c 5 e 6 b

c 2 It's hard to have a good time in this town.
3 It's fun to make new friends.
4 It's nice to help other people.
5 It doesn't hurt to smile.
6 It's normal to forget people's names sometimes.
7 It doesn't cost anything to be kind to other people.
8 It's wonderful to see other people smile.

2 **a** 1 trial 2 properly 3 wrong 4 struggled
5 out 6 heartedly 7 easy 8 lengths

b 2 go to great lengths 3 struggled
4 trial and error 5 done something wrong
6 half-heartedly 7 did the job properly

c 2 sweating 3 made 4 bothered
5 was 6 couldn't

3 **a** ▶ CD4 T15 TAPESCRIPT/ANSWERS
1 You and I have to talk about it. [w sound]
2 Our uncle sent it for me and my sister. [y sound]
3 I think I'm too old to play those games. [w sound]
4 I wish he'd go away. [w sound]
5 It's the easiest thing to do. [y sound]
6 She used to study more. [y sound]

4 **a** 2 a 3 f 4 h 5 b 6 g 7 c 8 e

b 2 'll 3 'll 4 shouldn't 5 can't 6 'll
7 can 8 shouldn't

c 2 can't 3 must 4 can 5 mustn't
6 wouldn't

d 1 must 2 can/may 3 can't
4 might/could/may 5 wouldn't 6 must

5 **a** 3 ✓ 4 who 5 of 6 ✓ 7 ✓ 8 which
9 ✓ 10 ✓ 11 been 12 more
13 the (before peace)

b 1 False. She has been in two bands.
2 False. They only had moderate success.
3 True.
4 False. She won it for a song on the soundtrack.
5 True.

c ▶ CD4 T16 TAPESCRIPT

Al Green was born in Forrest City, Arkansas in 1946. By the age of nine, he was already performing with his brothers in a gospel quartet called The Green Brothers. They played many shows in the south of the US. When he was 16, he started an R&B group, Al Green and the Creations, with several friends from his high school. They later changed their name to The Soul Mates and their first single, 'Back Up Train' became a surprise hit, climbing to number five on the R&B charts early in 1968. However, the band never managed to have another hit and in 1969 Al Green became a solo artist. Over the next few years, Al released a number of albums, each one becoming more successful than the previous one. He also enjoyed seven consecutive gold singles during this time.

On October 18, 1974, Green's life was hit by personal tragedy when his girlfriend killed herself after an argument at his home. Green says that this incident was a turning point in his life and in 1976 he became a pastor at his local church. He continued to release albums but his popularity was in decline. In 1979 he suffered an accident while on stage and he took this as a sign to stop recording soul music and concentrate solely on gospel music.

He returned to popular music in 1988 when he recorded 'Put a Little Love In Your Heart' with Annie Lennox for the film *Scrooged*. Since then Al Green has continued to release both popular and gospel music albums.

1 He played a lot of shows with a gospel quartet.
2 He released several successful album and had seven gold singles.
3 His girlfriend killed herself and he had an accident on stage.
4 He decided to stop recording soul music and to record only gospel.
5 In 1988.
6 He makes pop and gospel music.

6 **a** ▶ CD4 T17 TAPESCRIPT

Speaker 1: A strange thing happened to me the other day ...

Speaker 2: Yeah? What was that?

Speaker 1: Well, I was just walking down the road from my place, down towards the town centre, I just needed, erm, I was going to, to the bank and I needed to get a bit of money and buy a couple of things, and I was listening to some music on the MP3 player and sort of singing along a bit. And there was this song called 'Good People', it's by, er, Jack Johnson.

Speaker 2: Oh yeah, I know that one. It's good, eh?

Speaker 1: Yeah it's, I mean, I really like it. Anyway, I look over to the other side of the road and there's a man trying to push his car over to the side of the road, he's broken down, you know, and he's trying to get his car out of the traffic, and he's doing it on his own ...

Speaker 2: Wow, that's tough ...

Speaker 1: Yeah, steering and pushing at the same time, it's not easy. And anyway, I thought that, I thought, you know, about the song I was listening to, you know, 'Good People' and he sings 'Where did all the good people go?' and I thought 'Good question!'

Speaker 2: Right!

Speaker 1: Yeah, and I kind of thought, 'Come on, why not? If that was me, I'd love someone to come and help me push the car,' so I crossed over and went up to him and said 'Can I give you a hand?' and he said 'Yeah, thanks mate, if you give the car a push maybe it'll start' so I said 'OK'. Then the guy looked inside the car and said 'Go and help him to push,' and I didn't know who he was talking to at first but then this small boy got out of the car and came to the back beside me. He was only about ten I think, a little kid, you know, so I said 'Come on, let's get your dad's car going – let's push!' and we started pushing and the car kind of started to move a bit ...

Speaker 2: Where was the man?

Speaker 1: Oh he was back inside the car behind the wheel, of course. Anyway, after about 50 metres pushing, I don't know, maybe 50 or 60 metres, the car started! Great! So I stood up and then the man leaned out of the window and shouted 'You! Get back in the car!' and the little boy ran and jumped in. And I started to walk up to the driver's window to say something – and the guy just drove away! I was so surprised! No wave, no 'Thank you', no nothing!

Speaker 2: You're kidding!

Speaker 1: No, honestly – there I am, standing in the middle of the road, all hot and sweaty, I've helped him get his car started, and he just drives away!! I mean, can you believe it!

Speaker 2: So you'll never push a car again then?

Speaker 1: Oh, no, I'd do it again. I mean, not everyone's like that, are they? You can't stop trying to help just because some people are horrible!

Speaker 2: I suppose not, but even so, it's kind of ...

The correct order is: picture A, B, F, D, E, C. Pictures G and H are not used.

b
1 He was going to the bank to get some money.
2 'Good People'
3 The car had broken down.
4 He was about ten.
5 50 or 60 metres
6 The man didn't say thank you.

Unit check

1 2 find 3 arguments 4 lengths 5 couldn't 6 wrong 7 properly 8 must 9 struggled 10 half-heartedly

2 2 a 3 c 4 c 5 a 6 a 7 c 8 a 9 b

3 2 found 3 great 4 of 5 sweat 6 endeavour 7 over 8 into 9 bothered

9 Language

1

a 2 f 3 a 4 e 5 b 6 d

b 2 brought about 3 look ... up 4 go for 5 came across 6 takes off 7 gets away with it 8 come up with

c
2 I'm trying to find out.
3 They got away with being rude.
4 Which dress do you think I should go for?
5 £1,000 would bring all my problems to an end. / £1,000 would bring an end to all my problems.
6 She comes across as being a bit superficial.
7 I looked it up but I still don't know what it means.
8 Who came up with that great idea?

d
2 I never found them out.
3 I came across them in my garden.
4 I got away with it.
5 I looked it up in my dictionary.
6 He came up with it in the bath.

2

a 2 work out 3 go for 4 took off 5 look ... up 6 came across 7 come across 8 taking off 9 went for

b Across: 1 sign 3 slang 4 bad 6 terminology
Down: 1 slogan 2 jargon 3 swear 5 cliché 7 idiom

3

a enough, tough, rough = stuff; through = blue; cough = off; though = know

4

a 2 gist 3 lost 4 totally 5 out 6 get

b 2 I'm managing to understand most of it.
3 I can just about catch the gist.
4 I understand a lot of what he's saying.
5 I can't make out very much.
6 The talks he gives are totally incomprehensible.

c 1 might say 3 and 5 2 might say 2 and 4
3 might say 1 and 6

5 **a** It's called Bannzish.

b 1 b 2 d 3 a 4 c 5 b

6 **a** Paragraph order: 5, 2, 4, 1, 3

b 1 T 2 T 3 F (It was popular with old people, university students and other people with not much to do in the afternoons.) 4 T 5 T 6 F (The winner from the previous day's show stays on to face a new contestant.)

Unit check

1 2 speaks 3 to speaking 4 would 5 trying
6 paid 7 to speak 8 make 9 get 10 which

2 2 c 3 b 4 a 5 c 6 a 7 c 8 b 9 b

3 2 word 3 Idioms 4 gist 5 swears 6 slang
7 make 8 sign 9 incomprehensible

10 Using fame to help

1 **a** 2 ✓ 3 ✓ 4 ✓ 5 ✗ 6 ✗ 7 ✓

b 2 Here is an extract ↑ taken from the first chapter of the book. which was
3 The Great Sphinx is a famous statue, half human, half lion, ↑ built by the Egyptians. which was
4 Harry Potter is a fictional character ↑ created by J. K. Rowling. who was
5 The A380 plane, ↑ built by Airbus Industries, can seat over 550 passengers. which was
6 The Live 8 concert ↑ attended by 15,000 people was a success. which was

2 **a** 2 c 3 a 4 c 5 b 6 a

b 2 sensation 3 household 4 made
5 made 6 enjoyed

3 **a** 2 thought 3 way 4 concerned
5 mind 6 ask

b and **c**
2 I couldn't care less. ∅
3 It doesn't really matter. ∅
4 It's not a good idea. ✗
5 I'm completely against it. ✗
6 It can't be a bad thing. ✓

d 2 express 3 considered 4 difference
5 second 6 high 7 poll 8 public

4 **a** 3 ✗ are you? 4 ✗ doesn't she? 5 ✗ didn't he? 6 ✓ 7 ✗ did it? 8 ✗ didn't they?
9 ✓ 10 ✓

b 2 isn't it 3 have they 4 does she
5 won't she 6 didn't they 7 shouldn't we
8 could they

c ▶ CD4 T20 TAPESCRIPT

Harry: Did you see the programme about celebrity charity work last night?

Carol: Yes, it was interesting, wasn't it?

Harry: Not really. It didn't tell you much you didn't already know, did it?

Carol: What do you mean?

Harry: I mean, we know everything there is to know about Brad Pitt, don't we? People don't want to see his face on TV again, do they?

Carol: Oh Harry – you can be really boring sometimes.

Harry: Sorry, but you asked me what I thought.

Carol: Well, yes – but if you always talk like that, people won't ask you for your opinion very often, will they?

Harry: OK, I'm sorry. Let's talk about something else. I mean, we shouldn't fall out over something as silly as this.

Carol: But Harry, you don't really think charity work's silly, do you?

2 did it 3 don't we 4 do they 5 will they
6 do you

5 **a** ▶ CD4 T21 TAPESCRIPT/ANSWERS
1 You're new here, aren't you? ↙ B
2 You speak French, don't you? ↗ A
3 I'm being boring, aren't I? ↙ B
4 It was an interesting programme, wasn't it? ↗ A
5 You didn't enjoy it very much, did you? ↙ B
6 This is a great party, isn't it? ↗ A
7 They won't be late, will they? ↙ B
8 You don't like this kind of music, do you? ↙ B

6 **a** 2 We might as well. 3 What do you reckon?
4 Leave it out 5 I couldn't care less.
6 I thought as much.

b b 4 c 2 d 1 e 5 f 6

c 1 I couldn't care less 2 I bet 3 What do you reckon? 4 Leave it out 5 I thought as much 6 we might as well

7 **a** ▶ CD4 T22 TAPESCRIPT

Interviewer: First of all, can you tell me, erm ... what is it that qualifies someone to represent UNICEF?

Expert: Well, UNICEF's celebrities have a wide range of talents and achievements, you know – there are singers, writers, actors, musicians, erm, footballers of course, erm, photographers – all kinds of people. But they all share a commitment, erm, a commitment to improving the lives of children all over the world.

Interviewer: I see. And how does UNICEF pick the people to be ambassadors?

Expert: Well, in each case a celebrity working with UNICEF happens because he or she has already ... erm ... shown some commitment. For example, Youssou N'Dour, the singer from Senegal, erm, he became a Goodwill Ambassador in 1991 but before that, in 1987 I think, he had already worked on a programme in his own country to immunise children, you know, protect them from diseases. And he'd also, if I'm not wrong, he also took part in concerts to raise money for kids in Africa.

Interviewer: Uh huh.

Expert: And Shakira, the Colombian singer, had also done a lot of work and shown a lot of interest in children, especially education for children, before she became an ambassador in, erm, in 2003.

Interviewer: Right. And, it's always important that they're famous, isn't it? I mean, you always ask famous people to become ambassadors.

Expert: That's right. But they don't need to be famous worldwide. I mean, there are many ambassadors who are best known in the parts of the world where they are going to work, and that's extremely useful. Erm, but the important thing, you see, the really important thing is that celebrities do two things. That they attract attention, when they travel and visit places, there are cameras behind them and in front of them because they're so well-known. And so the needs of children and the work of UNICEF get publicity, people know about it, this is very important ...

Interviewer: And the second thing?

Expert: Well, the second thing is access – I mean, very often the fact that these people are famous means that they get access to presidents and prime ministers. These are the kinds of people who make the big decisions, who make changes. And the ambassadors can talk to them, and, you know, maybe the ambassadors can have some influence. They can argue for children, they can argue for children's rights.

Interviewer: Uh huh.

Expert: And that's important, I mean, don't forget that children can't vote, they don't get to choose the leaders of the country. So it can be easy sometimes for leaders, erm, politicians to, erm, not to pay much attention to children.

Interviewer: Yes, indeed. And what is it that UNICEF wants children to have?

Expert: Four things, basically – health, education, equality, protection. UNICEF believes that all children all over the world have the right to these four things, but in so many places they don't get it. UNICEF wants to improve that situation and the ambassadors work to achieve that.

Interviewer: Is this a new idea, this idea of Goodwill Ambassadors?

Expert: Not really – erm, the first person to do it was Danny Kaye ...

Interviewer: The film star in the 1950s?

Expert: Yes, he became 'Ambassador at Large' in 1954, so he started everything. And then later the great Audrey Hepburn, the film actress, she took the role on, and she was incredible, she worked so hard, all the years up to when she died in 1993.

Interviewer: And there have been many other famous people too, haven't there?

Expert: Oh, yes, the list is a very long one ...

1 F 2 F 3 F 4 T 5 F 6 T 7 T 8 T

b ▶ CD4 T22 (possible answers)

1 They all share a commitment to improving the lives of children.
2 He took part in concerts to raise money for African children.
3 They can have some influence and argue for children's rights.
4 Because children don't have votes.

Unit check

1 2 borrowed 3 won't 4 make 5 see 6 household 7 bad 8 enjoying 9 will 10 concerned

2 2 a 3 c 4c 5 c 6 a 7 b 8 c 9 b

3 2 made a name for himself
3 had a difference of opinion
4 get a second opinion
5 The way I see it

6 have a high opinion of himself
7 He's a household name.
8 was big
9 enjoyed a lot of success

11 Music is everywhere

1 **a** 2 Do you know how much this costs?
3 Can you tell us what time the film starts?
4 Can you ask him what mark he got in the test?
5 Do you know when they arrived? / Do they know when you arrived?
6 Do you know who I can speak to?
7 Can you tell them who the teacher will be?
8 Do you know what his name is?

b 2 How much does this cost?
3 When does the film start?
4 What mark did he get in the test?
5 When did they/you arrive?
6 Who can I speak to?
7 Who will the teacher be?
8 What's his name?

c 2 b 3 c 4 g 5 d 6 h 7 e 8 a

d 2 what type of music is popular in the early mornings?
3 what you played this morning when you opened the gym?
4 what people like to listen to while they exercise in the afternoons?
5 what time it starts getting busy again?
6 what kind of music we can hear then?
7 how many clients the gym has got at the moment?
8 how many complaints you have had about the music you play?

2 **a** 2 Elvis Costello 3 Coldplay 4 Keane
5 Echo and the Bunnymen 6 New Order
7 The White Stripes 8 Fat Boy Slim

b 2 nearly 3 lot 4 just 5 far 6 a
7 nothing 8 better

3 **a** ▶ CD4 T23 TAPESCRIPT/ANSWERS
1 We export a lot of coffee to Europe.
2 Sugar is our biggest export.
3 There's been an increase in car theft recently.
4 The graph shows that the number of university students increases every year.
5 I'm sorry. I didn't mean to insult you.
6 Don't do that with your hand. It's considered an insult here.
7 What a lovely present. Thank you.
8 We'd like to present you with the 'student of the month' certificate.

4 **a** 2 lyrics 3 live 4 tune 5 hum
6 muzak 7 recorded 8 Instrumental

b 2 album 3 singer-songwriter 4 compose
5 soundtrack 6 track 7 cover

5 **a** 2 when 3 how 4 where 5 why 6 what

b 2 c ... that? 3 h ... live? 4 f ... year.
5 d ... party? 6 b ... went. 7 a ... works.
8 e ... went?

6 **a** 1 It used to take a bit of time to warm people up,
2 .. there's a terrible whine which for a moment I fear is their opening number.
3 ... everyone in the place goes mad. And Barry can sing. The crowd are so pleased ...
4 ... a crowd of thritysomethings ...

b 1 b 2 c 3 a 4 c 5 b

c (possible answers)
1 Being able to DJ successfully.
2 He is embarrassed to say the words Barry wants him to.
3 The crowd are tired/ excited from dancing to the band and don't want to dance.
4 students' own answers

7 **a** 1 The Rolling Stones, The Black Eyed Peas
2 Keith Richards, Mick Jagger
3 'Start Me Up', 'Rough Justice', 'Miss You', 'Satisfaction', 'Jumping Jack Flash', 'You Can't Always Get What You Want', 'It's Only Rock 'n' Roll'

b A 5 B 6 C 1 D 2 E 3

Unit check

1 2 sensation 3 charts 4 best 5 far
6 household 7 name 8 live 9 which
10 huge

2 2 c 3 a 4 a 5 b 6 b 7 b 8 c 9 a

3 2 along 3 live 4 canned 6 label
7 tune 8 cover 9 just

12 Nature's best

1 **a** 4, 5 and 7 are correct.

b 2 Hugging the hillsides behind me, the city of Rio de Janeiro is one of the most beautiful places I've ever seen.
3 Having booked into a cheap hotel in the Gloria district, we made our way immediately to the beach.

4 Having spent all day in the sun, Dave spent all night complaining about sunburn.
5 Having hired a deck-chair and an umbrella on the beach, I spent most of the time reading my Rio de Janeiro guide.

2 **a** 2 Lake 3 Canyon 4 mountain range 5 cliffs 6 Desert

b 2 Bolivia and Peru 3 the USA 4 South America 5 England 6 China

3 **a** 1 a 2 a 3 b 4 a 5 a 6 b

b 2 f 3 a 4 d 5 c 6 b

4 **a** 2 away 3 on 4 on 5 to 6 off 7 for 8 in 9 off 10 out 11 for 12 on 13 off

b 1 excursion 2 trip 3 tour 4 stopover 5 journey 6 commute 7 cruise 8 expedition

5 **a** ▶ CD4 T24 TAPESCRIPT/ANSWERS

1 She bit her sandwich.
2 I'll heat the chicken.
3 Can you feel it?
4 The ship is leaving in the morning.
5 The pitch was in bad condition.
6 Where did you put the beans?
7 Did he leave in the car?
8 Don't slip!

6 **a** 2 most 3 which 4 example 5 between 6 could 7 heart 8 sing 9 recent 10 instead 11 call 12 keep

b ▶ CD4 T25 TAPESCRIPT

1 Join the whales and dolphins on their voyage across the mighty Pacific Ocean. The songs, clicks and whistles of these amazing mammals are accompanied by beautiful original musical arrangements and vocals provided by the Pacific islanders. *Pacific Blue* will take you on an amazing journey to the mysterious world of the Pacific Ocean.
2 The beautiful but contrasting harmonies of the flute and didgeridoo combine to amazing effect and bring alive the hidden mysteries of The Great Barrier Reef. The relaxing tunes on *Coral Reef* will take you there and leave you in a world of fish and underwater beauty.
3 A combination of the awesome power of a thunderstorm and some of the most beautiful classical music ever written. This is *Classical Thunder*, an album to inspire and motivate.
4 Deep in the forest, where time has no meaning, the incredible waterfall descends endlessly over the rocks. In the distance, the birds sing their approval as the rain begins to fall. Relax and enjoy this visit, as the magical sounds of nature and dreamy modern music on the CD Eternal Forest make everything right in your world.

2 Reef 3 Thunder 4 Forest

c 2 CD 2 3 CD 4 4 CD 1

7 ▶ CD4 T26 TAPESCRIPT

Speaker: It's official – the beach is America's favourite place for a quick getaway. In an online survey of 1,023 people, three quarters of those who completed the questionnaire said that they would definitely or very likely visit a beach in the coming year. That's 75% – about 700 people – that's a lot of people! What's really interesting is that 43% chose the beach as their ideal destination for a perfect holiday, just higher than the number of people who chose the mountains. Holidays shopping in the city don't seem to interest people so much according to this questionnaire! Big cities had a much lower score. And we have even more holiday information from the survey. When asked if they would be going into the sea for a swim, 68% of the questionnaire respondents said they definitely would, while 27% said they would at least put their toes into the water. This means that 5% of everyone who replied have no intention at all of getting anywhere near the water! But when you look at the results for favourite activities, you realise there is more to do at the beach than just swim in the sea. The most popular beach activity is to have a beach party or a barbeque, with 44% choosing this. This was followed by building a sandcastle – 39% of all the people who replied said they would definitely make one of these. For themselves or for their children, we'd like to know! Relaxing was quite high on the list too. 32% said they would just like to lie on the beach with a good book. 21% of all the people who replied said they would like to be with their friends – aaaah! And flying a kite was a choice for 17%. They'll have to find somewhere windy! Maybe another reason why those 5% don't fancy getting into the sea at all, is because 39% of Americans are afraid of jellyfish when they go swimming. This was the top answer in the 'beach fears' category. Amazingly, people are more afraid of jellyfish than they are of sharks. Only 37% said they wouldn't swim because of the risk of becoming shark food! The sting, it seems, is mightier than the bite. Finally, internet users were asked what they look for in a beach. Here they were allowed to choose more than one category. A clean beach was the top answer. This was chosen by just under half of all the people who replied. Just one percent below, with 46%, was having a good view. Good weather was thought to be very important by 34% and warm water by 23%. We imagine this was not that 5% who refuse to get into the sea at all! Oh, and before I forget, the nation's favourite beach is Waikiki in Hawaii – now there's a surprise! OK, I'm packing my barbecue and beach hat – hope to see you there!

1 1,000 2 75 3 43 4 toes 5 sandcastle 6 friends 7 17 8 47 9 Good weather 10 Hawaii

Unit check

1 2 islands 3 ever 4 beaches 5 reefs 6 on 7 for 8 thunder 9 off 10 in

2 2 a 3 b 4 b 5 b 6 a 7 c 8 b 9 b

3 2 packing 3 back 4 reef 5 over 6 lake 7 voyage 8 cliff 9 on

13 Natural health

1 **a** 1 are known to be 2 is believed to be used 3 are also thought to have 4 is believed to have 5 is known to be 6 are known to be able

b 2 past 3 past 4 past 5 present 6 past

c 2 ... is said to be good at helping you relax.
3 ... are thought by scientists to have good memories.
4 ... is believed by experts to have been used by our ancestors to cure headaches.
5 ... is said by scientists to have been cut down more than 100 years ago.
6 ... are known to actually do us harm.

2 **a** 1 operating theatre 2 local anaesthetic 3 surgeon 4 diagnosis

b 2 check up 3 symptoms 4 suffer 5 recovering 6 diagnosed 7 diet 8 get better

3 **a** ▶ CD4 T27 TAPESCRIPT

1 A placebo is a substance with no active ingredients that is given to a patient.
2 A scientist is someone who does research, usually in a laboratory.
3 A diagnosis is a doctor's opinion about a patient's illness.
4 A symptom is a sign of illness in the body.
5 A general anaesthetic is a drug that makes you sleep during an operation so you do not feel anything.

1 d 2 e 3 a 4 c 5 b

4 **a** ▶ CD4 T28 TAPESCRIPT

Speaker 1: Tell me, how is everyone?

Speaker 2: Well Katy's in London and she's feeling very sorry for herself.

Speaker 1: That's because she's feeling homesick, I suppose.

Speaker 2: Yes. And poor Dilshan's exhausted.

Speaker 1: Why's that?

Speaker 2: He's working on a big project at university and he's over anxious.

Speaker 1: What about Nick?

Speaker 2: His usual guilty self.

Speaker 1: Why does he always feel so guilty?

Speaker 2: He gets very jealous over Julia and then he feels guilty.

Speaker 1: What about Julia?

Speaker 2: She's depressed.

Speaker 1: Because of Nick?

Speaker 2: No. She's got no confidence in herself and then that gets her down. She cries a lot, and she isn't sleeping very well.

Speaker 1: The poor thing. And how's your grandma?

Speaker 2: Poor Grandma's really inattentive. You never get the impression that she's really with you, it's like she's in another world.

Speaker 1: Is there something on her mind?

Speaker 2: I don't think so. I just think she lives in the past. She's so nostalgic about the past, especially the 1940s when she was a teenager. She thinks life was so much better then.

Speaker 1: And that leaves Abby ...

Speaker 2: Oh, Abby's always in a panic.

Speaker 1: What makes her panic?

Speaker 2: Everything! She's so absent-minded, she forgets everything and then panics. What a bunch, eh?

1 e 2 a 3 d 4 c 5 f 6 b

b 3 can 4 on 5 that 6 very 7 that 8 ✓ 9 to 10 ✓ 11 to 12 at 13 ✓

c 2 down 3 uneasy 4 on top of the world 5 uptight 6 over the moon 7 livid 8 irritable

5 **a** tuberculosis, dysentery, diphtheria, typhoid, measles, smallpox, cholera

b 1 A shortlist was made and members of the public voted for the most important medical breakthrough.

2 It includes all aspects of delivering clean water to homes and taking the dirty water away.
3 Huge factories opened and people moved from the country to cities.
4 Because the lack of sanitation caused illnesses and infectious diseases.
5 He showed that cutting off a particular pump in London stopped the spread of cholera.
6 Sewers and piped drinking water linked to people's houses.
7 Deaths from diarrhoea and dysentery fell by 12%.
8 It said to account for 88% of the 1.8 million deaths in developing countries.

6 2 c 3 a 4 d 5 d 6 b 7 c

Unit check

1 2 was prescribed 3 condition 4 was performing 5 felt 6 specialised 7 taking 8 symptoms 9 is believed 10 medicine

2 2 b 3 a 4 a 5 a 6 b 7 c 8 c 9 a

3 2 We were over the moon when we heard the news.
3 I'm on top of the world.
4 Don't be so anxious.
5 He made a quick recovery.
6 She was suffering from a bad headache.
7 He's very absent-minded.
8 The doctor wants to operate on the tumour.
9 I went to the doctor for a check-up.

14 Movie magic

1 **a** 2 e 3 a 4 c 5 f 6 d

b 2 so as to 3 in order not to 4 in order to 5 to 6 so as not to 7 in order not to 8 to

c 2 We got to the stadium early in order not to miss the start of the game.
3 I phoned Michelle so as to invite her to my party.
4 I didn't tell Ahmed about the accident so as not to worry him.
5 I took the train in order not to get caught in a traffic jam.
6 I'd like to speak to her so as to apologise.
7 He's saving all his money to buy a new computer.
8 Can you speak quietly so as not to disturb other people?

2 **a** 2 such 3 so 4 so 5 so 6 such

b 2 so 3 so 4 such 5 such 6 so 7 so 8 so

c 2 Nigel's so careless that he breaks something every time he comes to my house.
3 We set out so late that we didn't arrive until midnight.
4 That's such a nasty cough that you should see a doctor.
5 United played so badly that they were beaten five to one.
6 Rob's such an intellectual person that it's difficult to understand everything he talks about.
7 The sponsored walk was such a great success that we're going to organise another one.
8 He snored so loudly that I couldn't get to sleep.

3 **a** ▶ CD4 T29 TAPESCRIPT/ANSWERS
1 million 2 millionaire 3 confront
4 confrontation 5 problem
6 problematic 7 adapt 8 adaptation
9 recommend 10 recommendation

4 **a** 1 f 2 c 3 h 4 d 5 a 6 g 7 e 8 b

b Students' own answers

c 2 laughing 3 screaming 4 sitting 5 chuckling 6 biting 7 crying 8 jumping

d 1 goose 2 lip 3 hair 4 joy 5 face 6 laugh 7 hands 8 nails

5 **a** b It's on the tip of my tongue. c That rings a bell. d This and that. e Got anything in mind? f … it all the way through

b 1 d 2 e 3 a 4 b 5 c 6 f

6 **a** *The Purple Rose of Cairo*: director – Woody Allen; leading actors – Mia Farrow, Jeff Daniels
The Truman Show: director – Peter Weir; leading actors – Jim Carrey, Laura Linney, Ed Harris
EDtv: director – Ron Howard; leading actors – Ellen DeGeneres, Matthew McConaughey

b A 5 B 4 C 6 D 2 E 3 F 1

Unit check

1 2 order 3 so 4 a 5 about 6 such 7 not 8 which 9 chuckled 10 should

2 2 c 3 b 4 c 5 a 6 a 7 b 8 b 9 c

3 2 biting 3 goose-bumps 4 chuckling 5 yawning 6 horror 7 jumped 8 nails 9 screaming

Name ....

Class .... Date ....

ENTRY TESTS

1 Present simple vs. present continuous

Complete the sentences. Use the present simple or present continuous form of the verbs in the box.

~~like~~ spend have learn not understand think

0 *Do* you *like* surfing the Internet?

1 I .... what you mean. Could you explain once again please?

2 More and more people .... English these days.

3 Simon .... at least two hours a day on the phone.

4 I .... professional footballers get too much money. It's ridiculous.

5 you .... a good time? You look a bit sad.

[ ] 5

2 Making new friends

Complete the sentences with the expressions in the box.

fit in bond with feel left out settle in ~~stand out~~ join in

0 Jack always *stands out* because he wears very brightly coloured clothes.

1 Mary often .... at home because she has five brothers.

2 One way of .... is to listen to the same music as everyone else.

3 I usually .... quickly because I've changed schools so many times so I make friends easily.

4 Claudia .... her baby sister as soon as she was born.

5 Why are you standing on your own? Come and .... We need a good player on our team.

[ ] 5

3 *say* and *tell*

Complete the expressions with *say* or *tell*.

0 *say* a prayer

1 .... goodbye

2 .... the time

3 .... the difference

4 .... thank you

5 .... someone off

6 .... a secret

7 .... (it) again

8 .... sorry

9 .... the truth

10 .... a lie

[ ] 10

4 Past simple vs. present perfect simple

Complete the sentences. Use the past simple or present perfect simple form of the verbs in the box.

~~live~~ buy go eat be study

0 I *'ve lived* in the same house since I was a child.

1 I .... French at university before I became a teacher.

2 We .... a new computer last week.

3 Tom .... my best friend for two years but we still fight sometimes!

4 .... you ever .... a really hot curry?

5 Where .... you .... on your last holiday?

[ ] 5

5 Present perfect simple vs. present perfect continuous

Circle the correct words.

0 I've (seen) / been seeing three films this month.

1 How long *have you known / have you been knowing* Steve?

2 Max *has had / has been having* an iPod since last year.

3 I'm so tired! I've *written / been writing* 'thank you' letters all day.

4 We've *worked / been working* in the garden for hours and it still looks terrible!

5 Mum *has made / has been making* five cakes for my birthday party.

| | 5 |

6 Phrasal verbs with *up*

Complete the sentences. Use the correct form of the phrasal verbs in the box.

~~look up~~ meet up break up
break up look (someone) up turn up

0 When you come to London again, please *look* me *up* .

1 Don't worry about Tim. He finally .... at 10 o'clock last night.

2 Joanne and Ben .... last week. They both look really unhappy now.

3 I .... Matt .... when I was in town last week, but he was busy so we couldn't meet.

4 If you're free this evening, how about .... for a coffee?

5 It's very hard when two people ....

| | 5 |

7 Past simple vs. past continuous

Complete the sentences. Use the past simple or past continuous form of the verbs in brackets.

0 While we *were eating* (eat), the storm *started* (start).

1 As we .... (drive) along, they .... (play) my favourite song on the radio.

2 When Mary .... (hear) the news, she .... (cook) dinner.

3 John .... (leave) the concert while the band .... (play).

4 Katie .... (break) a tooth while she .... (eat) a piece of toast.

5 The boys .... (play) football when a dog .... (run) onto the pitch.

| | 5 |

8 Friends and enemies

Circle the correct words.

0 It's really bad to (tell on) / *stand by* a good friend.

1 Mark never does what he says he's going to do. He's always *letting me down / sticking up for me.*

2 I'm very lucky because I *fall out / get on well* with my sister.

3 You're my best friend, so I promise to *let you down / stand by you.*

4 Matt and David *fell out / got on well* because Matt used David's computer without asking.

5 Julia always *tells on / sticks up for* her younger sister because she loves her.

| | 5 |

9 Past simple vs. past perfect simple

Complete the sentences. Use the past simple or past perfect simple form of the verbs in brackets.

0 When I ___got___ (get) home, my parents ___had___ already ___gone___ (go) to bed.

1 Sally .... (not have) any lunch because she .... already .... (eat).

2 I .... (realise) I .... (forget) my keys while I was waiting for the bus.

3 Dave .... (miss) the concert because he .... (not hear) it was on.

4 Liz and Jack .... (know) each other for years before they .... (get) married.

5 When we .... (arrive), the party .... just .... (start).

[ ] 5

10 Jobs and work

Complete the sentences. The first letter of each word will help you.

0 Bob has been u*nemployed* for six months as there are no jobs in his town.

1 Sam left school without any q............... .

2 I have a p............... job, working 15 hours a week.

3 Tom was very unhappy in his job so he r............... last week.

4 What is the average monthly s............... in Italy?

5 I a............... for 50 jobs before I found the one I wanted.

[ ] 5

11 Future review: *going to*, present continuous and *will*

Complete the sentences. Use the correct form of the verbs in brackets.

0 Next term's timetable ___will be___ (be) ready on Friday.

1 Look at the sky! It .... (rain) soon.

2 I've arranged to see Tom later. We .... (meet) in town this evening. Do you want to come?

3 I .... (go) to the shops for you if you're busy.

4 I really want to buy a car so I .... (save) some money every month.

5 Mr Brown's going to the dentist this afternoon, so he .... (not be) in the office again until tomorrow.

[ ] 5

12 Travel

Complete the sentences with the words in the box. You won't need to use all of them.

check-in desk ~~platform~~ journey terminal customs cruise departure lounge boarding card

0 The train leaves from ___platform___ 7.

1 Your .... shows you your seat number on the plane.

2 You should wait for your flight in the ....

3 My parents went on a two-week .... around the islands of the Mediterranean.

4 It's good to see you again. I hope you had a good ....

5 You have to show your passport and ticket at the ....

[ ] 5

ENTRY TESTS

13 Verbs with prepositions

Complete the sentences with a suitable preposition.

0 Most teenagers argue ....*with*.... their parents from time to time.

1 I need to think .... what to wear to Jenny's wedding next month.

2 Why are you worrying .... your exam results? There's nothing you can do now.

3 Hurry up and get ready .... school. You're already late.

4 I bumped .... an old friend of mine in town yesterday. I hadn't seen him for years.

5 I must start revising .... my exams. I want to do well this year.

	5

14 The passive: present, past, present perfect and future

Complete the sentences. Use the correct form of the verbs in brackets.

0 ....*Is*.... rice ....*grown*.... (grow) in Europe?

1 A lot of new houses .... (build) in the village since the 1990s.

2 David Beckham .... (interview) on television last week.

3 The Amazon rainforests .... (destroy) completely if we don't take action now.

4 Millions of emails .... (send) around the world every day.

5 Not enough money .... (spend) on improving public transport over the last 20 years.

	5

15 *make* and *do*

Complete the expressions with *make* or *do*.

0 ....*do*.... business

1 .... money

2 .... your best

3 .... progress

4 .... a lot of good

5 .... a mess

6 .... room

7 .... a difference

8 .... sense

9 .... an effort

10 .... fun of (someone)

	10

16 Causative *have* (*have something done*)

Rewrite the sentences. Use the correct form of causative *have*.

0 The gardener cut the grass yesterday.
We *had the grass cut yesterday* .

1 Alice is cutting my hair on Saturday.
I ....

2 The boys have just decorated the kitchen.
We ....

3 The mechanic will fix the car at the weekend.
I ....

4 The optician tests my eyes every year.
I ....

5 Polly is organising a big party for us.
We ....

	5

17 *make / let / be allowed to*

Complete the sentences. Use the correct form of *make*, *let* or *be allowed to*.

0 You *are not allowed to* talk during exams.

1 My parents always .... me do my homework before I could watch television.

2 Would you .... me borrow your bicycle tomorrow?

3 When I was little, my parents often .... me stay up late on Saturdays.

4 Sam .... use his dad's computer unless he asks first.

5 You .... go home as soon as you finish your work.

[ ] 5

18 Television

Complete the sentences. The first letter of each word will help you.

0 The v*iewing* f*igures* for *Big Brother* are beginning to fall now.

1 So many s .... are just not funny.

2 The new p .... of the six o'clock news is really good-looking.

3 I'd hate to be a c .... on *Who Wants to Be a Millionaire?*. I'd be so nervous.

4 I'm so annoyed because I missed the last e .... of *Planet Earth* on television yesterday.

5 It would be fun to be in the a .... of a quiz show or a comedy series.

[ ] 5

19 Extreme adjectives and modifiers (*very, really, absolutely*)

Circle the correct words.

0 I'm feeling *absolutely* / (*very*) hungry.

1 It's *very* / *really* boiling in here. Can you open a window, please?

2 You must be *absolutely* / *very* exhausted after your long journey.

3 Wow – that's *very* / *really* fantastic news!

4 I thought the film was *very* / *absolutely* good.

5 Our dog was *really* / *absolutely* small when we got her.

[ ] 5

20 Modal verbs of obligation, prohibition or permission

Write *obligation*, *prohibition* or *permission* after each sentence.

0 You mustn't talk in the library. *prohibition*

1 We had to help our grandmother yesterday. ....

2 Of course you can use my dictionary. ....

3 I must remember to buy some bread on the way home. ....

4 You can't use your mobile phone on the plane. ....

5 You can go home as soon as you've finished. ....

[ ] 5

ENTRY TESTS

21 Verbs + gerund (*-ing*) / verbs + infinitive

Complete the sentences. Use the gerund or infinitive form of the verbs in the box.

~~go~~ stay tell talk help see

0 My brother wants *to go* to university.
1 Please stop .... and listen.
2 I hope .... you again soon.
3 Don't you remember .... Jack about the party?
4 Paul offered .... the old lady.
5 I don't mind .... at home if you don't feel like going out.

[ ] 5

22 Noun suffixes

Make nouns from the verbs and adjectives.

0 imagine *imagination*
1 agree ....
2 different ....
3 kind ....
4 possible ....
5 react ....
6 entertain ....
7 protect ....
8 prepare ....
9 popular ....
10 relax ....

[ ] 10

23 *I wish / If only ...* + past simple

Rewrite the sentences.

0 I don't like sports.
I wish *I liked sports* .
1 I can't speak German.
If only ....
2 We have so much homework every day.
I wish
....
3 I don't have enough money to buy Mum a birthday present.
If only
....
4 Tom is so good-looking! He gets all the girls!
I wish
.... !
5 We have an exam tomorrow.
If only
....

[ ] 5

24 Crime

Complete the sentences with the words in the box. You won't need to use all of them.

~~commit~~ arson do joyriding pick-pockets vandalism burglaries shoplifting pay send

0 If you *commit* a crime, you'll be punished.
1 When you're in a crowded place, you have to be careful of ....
2 If the crime isn't serious, you may just .... a fine.
3 Jim was arrested for .... last week. He'd stolen a shirt and tie from a department store.
4 The police think that the fire at the local school was ....
5 There has been an increase in the number of .... in our street over the last year.

[ ] 5

25 Phrasal verbs

Complete the sentences. Use the phrasal verbs in the box, in the correct form. You won't need to use all of them.

get (someone) down ~~turn down~~ call off pay off go out break down slow down come across pass away start out

0 Sally *turned down* the job .... because she didn't want to leave the company.

1 I'm sure all your hard work .... in the end. You'll do really well.

2 They .... the match yesterday because of the bad weather.

3 If you .... my new Franz Ferdinand CD, please tell me! I can't find it anywhere.

4 There was a loud noise and then the lights ....

5 Peter's car .... twice this year – and it's new!

☐ 5

26 Linkers of contrast: *however / although / even though / in spite of / despite*

Circle the correct words.

0 *(Although) / Despite* John was good-looking, he was very shy.

1 Tim speaks very good English. *Even though / However,* he doesn't think so.

2 Everyone enjoyed the picnic *in spite of / although* the bad weather.

3 I love playing tennis *even though / however* I'm not good at it.

4 My uncle has a lot of money. *However / Despite,* he isn't happy.

5 I enjoyed the meal *although / despite* not being hungry.

☐ 5

27 Problems

Complete the sentences. Use the correct form of the words in the box.

~~sleep on~~ ignore come up talk over sort (something) out come up with

0 It's usually best to *sleep on* a problem as things always look better in the morning.

1 My best friend always .... a solution to my problems.

2 The problem won't go away if you .... it.

3 A serious problem .... at work yesterday.

4 Is there anything you want to .... with me? I can see you're upset about something.

5 Don't worry about the mess. I'll .... it .... later.

☐ 5

28 Modal verbs of deduction (present)

Complete the sentences with *must be, can't be* or *might be*.

0 Tony *must be* very rich because he owns five cars.

1 That .... Ben at the door. He's in Spain at the moment.

2 Sarah .... at work. She sometimes works late on Mondays.

3 You .... hungry. You've just had a huge pizza.

4 You .... exhausted! You haven't slept for 48 hours.

5 I think Louisa .... annoyed with me. She hasn't even said 'good morning'.

☐ 5

29 Modal verbs of deduction (past)

Complete the sentences, using *must have*, *can't have* or *might have* with the correct form of the verbs in brackets.

0 Where are the car keys?
Oh no! I *must have left* (leave) them at home.

1 You .... (forget) my birthday! I reminded you yesterday.

2 I don't know where Ben is, but he .... (go) to the gym after work.

3 The film .... (be) really bad because a lot of people left before the end.

4 Jack .... (fail) his driving test. He's had so many lessons.

5 I wonder why Laura is so quiet. I guess she .... (have) a bad day at work.

[ ] 5

30 Expressions with *be* + preposition

Complete the sentences. Use suitable prepositions.

0 A: Where shall we go this evening?
B: I don't mind. It's *up to* you.

1 I'm really .... chocolate at the moment. I had much too much at the weekend!

2 Be careful! I'm sure Miss Jones is .... us. She's been looking at us very strangely!

3 Look at the sky. I'm sure it's .... to rain.

4 I'm totally .... using animals for experiments. It's cruel and unnecessary.

5 It's .... you if you decide to accept the job or not.

[ ] 5

31 Reported statements and questions

Write the direct statements and questions in reported speech.

0 'I didn't enjoy the film.'
Matt said he *hadn't enjoyed the film* .

1 'We can't come to the party.'
They said ....

2 'What time does the exam start?'
Sarah asked ....

3 'Have you seen my MP3 player anywhere?'
Louise asked John
....

4 'I'll help Tom later.'
Mary said ....

5 'Why didn't you say something?'
Rose asked Jack
....

[ ] 5

32 Appearance

Put the words in the box in the correct columns.

~~clean-shaven~~ ~~wavy~~ ~~slim~~ tall
freckles highlights broad-shouldered
rosy cheeks wrinkles medium height
straight a fringe plump

face	hair	height and build
clean-shaven	*wavy*	*slim*
....	....	....
....	....	....
....	....	....
		....

[ ] 10

33 Personality

Complete the sentences with the words in the box. You won't need to use all of them.

bad-tempered	~~bossy~~	sensible
considerate	imaginative	independent
determined	sensitive	insensitive

0 Janet is so *bossy*. She just loves telling people what to do.

1 Mum always thinks of other people first. She's so ....

2 It's impossible to help Ben. He's so .... and always wants to do everything by himself.

3 I'm sure Claire will get to the top as she's very ....

4 Now, if you were ...., you'd go to bed early as you have an important exam tomorrow.

5 Sally is one of the most .... people I know. She always creates such fantastic things.

[ ] 5

34 *I wish / If only* + past perfect

Rewrite the sentences.

0 I feel really tired because I went to bed late.
I wish *I hadn't gone to bed late*.

1 I missed the bus because I didn't hear my alarm clock.
I wish ....

2 I've got a stomach ache because I ate so much yesterday.
If only ....

3 I forgot my money so I walked home.
If only ....

4 I told my brother to get out of my room and now he's really upset.
I wish ....

5 I left my homework at home so my teacher was angry.
If only ....

[ ] 5

35 Anger

Match the definitions with the words.

0	quite angry	a	calm
1	get angry suddenly and shout	b	a tantrum
2	someone who gets angry really quickly	c	cross
3	childish display of anger	d	bite someone's head off
4	really, really angry	e	hot-headed
5	not angry	f	furious

[ ] 5

36 Non-defining relative clauses (giving extra information)

Join or rearrange the two sentences to make one. Use the words in brackets.

0 My neighbour is very friendly. He's a doctor. (who)
My neighbour, who is a doctor, is very friendly.

1 Our house is by the sea. It is 200 years old. (which)
....

2 Jack is very popular. His friends call him Jacko. (whose)
....

3 Mandy loves animals. She wants to be a vet. (who)
....

4 Dan Brown's last book was very good. I really enjoyed it. (which)
....

5 Bulgaria is a beautiful country. I went there last summer. (where)
....

[ ] 5

37 Definite, indefinite and zero article

Complete the sentences with *the*, *a*, *an* or *nothing*.

0 How can you spend so much time on *the* Internet?
1 Neil plays .... guitar really well.
2 My dad's .... engineer.
3 Our teacher's been in .... hospital for a month now. I hope she gets better soon.
4 I love listening to .... rock music.
5 I think the children are in .... garden.
6 What time do you usually get to .... school?
7 I love .... jacket you bought last week.
8 Could you buy .... carton of milk on your way home?
9 Did you like .... CD I gave you for your birthday?
10 We're getting .... new car at the weekend.

☐ 10

38 Adjectives with prefixes

Rewrite the adjectives with the correct prefix to make their opposites.

0 afraid *unafraid*
1 formal ....
2 patient ....
3 comfortable ....
4 logical ....
5 expensive ....
6 legal ....
7 responsible ....
8 possible ....
9 helpful ....
10 regular ....

☐ 10

39 *be used to* vs. *used to*

Complete the sentences. Use the correct form of *be used to* or *used to*.

0 I *used to* (live) in London but now I live in Berlin.
1 I start work at 8am so I .... (get up) early now.
2 I .... (play) tennis regularly but now I'm too lazy.
3 We .... (spend) time together because we both work from home.
4 Robert .... (be) very ambitious but now he knows it's more important to be happy.
5 We have a huge family so I .... (cook) for lots of people!

☐ 5

40 *feel*

Complete the sentences. Use the expressions in the box, in the correct form.

~~feel sorry for~~	feel up to	feel confident
feel stupid	feel the need	feel strange

0 I *feel sorry for* Matt because he has no friends.
1 I .... when I realised my mistake!
2 Claudia has been studying really hard so she .... about the exams.
3 Steven always .... to tell everyone how happy he is and how well he's doing.
4 It .... going back to my old primary school after so many years, but I'm glad I did.
5 I've got a terrible cold, so I .... going out this evening. I hope you don't mind.

☐ 5

Entry test key

1 1 don't understand 2 are learning 3 spends 4 think 5 Are ... having

2 1 feels left out 2 fitting in 3 settle in 4 bonded with 5 join in

3 1 say 2 tell 3 tell 4 say 5 tell 6 tell 7 say 8 say 9 tell 10 tell

4 1 studied 2 bought 3 has been 4 Have ... eaten 5 did ... go

5 1 have you known 2 has had 3 been writing 4 been working 5 has made

6 1 turned up 2 broke up 3 looked ... up 4 meeting up 5 break up

7 1 were driving / played 2 heard / was cooking 3 left / was playing 4 broke / was eating 5 were playing / ran

8 1 letting me down 2 get on well 3 stand by you 4 fell out 5 sticks up for

9 1 didn't have / had ... eaten 2 realised / had forgotten 3 missed / hadn't heard 4 had known / got 5 arrived / had ... started

10 1 qualifications 2 part-time 3 resigned 4 salary 5 applied

11 1 's going to rain 2 're meeting 3 'll go 4 'm going to save / 'm saving 5 won't be

12 1 boarding card 2 departure lounge 3 cruise 4 journey 5 check-in desk

13 1 about 2 about 3 for 4 into 5 for

14 1 have been built 2 was interviewed 3 will be destroyed 4 are sent 5 has been spent

15 1 make 2 do 3 make 4 do 5 make 6 make 7 make 8 make 9 make 10 make

16
1 'm having my hair cut on Saturday
2 've just had the kitchen decorated
3 'll have / 'm having the car fixed at the weekend
4 have my eyes tested every year
5 're having a big party organised (for us)

17 1 made 2 let 3 let 4 isn't allowed to 5 will be / 're allowed to

18 1 sitcoms 2 presenter 3 contestant 4 episode 5 audience

19 1 really 2 absolutely 3 really 4 very 5 really

20 1 obligation 2 permission 3 obligation 4 prohibition 5 permission

21 1 talking 2 to see 3 telling 4 to help 5 staying

22 1 agreement 2 difference 3 kindness 4 possibility 5 reaction 6 entertainment 7 protection 8 preparation 9 popularity 10 relaxation

23
1 I could speak German
2 we didn't have so much homework every day
3 I had enough money to buy Mum a birthday present
4 Tom wasn't so good-looking / I was as good-looking as Tom
5 we didn't have an exam tomorrow

24 1 pick-pockets 2 pay 3 shoplifting 4 arson 5 burglaries

25 1 will pay off 2 called off 3 come across 4 went out 5 has broken down

26 1 However 2 in spite of 3 even though 4 However 5 despite

27 1 comes up with 2 ignore 3 came up 4 talk over 5 sort ... out

28 1 can't be 2 might be 3 can't be 4 must be 5 might be

29 1 can't have forgotten 2 might have gone 3 must have been 4 can't have failed 5 might have had

30 1 off 2 on to 3 about 4 against 5 up to

31
1 they couldn't come to the party
2 what time the exam started
3 if he had seen her MP3 player anywhere
4 she would help Tom later
5 why he hadn't said something/anything

32
face: freckles, rosy cheeks, wrinkles
hair: highlights, straight, a fringe
height and build: tall, broad-shouldered, medium height, plump

33 1 considerate 2 independent 3 determined 4 sensible 5 imaginative

ENTRY TEST KEY

34

1 I had heard my alarm clock
2 I hadn't eaten so much yesterday
3 I hadn't forgotten my money
4 I hadn't told my brother to get out of my room
5 I hadn't left my homework at home

35

1 d 2 e 3 b 4 f 5 a

36

1 Our house, which is 200 years old, is by the sea.
2 Jack, whose friends call him Jacko, is very popular.
3 Mandy, who wants to be a vet, loves animals.
4 Dan Brown's last book, which I really enjoyed, was very good.
5 Bulgaria, where I went last summer, is a beautiful country.

37

1 the 2 an 3 – 4 – 5 the 6 – 7 the 8 a 9 the 10 a

38

1 informal 2 impatient 3 uncomfortable 4 illogical 5 inexpensive 6 illegal 7 irresponsible 8 impossible 9 unhelpful 10 irregular

39

1 'm used to getting up 2 used to play 3 're used to spending 4 used to be 5 'm used to cooking

40

1 felt stupid 2 's feeling / feels confident 3 feels the need 4 felt strange 5 don't feel up to

Teaching notes for communication activities and grammar practice

Unit 1

Communication activity

Area practised

Relative clauses

- Copy and cut up enough cards for one set per four students. Divide the class into four groups. Give group 1 a copy each of card A, group 2 a copy each of card B, etc.
- Tell the students to look at the pictures. Allow time for the group members to make sure they all know the words. They should do this without students from other groups hearing them.
- Then regroup the students so that each new group has one student with card A, one with card B, one with C and one with D.
- In groups, students play 'Taboo' by describing the items on their card without saying the name of the item. For example, A – *It's a person who films for TV programmes.* (A cameraman.); B – *It's a place that has water on all sides.* (An island.) The groups can race each other to guess the six items first, or set a time limit and tell each group to count the words they guess correctly.

Grammar practice key

1

2 is a place where
3 is a person whose
4 is a thing which
5 is the person who is
6 is a thing/book that

2

2 The film that stars Johnny Depp is on at the Odeon.
3 The maths exam that we have tomorrow is going to be difficult for me.
4 Matt, who lives next door to me, plays football three times a week.
5 The students who broke the window in the classroom have been expelled.
6 I saw that man whose wife is a presenter on TV today.

3

2 who are always late
3 is a book which/that tells you how to say words in another language
4 is a place where they try to make people better
5 is the man who created Microsoft
6 is a woman whose husband has died

4

3 which
4 who
5 ✓
6 that
7 ✓
8 that
9 ✓
10 which
11 ✓
12 ✓
13 who
14 ✓

Unit 2

Communication activity

Areas practised

Verbs + gerund / infinitive; *what* clauses

- Copy one worksheet for each student. Ask the students to read through the statements and then to write two more in the blank spaces at the bottom.
- Demonstrate with a stronger student how to make appropriate questions to find out the information. For example, in the first statement the question could be: *Do you like/hate shopping?*
- Tell the students that the column for extra information is very important. Check that they can make a follow-up question. For example, *What can't you stand about shopping? What do you enjoy about learning English? When do you hope to go to the cinema this week?*
- When you are confident that the students understand the task, tell them they must speak to as many classmates as possible.
- Set a time limit and ask students to stand up and ask each other the questions.
- When they have completed the task, ask some students what they found out about

TEACHING NOTES

their classmates. Encourage them to use *what* clauses. For example: *What Mario remembers about buying his first CD is that it was very expensive.*

- You could extend this task by asking students to write a summary of their extra information.

Grammar practice key

1

2 to speak
3 watching
4 playing
5 to lend
6 to buy
7 waiting
8 to drive

2

2 don't like about her is that she's rude to the teacher
3 need to remember is that English will be useful in the future
4 hate about shopping is waiting in queues
5 really need is a new pair of trainers
6 like about The Black Eyed Peas is that their music is original

3

2 to come
3 to buy
4 having
5 to do
6 to look for

4

3 ✓
4 for
5 ✓
6 ✓
7 a
8 with
9 ✓
10 of
11 for
12 ✓
13 to

Unit 3

Communication activity

Area practised

Reported speech

- Copy and cut up enough role cards for one set per four students.
- Divide the class into groups of four. You can also have groups of three with only one parent.
- Tell the students to imagine an English speaker is coming to stay in their home for two weeks. Discuss what problems may arise. Ask them if their parents speak English well.
- Give out the role cards and give the students time to understand and think about their role.
- Allow all the students with the same role card to discuss the role and make notes.
- Tell the students they have ten minutes to do the roleplay. Monitor closely and help when needed. Make sure the students with card A use reported speech when they interpret the parents' comments. For example, *My father asked if you had a good journey. My mother would like to know if you need any towels.*
- If time allows, repeat the roleplay but change the students' roles so that those who were speaking L1 (the parents) get a chance to do the more challenging roles.

Grammar practice key

1

2 a
3 a
4 b
5 c
6 b

2

2 suggested going to the cinema on Thursday
3 encouraged me to apologise to her
4 denied eating the last chocolate
5 recommended that Paula took more exercise
6 stated that the nation was in crisis

3

2 'I've never been happier.'
3 'How are you and the team going to celebrate winning the league?'
4 'We're not going to celebrate today because we have to concentrate on training for the Champions League final.'
5 'Good luck for the final.'
6 'Thank you. Can I say hello to my mum? She'll be watching the interview on TV.'
7 'Of course you can. Tonight you're the hero of thousands of Barcelona fans!'

4

2 (that) she had been to the doctor's the day before / the previous day
3 (that) they would be there by the following/next day
4 (that) she was going to Paris the following week
5 (that) he had had the worst morning of his life that day
6 (that) she was going to Amsterdam the following weekend

Unit 4

Communication activity

Areas practised

Common adverbial phrases; *used to* and *would*

- Copy and cut up several sets of cards. Ensure there are two or three cards for each student.
- Form a circle with the students. Tell them you are going to make up a story as a class.
- Give each student two or three cards and tell them that they must use the words on one of the cards as they're telling the story.
- Start the story and, if possible, connect it to a topic you want to revise from a previous class. Tell the students that it doesn't matter how absurd the story is. As you say the words on your card, hold it up to show the class. The student on your right must then continue the same story, using the words on one of their cards.
- Continue round the circle until all the students have added to the story and used a card.
- If time allows, make up two or three stories with the class so that they use all their cards.

Grammar practice key

1

2 used to be a fantastic football player
3 we would / used to listen to the radio every Saturday afternoon
4 I used to love going to the beach
5 that people used to / would work without computers in the past
6 I didn't use to enjoy reading, but I do now

2

2 [✓]
3 [✗] No. I didn't use to like them.
4 [✓]
5 [✗] I used to think they were the best pop group in the world.
6 [✗] Did you (use to) have a Rubik's Cube when you were younger?
7 [✓]

3

2 Did you use to have long hair?
3 Didn't you use to ride a bicycle?
4 Did you use to eat fast food?
5 Didn't you use to watch TV?

4

2 annoys me on purpose
3 in secret
4 by accident
5 in a row
6 in a panic

Unit 5

Communication activity

Area practised

Conditionals review

- Before you copy the cards, complete the three blank ones with topics that are appropriate for your students. Personalise or localise the themes.
- Copy and cut up a set of cards for each group of three or four students.
- Divide the class into groups of three or four and give each group a set of cards.
- Ask the students to take one card at a time and discuss it with their group.
- If necessary, set a time limit of two minutes per card.
- Monitor and check that students are using conditionals correctly. Then have class feedback on the main ideas raised.

Grammar practice key

1

2 0
3 2
4 M
5 3
6 3

2

3 had
4 to
5 it
6 ✓
7 for
8 would
9 ✓
10 ✓
11 have

3

2 had enough money we'd buy a flat
3 (love to) go swimming if I had more time
4 write to Jonathan if he (ever) replied to my emails
5 played hip-hop I'd go to that club
6 wasn't bad for my skin I'd eat more / a lot of it

4

2 b
3 d
4 a
5 c
6 a

Unit 6

Communication activity

Areas practised

Future perfect; future continuous; time expressions

- Copy one worksheet for each student.
- Ask the students if they know anything about fortune-tellers, crystal balls etc.
- Tell the students they are going to be fortune-tellers and to think about their future, the future of the world and the future of a friend or famous person. They should specify who the friend / famous person is.
- Give out the worksheets and ask the students to think about the future. They should make notes in the different sections and time zones. Give some examples: *In two years' time I'll have left school. By 2050 we'll have used up most of the world's resources. Ten years from now Antonia will be living in London and working in a bank.*
- When the students have made notes, divide the class into groups of three or four and ask them to tell each other about their predictions.
- Monitor and check that the students are using the future forms and time expressions correctly.

Grammar practice key

1

2 In two years' time
3 from now
4 for
5 By
6 during

2

2 will be looking for
3 will be making
4 will have fished
5 will have planted
6 will be teaching

3

3 ✓
4 be
5 during
6 by
7 ✓
8 for
9 ✓
10 the
11 being
12 ✓
13 ✓

4

2 government
3 reduction
4 pollution
5 recycle
6 unplug

Unit 7

Communication activity

Area practised

Past perfect continuous

- This activity would be good practice for part 2 of the FCE writing paper in which students may have the option of writing a story that begins or ends with a given line.
- Copy and cut up enough cards so that there is one opening line card and one time card for each pair of students.
- Ask the students how they usually find out about what's happening in the news.
- Ask them if they can remember any strange or unusual news items they've heard recently. Give some examples of your own (include the past perfect continuous tense). For example, *A group of miners was rescued today from a mine in Tasmania. They had been waiting for a week to be rescued.* Encourage students to ask you questions about the event.
- Divide the class into pairs or groups of three and tell them they are going to invent a news story.

- Give each pair or group an opening line card and a time card. Set a time limit for the students to plan the story around the line and then ask different groups to tell the rest of the class their news story.
- As an extension activity, stronger students could write up the story as a news article.

Grammar practice key

1

2 had / 'd been working
3 had been losing
4 had / 'd been crying
5 had been studying
6 had / 'd been driving

2

2 had been made
3 had been cooked
4 had been done
5 had been prevented
6 had been invited
7 had been told

3

2 had (already) been sent
3 had been celebrating
4 hadn't been invented
5 had been waiting
6 had been hoping

4

2 He'd been looking for a job for six months when he finally got an interview.
3 They'd been playing tennis for five minutes when the rain started / it started to rain.
4 She'd been doing her homework when she got the text message.
5 They'd been queuing for three hours by the time they bought the concert tickets.
6 He'd been training for two years before he ran a marathon.

Unit 8

Communication activity

Areas practised

Modals review; dummy *it*

- Copy and cut up one set of cards for each group of three or four students.
- Ask the students what jobs they'd like to do in the future and ask them how they could start to prepare themselves for their dream job.
- Show the students one of the careers advice cards and elicit answers to fill the gaps. For example, *If you want to be a pop star you should have singing lessons. You could learn to play an instrument. It's a good idea to start a band with friends.*
- Divide the class into groups of three or four and give each group a set of cards. Ask the students to complete the cards in their groups. They should choose four more jobs for the blank cards.
- When they have finished, ask each group to read out the advice on one or more of their cards, without saying what the job is. The other groups have to guess.
- This could lead to a discussion to see if the groups agree with each other's careers advice.

Grammar practice key

1

2 important to speak foreign languages well these days
3 forbidden to skateboard in the city centre
4 wonderful to see Rachel at the weekend
5 bad for your eyes to watch too much TV
6 a great feeling to wake up late on a Saturday morning

2

2 [✓]
3 [✗] He can speak Japanese.
4 [✓]
5 [✗] We should listen to his opinion.
6 [✗] I might go to the party on Saturday.

3

2 You shouldn't revise the new vocabulary at home.
3 He can't speak Japanese.
4 It won't be sunny tomorrow.
5 We shouldn't listen to his opinion.
6 I might not go to the party on Saturday.

4

2 don't have to
3 must not smoke
4 could swim when
5 you should apply
6 do you think will

Unit 9

Communication activity

Area practised

Phrasal verbs

- Copy one set of dice for each group of four or five students. Copy onto card, or paper and glue onto a piece of card. Ask two students in each group to cut out and make one dice each.

- Demonstrate the activity by asking a stronger student to roll a dice and to make a sentence using the phrasal verb that comes up.
- Divide the class into groups of four or five. The students take it in turns to roll one of their dice. They get one point for each correct sentence.
- When the activity is finished, ask the groups to roll both dice. Two members of the group have to make a quick dialogue using both the phrasal verbs. It may help students if you give them a starting point such as *at the airport* or *in the supermarket*.
- As an extension activity, students could make their own dice with other phrasal verbs.
- The dice could also be used to create circle stories. This could be done as a class activity, or in groups. Students take it in turns to roll a dice and to make an interesting sentence with the phrasal verb that comes up. The next student has to make another sentence to continue the story, and so on.
- The dice could also be used to play a guessing game. One student sits with their back to the class. The other students roll the dice and have to define the phrasal verb so the student with their back to the group guesses the phrasal verb on the dice.

Grammar practice key

1

2 [✓]
3 [✗] When he arrives late he always tries to make up for it, but it's not good enough.
4 [✓]
5 [✗] The doctors were trying to bring her round for an hour.
6 [✗] She always gets away with it when she cheats in exams.

2

2 find out
3 look it up
4 put up with
5 send off
6 going up

3

2 to make up for
3 bring your mum round
4 goes up
5 looking into
6 look it up

4

3 the
4 if
5 ✓
6 it
7 it
8 ✓
9 on
10 ✓
11 for
12 ✓
13 on

Unit 10

Communication activity

Area practised

Question tags

- Copy and cut up one set of cards for each group of three or four students.
- Divide the class into groups of three or four and tell the students to write sentences with question tags in the speech bubbles. Monitor and check they are using the question tags correctly.
- Ask each group to read out their speech bubbles one by one. The other groups have to guess which picture each one belongs to. The first group to guess correctly gets a point.
- Stronger classes could be shown how we often use question tags to express sarcasm. For example, in picture 8, the sentence could be, *They look really poor, don't they?*
- As an extension activity, stronger students could be asked to draw a new situation with a speech bubble for the others to complete.
- Alternatively, copy and cut up one set of cards (enlarged, if possible) or use an overhead projector. Divide the class into four groups and show the pictures one at a time. The first group to think of a suitable sentence and question tag gets a point.

Grammar practice key

1

2 isn't he
3 would they
4 haven't I
5 aren't you
6 couldn't she

2

2 You've dyed your hair, haven't you?
3 It was a great film, wasn't it? / The film was great, wasn't it?
4 You won't be late, will you? / You're not going to be late, are you?
5 It doesn't look good on me, does it?
6 You're not hungry yet, are you?

3

2 which
3 ~~which were~~
4 who
5 ~~who were~~
6 who

4

2 *Marina d'Or*, which is famous for its sea-water spa, is one of the biggest holiday complexes in Europe.
3 MP3 players, which were designed to be the modern-day 'Walkman', are really popular.
4 Television, which was invented in the 1920s, really changed the way people viewed the world.
5 Muhammad Ali, who was once the best boxer in the world, has been a peace ambassador for the UN.

Unit 11

Communication activity

Areas practised

Indirect questions

- Copy one questionnaire for each student.
- Tell the students they are reporters for a local radio/TV station and they are going to collect *vox pops* about topics of their choice. Explain that *vox pops* are short interviews that are usually carried out on the street or in a public place to gather public opinion about a topic. They are often used on radio broadcasts or TV programmes.
- Brainstorm possible topics as a class. Ask the students to complete questions 1–3 and then to write one extra question for 4. Encourage them to write controversial questions that will provoke discussion.
- Monitor and check that the students are forming the questions correctly.
- Divide the class into two groups: reporters and passers-by. The reporters should have their questionnaire with them.
- Tell the passers-by to walk around the class as if they are walking along the street. The reporters have to stop the passers-by, ask them their questions and write their answers on the questionnaire.
- After a set time, the students change roles.
- When all the questionnaires have been completed, students report back to the class the more interesting answers.

Grammar practice key

1

2 Where was the first computer invented?
3 What's the time?
4 When are you planning to tidy your bedroom?
5 Where did I leave my keys?
6 What do you think about the election results?

2

2 me whether or not
3 know where the teacher has
4 idea why she's behaving
5 wonder why George didn't
6 which your favourite band is

3

2 I don't know where they will build new houses when there's no land left.
3 It's important to think about how we should protect our planet for future generations.
4 It's difficult to find out what happened to all the money from the charity concert.
5 I'm not sure how often it rains in the south of Spain.

4

2 what time she left
3 who she went with
4 when / what time she's going to be home/ back
5 if she's going to Teresa's party
6 if/whether Alba is going out with Chris

Unit 12

Communication activity

Areas practised

Participle clauses; *didn't need to / needn't have*

- Copy one worksheet for each student.
- Ask the students to imagine they are travelling abroad for six months. Choose an exotic location that will appeal to most of your students.

- Tell them the best way to keep in touch with family and friends is by writing a weblog. They are in a town with an Internet café so they are going to update their blog.
- Tell the students to use the information on the top half of the page to write an update on their weblog on the bottom half of the page. Their blogs might include, for example: *Thanks to everyone for your emails. It's great to get news from home. Mum and Dad, you sounded worried in your message last week. You don't need to worry about me, I'm having a great time and taking care. Thanks too for the magazines you sent. You needn't have sent them though as they sell them here!*
- Encourage the students to use participle clauses to describe the events. For example, *Having arrived at the island, we had a picnic and a monkey stole some food. Having eaten my sandwiches, I was attacked by mosquitoes! Snorkelling with the fish was an amazing experience that I'll never forget. Having watched the sunset, I played the guitar.*
- Monitor and check the students' work.

Grammar practice key

1

2 B
3 A
4 B
5 A
6 B

2

2 He didn't need to confirm the reservation.
3 She needn't have phoned her friend.
4 I needn't have taken my mobile phone.
5 We didn't need to pay to go in the museum yesterday.
6 She needn't have spent hours doing her hair.

3

2 unemployed, he hasn't got any money
3 had a good breakfast, she felt energetic all morning
4 down the street, he fell over
5 exhausted, I went to bed early
6 ridden her bike to work, she needed a shower

4

2 Having done a Thai cookery course, we prepared a delicious green curry.
3 Having ridden elephants all afternoon, we had a quiet evening in the hostel.
4 Having trekked through the jungle, we slept really well that night.
5 Having learned some Thai, we practised our new phrases at the night market.
6 Having studied the map carefully, they set off.

Unit 13

Communication activity

Area practised

Passive report structures

- Copy and cut up one worksheet for each pair of students.
- Divide the class into two groups. Give a copy of card A to each student in one group and a copy of card B to each student in the other group.
- Give the groups time to prepare their roles. Encourage group B (the presidents) to think of some further questions they could ask the investigator. For example, they could find out more about the Tindi family.
- Monitor group A (the investigators) and encourage them to use passive report structures. For example, *It is believed that oil supplies will run out ... There is thought to be no clean water in rural areas ...* Check that group B (the presidents) are forming their questions correctly. For example, *When will the oil supplies run out? How many people don't have clean water?*
- When both groups are ready, make A and B pairs. They then roleplay the meeting between the president and the investigator.
- When the activity is finished, ask some of the presidents to report back to the class what they have learned from the investigators. Make sure they use passive report structures as far as possible.
- As an extension activity, the students could write up the investigator's findings as a report to be given to the president.

Grammar practice key

1

2 interest rates will go up again next month
3 kiwi fruit has a very high level of vitamin C
4 Mandarin Chinese is one of the most difficult languages to learn
5 too much fast food is bad for us
6 the Mediterranean diet to be one of the healthiest

2

2 [✓]

3 [✗] The film is said to be based on a true story.

4 [✓]

5 [✓]

6 [✗] This book is said to be her finest novel.

3

2 is estimated to be

3 is thought to be

4 are presumed to have

5 is reported to be

4

2 It is considered to be the best restaurant in London.

3 It is reported / said to be the worst road accident this year.

4 It is believed to be the most challenging race of all time.

5 It is expected to be the busiest shopping day before Christmas.

Unit 14

Communication activity

Area practised

Clauses of purpose

- Copy one game for each group of three or four students.
- Explain the expression, *Why on earth …?*. Ask them to practise saying the expression with exaggerated intonation to express disbelief.
- Students play the game in groups of three or four. They should use a coin, not a dice, to move around the board. (Heads = two spaces, tails = one space.)
- When they land on a square, the person on their right has to ask them the question in the role of an angry parent, *Why on earth …?*
- The student on that square has to try and justify why they were doing whatever it is. They should use the language in the speech bubbles to help them talk their way out of the situation. Ask a stronger pair to demonstrate:

  A: *Why on earth haven't you tidied your room for six months?*

  B: *In order not to waste valuable studying time.*

  Set a time limit of one minute for this. If they succeed, they stay where they are. If not, they move back a square.
- Monitor and check that students are forming the sentences correctly.
- The winner is the first person to reach the *Why on earth … ?* square in the centre.

Grammar practice key

1

2 a He is such a kind person that he gets on well with everybody.

3 d The children were so tired that they fell asleep on the sofa.

4 b The boss made such a big mistake that he apologised to all the employees.

5 c He earned so little money as an actor that he couldn't pay the rent.

2

2 She always arrived home on time so as not to get in trouble with her parents.

3 He put on sun cream so as not to get burnt.

4 He set his alarm clock in order not to oversleep.

5 He wrote himself a shopping list so as not to forget anything important.

3

2 People eat in restaurants so as not to have to cook at home.

3 I use the Internet to find out information for school projects.

4 He's bought a new car in order to drive to his new job.

5 People travel so as to learn about different cultures.

4

2 so as to be fit

3 such a good party

4 in order to pass

5 to meet

Communication activity 1

A

B

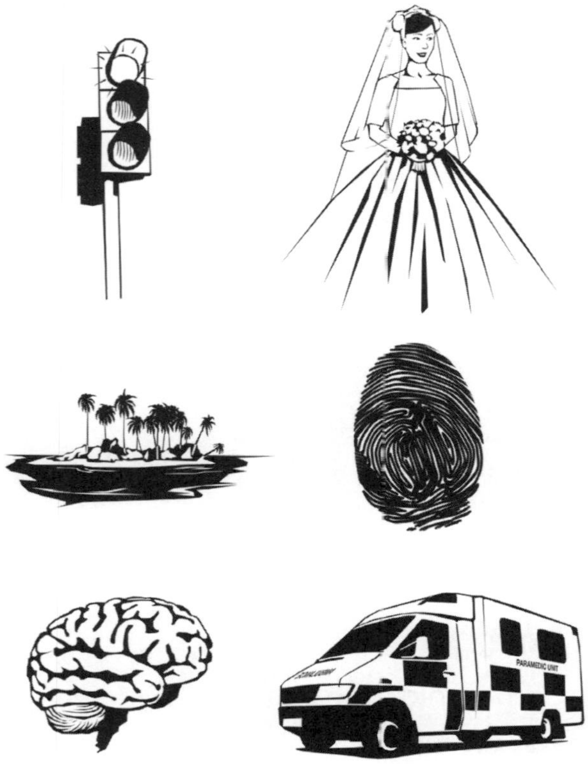

C

D

PHOTOCOPIABLE

Grammar practice 1

1 Rewrite the sentences using the word given. Do not change the word. Use between two and five words, including the word given.

1 Surgeons save lives.
who
A surgeon is *a person who* saves lives.

2 You can study in libraries.
where
A library .... you can study.

3 A researcher's job is to investigate.
whose
A researcher .... job is to investigate.

4 We can use an MP3 player to listen to music.
which
An MP3 player .... we can use to listen to music.

5 The coach is responsible for leading the team.
who
The coach .... responsible for leading the team.

6 A dictionary is useful for finding the meanings of new words.
that
A dictionary .... we use to find the meanings of new words.

2 Join or rearrange the two sentences to make one. Use the word at the end.

1 My sister lives in London. She has just had a baby. (who)
My sister, who lives in London, has just had a baby.

2 The film is on at the Odeon. It stars Johnny Depp. (that)
....
....

3 We have a maths exam tomorrow. It's going to be difficult for me. (that)
....
....

4 Matt plays football three times a week. He lives next door to me. (who)
....
....

5 The students broke the window in the classroom. They have been expelled. (who)
....
....

6 I saw that man today. His wife is a presenter on TV. (whose)
....
....

3 Complete the sentences with the endings in the box.

> they are always late / they try to make people better / it tells you how to say words in another language / ~~he lives in New York~~ / he created Microsoft / her husband has died

1 The film is about a man *who lives in New York* .
2 I can't stand people ....
3 A bilingual dictionary ....
4 A hospital ....
5 Bill Gates ....
6 A widow ....

4 Read the text. Some of the lines have an extra, unnecessary word. Write the words at the end of the line. If the line is correct, put a tick (✓).

I've just read a book which was all about the	1	✓
differences that between men and women. At	2	*that*
first which I thought it was all rubbish, and that	3	....
the author who was talking about the typical	4	....
stereotypes, but as I read it I started to believe it!	5	....
The other day I was looking that at my little	6	....
cousin, who is only two, and she loves playing	7	....
with dolls. It's strange because that she has an	8	....
older brother so there are plenty of cars and	9	....
building toys which for her to play with but she's	10	....
just not interested. The author who wrote the	11	....
book claimed that men and women's brains are	12	....
different and I'm starting to believe he who is	13	....
right, which is really surprising!	14	....

RESOURCES

UNIT 1

Communication activity 2

Find somebody who:	Name	Extra information (What they like / hate / think about it.)
can't stand shopping. 		
enjoys learning English. 		
doesn't mind waiting in queues. 		
is learning to speak two or more foreign languages. 		
remembers buying their first CD. 		
expects to pass all their subjects this year. 		
hopes to go to the cinema this week. 		
likes listening to the same music as you. 		

UNIT 2

RESOURCES

Grammar practice 2

1 Complete the sentences with the gerund or infinite form of the verbs.

1 I really hate *being* (be) the youngest in the family.

2 I was late for the lesson because I stopped .... (speak) to a friend on the way.

3 My brother really loves .... (watch) science fiction films.

4 He had to stop .... (play) football when he injured his ankle.

5 She refused .... (lend) me her new jacket.

6 My dad promised .... (buy) me a motorbike if I pass my exams!

7 Jack's so impatient he can't stand .... (wait) in queues.

8 In Britain you can learn .... (drive) when you're 17.

2 Join the sentences to make one.

1 I hate it when people talk loudly on their mobiles on the bus. It really annoys me.
What really annoys me is when people talk loudly on their mobiles on the bus.

2 She's rude to the teacher. I don't like that about her.
What I ....
....

3 English will be useful in the future. You need to remember that.
What you ....
....

4 I hate waiting in queues when I'm shopping.
What I ....
....

5 I really need a new pair of trainers.
What I ....
....

6 I like The Black Eyed Peas because their music is original.
What I ....
....

3 Complete the email. Use the gerund or infinitive form of the verbs.

Hi Barney!

How are you? I know I promised [1] *to write* (write) sooner, but I've been really busy lately. I'm afraid I have some bad news. I won't be able [2] .... (come) and visit you this summer as planned. I lost my weekend job last week as the shop closed down and I can't afford [3] .... (buy) the train ticket. I can't stand not [4] .... (have) enough money to afford [5] .... (do) what I want! I promise [6] .... (look for) another job as soon as I can, but it's not easy. That's what I hate about this town!

Write soon or phone me later for a chat.

Lisa.

4 Read the text. Some lines have an extra, unnecessary word. Write the words at the end of the line. If the line is correct, put a tick. (✓)

What I love about the weekends is	1	✓
having of time to do what I want to	2	*of*
do. During the week I often feel	3	....
like going to the cinema for to	4	....
watch a film or meeting a friend for	5	....
a coffee and a chat but I don't	6	....
have a time. I don't mind going to	7	....
school and I quite enjoy with	8	....
studying the subjects I like, but I	9	....
can't stand not having enough of	10	....
free time! I've decided for to try	11	....
and organise my time better so I	12	....
can start to kick boxing classes.	13	....

RESOURCES

UNIT 2

Communication activity 3

A YOU

You met a British girl/boy of your own age on the Internet last year. You've been cyber-pals ever since. A few months ago you invited her/him to visit you for two weeks in your country and she/he accepted your invitation.

Now your friend has arrived in your home and is meeting your parents for the first time. The only problem is that your parents speak no English at all, so you have to help them. You will have to be the interpreter so that your British friend and your parents can communicate.

B THE BRITISH VISITOR

You're a British girl/boy. You made friends with someone on the Internet last year and you've been cyber-pals ever since. A few months ago your new friend invited you to visit him/her and to stay with his/her family for two weeks. You're very excited as you have never been abroad before. The only problem is that you don't speak their language at all, only English. (Don't forget, you are British!) Now you're in their home and about to meet your friend's parents for the first time. You have some things you want to say to them including:

- Thanks for the invitation.
- You're very happy to be able to visit their country for the first time.
- You will try to learn a bit of their language.
- You want to phone your parents to tell them you've arrived. Ask for permission to use the telephone.

C PARENT 1

Your son/daughter has invited a British friend who he/she met on the Internet to come and visit. This friend will stay in your home for two weeks. You are happy to meet people from other countries and you like your son/daughter to have English-speaking friends so his/her English will improve.

You don't speak any English so your son/daughter will have to help you to communicate with the British visitor. You want the visitor to be comfortable in your home so you want to ask him/her a few things.

- Did he/she have a good journey?
- How long did it take to get here?
- Is there anything he/she doesn't eat?
- Does he/she need any towels?

D PARENT 2

Your son/daughter has invited a British friend who he/she met on the Internet to come and visit. This friend will stay in your home for two weeks. You are happy to meet people from other countries and you like your son/daughter to have English-speaking friends so his/her English will improve.

You don't speak any English so your son/daughter will have to help you to communicate with the British visitor. You want the visitor to be comfortable in your home so you want to ask him/her a few things.

- Is he/she tired?
- Is he/she hungry?
- How is his/her family?
- What would he/she like to do tomorrow?

Grammar practice 3

1 Complete the sentences. Circle the correct answers, a, b or c.

1 The doctor .... me to take the medicine.

a stated b (advised) c said

2 He .... his son not to touch the hot pan.

a warned b emphasised c recommended

3 Jack .... me to lend him my new T-shirt, but I didn't really want to.

a persuaded b stated c denied

4 She .... sending me that horrible text message, but I don't believe her.

a convinced b denied c promised

5 My dad .... me to study a bit more for my English exam. He said if I passed the exam I could go to the concert on Saturday.

a recommended b suggested c convinced

6 My brother is so angry, he .... to talk to me.

a promises b refuses c claims

2 Rewrite the sentences. Use the correct form of the verbs in the box.

~~tell~~ suggest encourage deny recommend state

1 'I like your shoes, Jenny.'

She *told Jenny she liked her shoes.*

2 'Why don't we go to the cinema on Thursday?'

He ....

3 'Come on, I think you should apologise to her.'

He ....

4 'I didn't eat the last chocolate!'

He ....

5 'I think you should take more exercise, Paula.'

The doctor ....

6 'The nation is in crisis.'

The president ....

3 Put the reported speech into direct speech.

1 I asked Messi how he was feeling.

'How are you feeling, Messi?'

2 He replied that he had never been happier.

....

3 Then I asked him how he and the team were going to celebrate winning the league.

....

4 He told me that they weren't going to celebrate today because they had to concentrate on training for the Champions League final.

....

5 I wished him good luck for the final.

....

6 He thanked me and asked if he could say hello to his mum who would be watching the interview on TV.

....

7 I said of course he could. I told him that tonight he was the hero of thousands of Barcelona fans!

....

4 Put the direct speech into reported speech. Change the underlined words.

1 'I did it three weeks <u>ago</u>.'

He said *that he had done it three weeks before.*

2 'I went to the doctor's <u>yesterday</u>.'

She told me ....

3 'We'll be there by <u>tomorrow</u>.'

They said ....

4 'I'm going to Paris <u>next week</u>.'

She told me ....

5 'I've had the worst morning of my life <u>today</u>!'

He said ....

6 '<u>At the weekend</u> I'm going to Amsterdam.'

She told me ....

Communication activity 4

in a hurry	in a panic	in private	would (for past habit)
used to	with difficulty	on purpose	in secret
would	in a row	by accident	used to
with fear	in a really horrible way	in a very friendly way	with surprise

Grammar practice 4

1 Rewrite the sentences using *used to* or *would*.

1 I hated cheese when I was younger but now I love it.

I *used to hate cheese but now I love it.*

2 My dad was a fantastic football player.

My dad ....

3 When I was little we listened to the radio every Saturday afternoon.

When I was little ....

4 I loved going to the beach when I was a child.

When I was a child ....

5 It's strange to think that people worked without computers in the past.

It's strange to think ....

6 I didn't enjoy reading when I was a child, but I do now.

When I was a child ....

2 Right (✓) or wrong (✗)? Correct the wrong sentences.

1 I would have a red bike when I was little. ✗

I used to have a red bike when I was little.

2 Did you use to listen to The Spice Girls? ☐

....

3 No, I didn't used to like them. ☐

....

4 I used to listen to S-Club 7! ☐

....

5 I would think they were the best pop group in the world. ☐

....

6 Would you have a Rubik's Cube when you were younger? ☐

....

7 I used to love hula hoops. I would practise every day! ☐

....

3 Interview your grandmother for the school magazine. Write questions using *use to*.

1 do a lot of sport

Did you use to do a lot of sport?

2 have long hair

.... ?

3 (not) ride a bicycle

.... ?

4 eat fast food

.... ?

5 (not) watch TV

.... ?

4 Rewrite the sentences using the word given. Do not change the word. Use between two and five words, including the word given.

1 He told me I was late. He didn't say it in a nice way at all.

horrible

He told me I was late *in a horrible way.*

2 My little brother annoys me intentionally.

purpose

My little brother ....

3 He didn't tell anyone he had bought the engagement ring.

secret

He bought the engagement ring

....

4 They didn't mean to smash the window.

accident

They smashed the window

....

5 The students did all the activities one after another.

row

The students did all the activities

....

6 She never relaxes and she always seems so anxious.

panic

She's always ....

Communication activity 5

What would the world be like today if ...

... aeroplanes hadn't been invented?

What would the world be like today if ...

... the Internet hadn't been invented?

What would the world be like today if ...

... there was no poverty?

What would the world be like today if ...

... you had been elected as President or Prime Minister of your country in the last elections?

How would your life be different today if ...

... you had been born 100 years ago?

How would your life be different today if ...

... you had just won £1 million in the lottery?

How would your life be different today if ...

... you had been born in a different country? (You can decide where.)

How would your life be different today if ...

... mobile phones hadn't been invented?

How would your life be different today if ...

... you had been born as a member of the opposite sex?

How would your life be different today if ...

... you had always followed the advice people gave you?

How would you be feeling now if ...

... you had met your favourite film star on the way to this lesson?

How would you be feeling now if ...

... you had found £300 on the way to this lesson?

What would the world be like today if ...

How would your life be different today if ...

How would you be feeling now if ...

What would you be doing now if ...

... you weren't in this English lesson?

Grammar practice 5

1 **Write *0* (zero), *1* (first), *2* (second), *3* (third) or *M* (mixed) next to these conditional sentences, depending on their type.**

1 If you don't take an umbrella, you'll get wet. *1*
2 If water is heated to 100ºC it boils. ....
3 If you studied a bit more, you'd pass the exam. ....
4 If you told her, I'll kill you! ....
5 If you'd applied for the job, you would have got it. ....
6 If I'd known you were coming, I'd have made a cake. ....

2 **Read the text. Some of the lines have an extra, unnecessary word. Write the words at the end of the line. If the line is correct, put a tick (✓).**

Hi Rachel!
How are you? I'm a bit upset today as I — 1 ✓
failed my driving test yesterday. I think that — 2 ✓
if it hadn't had been raining so much I — 3 ....
would've passed. I couldn't to see properly — 4 ....
because of the rain and a dog it ran out into — 5 ....
the road! I would've hit it if the examiner — 6 ....
hadn't screamed at me for to watch out. — 7 ....
She says if I practise a bit more I'll would — 8 ....
pass next time, but I don't know. Just — 9 ....
imagine, if it hadn't been for the rain and — 10 ....
the dog I would have be a driver now! — 11 ....
Write soon, Fernando.

3 **Rewrite the sentences. Use the correct type of conditional.**

1 Tony didn't play and they lost the match.
If Tony *had played they wouldn't have lost / would have won the match.*
2 We want to buy a flat but we haven't got enough money so we won't buy one.
If we ....
....
3 I don't have enough time to go swimming but I love it.
I'd ....
....
4 Jonathan never replies to my emails, so I don't write to him.
I'd ....
....
5 I don't go to that club because they don't play hip-hop.
If they ....
....
6 I don't eat much chocolate because it's bad for my skin.
If chocolate ....
....

4 **How possible is it? Choose the right answers, a, b, c or d.**

a It's possible.	c It didn't happen.
b It's unlikely or impossible.	d It's true.

1 If I'd won the lottery I'd be in the Caribbean now. *c*
2 If I was rich I'd buy a helicopter. ....
3 If you sunbathe too much you damage your skin. ....
4 If you eat less you'll lose weight. ....
5 If I'd worked harder I would have passed the exam. ....
6 If you invite her to go for a coffee, I think she'll accept. ....

RESOURCES UNIT 5

Communication activity 6

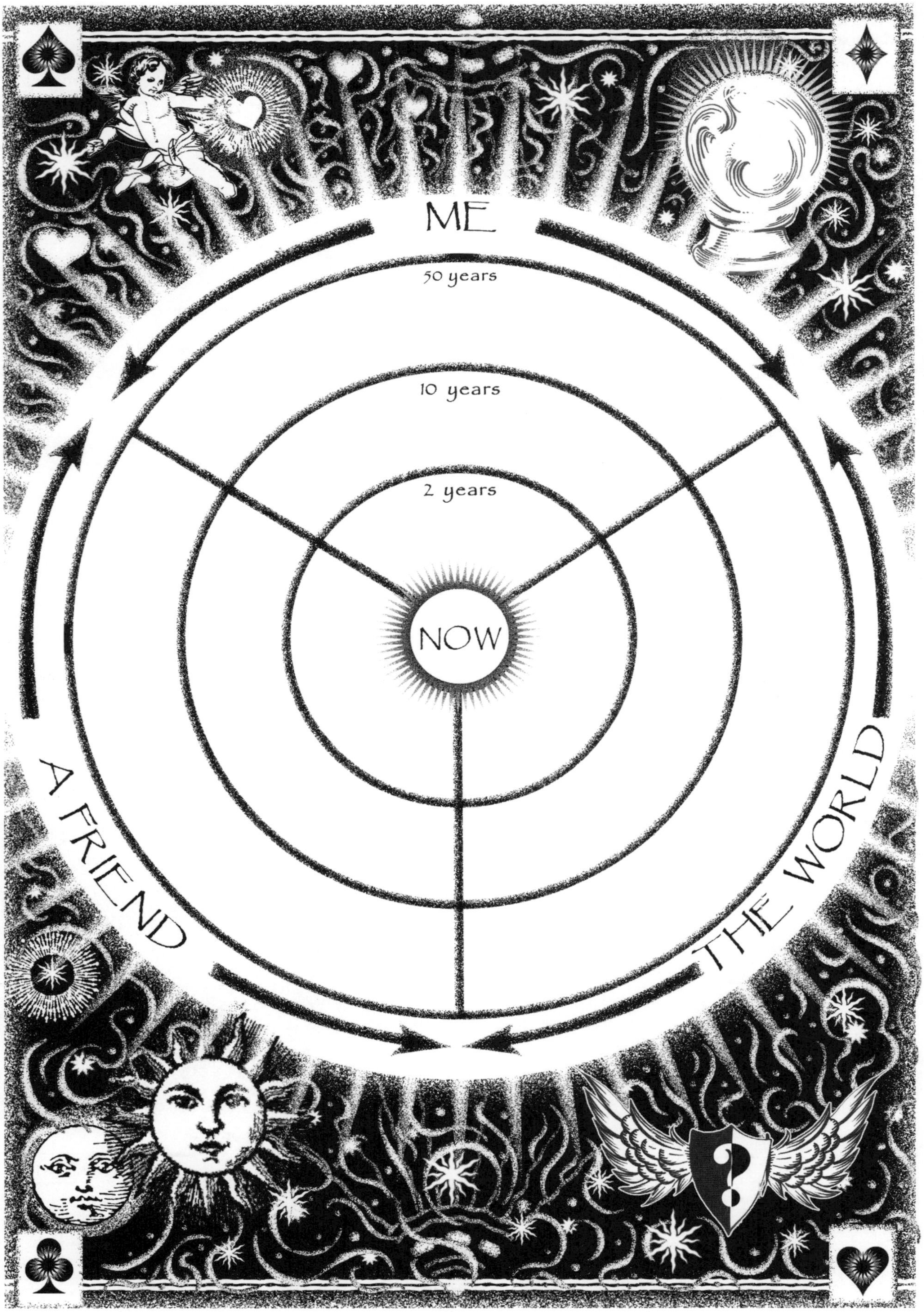

Grammar practice 6

1 Complete the sentences. Use the time expressions in the box.

by during for from now in two years' time ~~until~~

1 I'm going to stay at my cousin's house *until* next Wednesday.
2 .... I hope I'll be at university.
3 In a week .... I'll have finished all my exams.
4 I've been living here .... ten years.
5 .... next year I hope I'll have passed my driving test.
6 They met each other .... the summer holidays.

2 Circle the correct words.

1 By 2050 I think polar bears *will have become* / *will be becoming* extinct.
2 During the next decade scientists *will have looked for* / *will be looking for* solutions to all the environmental problems.
3 I think the government *will have made* / *will be making* lots more changes to the law from now on.
4 By 2020 we *will have fished* / *will be fishing* all the tuna from the Atlantic Ocean.
5 The local council *will have planted* / *will be planting* 50 new trees by next September.
6 From now on primary school teachers *will have taught* / *will be teaching* children about recycling.

3 Read the text. Some of the lines have an extra, unnecessary word. Write the words at the end of the line. If the line is correct, put a tick (✓).

Hi Sarah

How are you doing? Can you believe	1	✓
that in for two weeks' time I'll have	2	*for*
finished my exams. I can't wait! Summer	3	....
holidays will be have begun. I have a	4	....
plan. I'm going to work for during six	5	....
weeks in the local cinema. During by that	6	....
time I'll be saving all the money I earn	7	....
for to go inter-railing round Europe. So	8	....
in only two months' time I'll be travelling	9	....
to amazing places and meeting the new	10	....
people. What are being your plans for the	11	....
summer? Will you be staying in Bristol?	12	....
Write soon, or text if you're busy. Jo.	13	....

4 Complete the sentences. Use the correct form of the words in the box.

~~electric~~ govern plug reduce cycle pollute

1 You should always switch off all *electrical* appliances when you're not using them.
2 The .... needs to make stricter laws to protect the environment.
3 Waste .... is a big issue for all countries.
4 In some big cities the air .... is so bad it can cause breathing problems.
5 If you can, try to .... materials like plastic bags and glass bottles.
6 When you're not using your stereo or computer you should .... it.

Communication activity 7

They had been waiting ... to be rescued ...	He had been living there ... before he realised ...	The dog had been barking non-stop ...	She had been working there ... when she found out ...
He had been thinking about it ...	They had been studying ...	He had been looking for ...	She had been driving ...
He had been taking the medicine ...	They had been investigating the case ...	She had been hiding ...	He had been preparing for this day ...

for 20 years	since 1998	for ten minutes	since the summer	for a year	for six months	since 2006	for 30 seconds	for a decade	since New Year's Eve	for a week	since 1993

PHOTOCOPIABLE

Grammar practice 7

1 Complete the sentences. Use the past perfect continuous form of the verbs.

1 I finally found my purse. I *'d been looking for* (look for) it for ages.

2 Clare looked really tired. She .... (work) hard all day.

3 The business .... (lose) money for months and it finally closed down.

4 Luis looked upset. I think he .... (cry).

5 Marta .... (study) all week for the exam and she felt quite confident.

6 When the police stopped him they said he .... (drive) too fast.

2 Complete the sentences. Use the past perfect passive form of the verbs in the box.

tell ~~eat~~ cook prevent invite make do

1 When I got to the party all the food *had been eaten.*

2 They discovered that a huge mistake .... in the early stages of the plan.

3 The vegetables .... for too long and they weren't very tasty.

4 All the washing up .... before I could offer to help.

5 The man was angry because he .... from leaving the court.

6 We were upset to hear that everyone .... to the party except for us.

7 By 11 o'clock, all the students .... the news about the accident.

3 Complete the sentences. Use the past perfect continuous or the past perfect passive form of the verbs.

1 The decision *had been made* (make) before I was even consulted.

2 The invitations .... already (send) when he decided to call off the wedding.

3 They .... (celebrate) the good news when the police arrived.

4 Mobile phones .... (not invent) when I was a child.

5 I .... (wait) for the bus for half an hour when three arrived at once.

6 She .... (hope) he would send her a message when her phone beeped.

4 Write the sentences. Use the past perfect continuous and past simple form of the verbs.

1 He / make a cake / doorbell ring.
He had been making a cake when the doorbell rang.

2 He / look for a job / six months / finally get an interview.
....
....

3 They / play tennis / five minutes / rain start.
....
....

4 She / do homework / get the text message.
....
....

5 They / queue for three hours / by the time buy the concert tickets.
....
....

6 He / train for two years / before run a marathon.
....
....

Communication activity 8

Job: Pop star

You should ....
You could ....
You must ....
It's a good/bad idea to ....
It's important to ....

Job: Professional footballer

You should ....
You could ....
You must ....
It's a good/bad idea to ....
It's important to ....

Job: Surgeon

You should ....
You could ....
You must ....
It's a good/bad idea to ....
It's important to ....

Job: Astronaut

You should ....
You could ....
You must ....
It's a good/bad idea to ....
It's important to ....

Job: Vet

You should ....
You could ....
You must ....
It's a good/bad idea to ....
It's important to ....

Job: ....

You should ....
You could ....
You must ....
It's a good/bad idea to ....
It's important to ....

Job: Scientist

You should ....
You could ....
You must ....
It's a good/bad idea to ....
It's important to ....

Job: ....

You should ....
You could ....
You must ....
It's a good/bad idea to ....
It's important to ....

Job: Politician

You should ....
You could ....
You must ....
It's a good/bad idea to ....
It's important to ....

Job: ....

You should ....
You could ....
You must ....
It's a good/bad idea to ....
It's important to ....

Job: English teacher

You should ....
You could ....
You must ....
It's a good/bad idea to ....
It's important to ....

Job: ....

You should ....
You could ....
You must ....
It's a good/bad idea to ....
It's important to ....

Grammar practice 8

1 Rewrite the sentences.

1 Treating colleagues with respect is essential.
It's *essential to treat colleagues with respect.*

2 Speaking foreign languages well is important these days.
It's ....

3 Skateboarding in the city centre is forbidden.
It's ....

4 Seeing Rachel at the weekend was wonderful.
It was ....

5 Watching too much TV is bad for your eyes.
It's ....

6 Waking up late on Saturday morning is a great feeling.
It's ....

2 Right (✓) or wrong (✗)? Correct the wrong sentences.

1 He must to wear a uniform. [✗]
He must wear a uniform.

2 You should revise the new vocabulary at home. [ ]
....

3 He can speaks Japanese. [ ]
....

4 It'll be sunny tomorrow. [ ]
....

5 We should to listen to his opinion. [ ]
....

6 I might go the party on Saturday. [ ]
....

3 Rewrite the sentences in Exercise 2 in the negative.

1 *He doesn't have to wear a uniform..*
2 ....
3 ....
4 ....
5 ....
6 ....

4 Rewrite the sentences using the word given. Do not change the word. Use between two and five words, including the word given.

1 I haven't decided whether or not to go out tonight.
might
I *might go out* tonight.

2 It isn't necessary to spend a lot of money to have a good time.
have
You .... spend a lot of money to have a good time.

3 Smoking is prohibited in this building.
must
You .... in this building.

4 When he was three he was able to swim.
could
He .... he was three.

5 I think it's a good idea for you to apply for that job.
should
I think .... for that job.

6 Who do you think is going to win the match tonight?
will
Who .... win the match tonight?

RESOURCES

UNIT 8

Communication activity 9

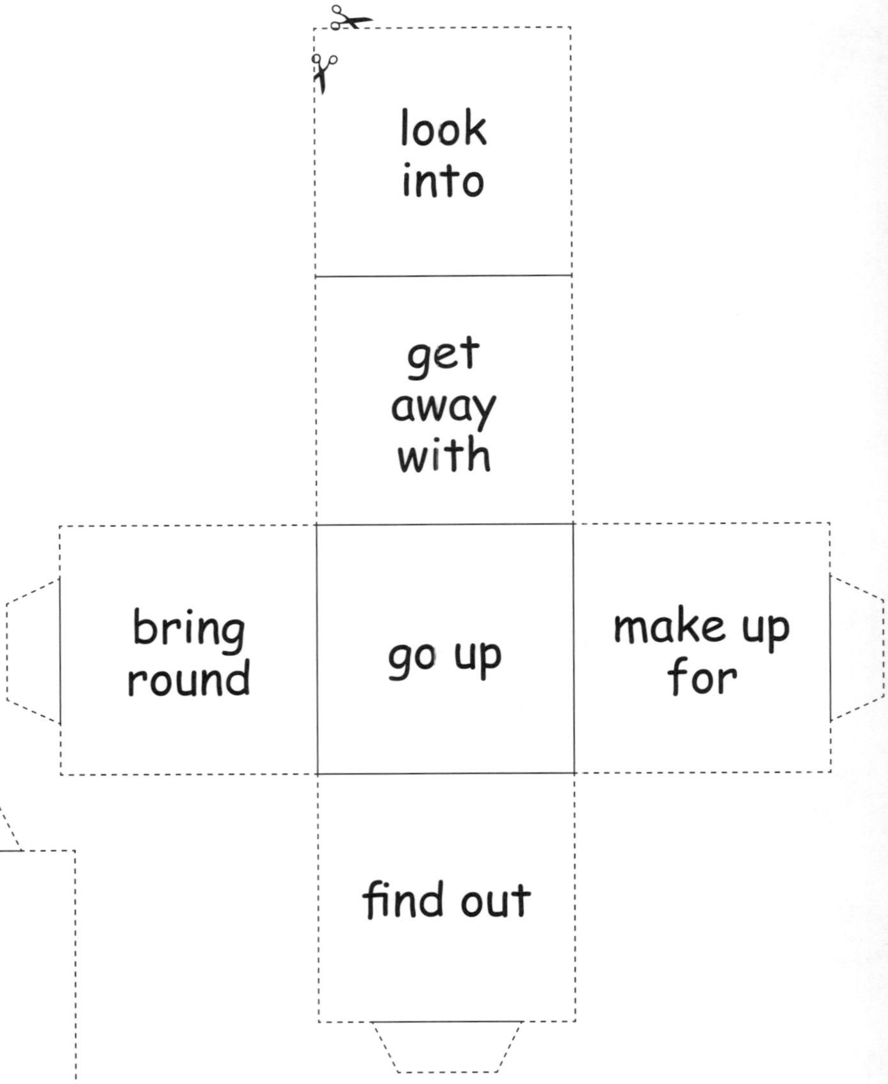

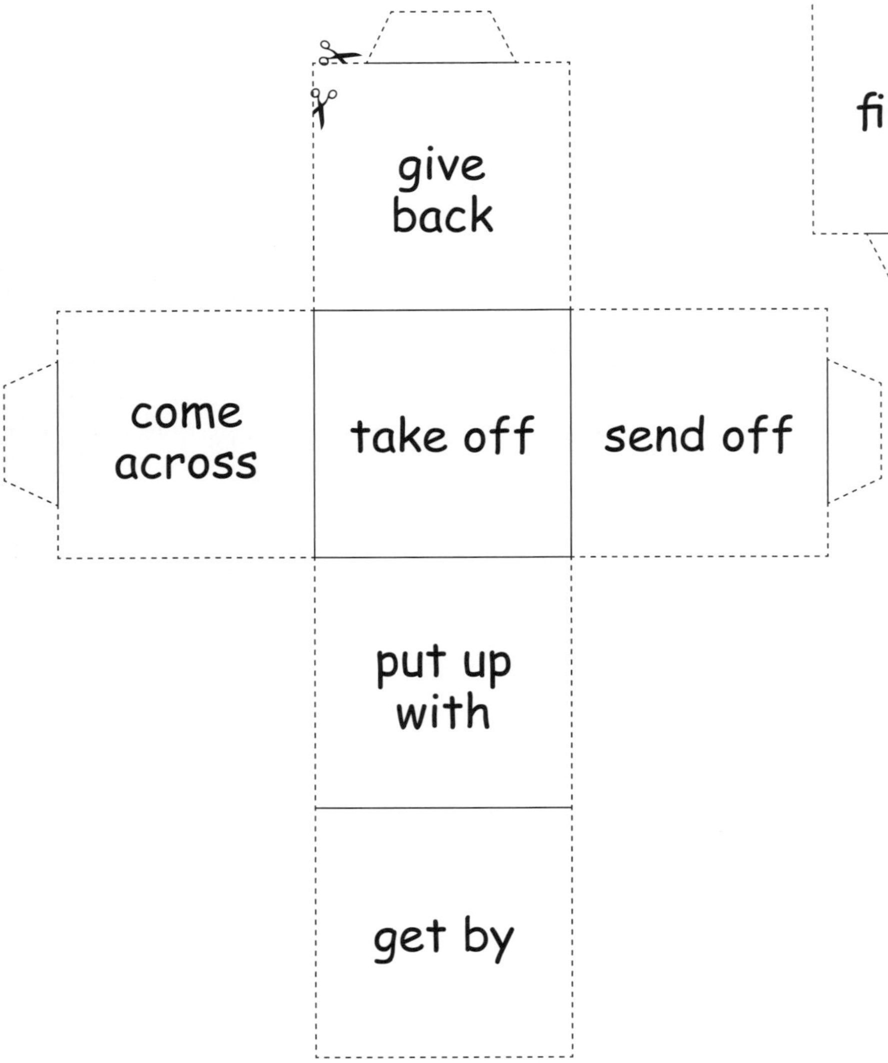

Grammar practice 9

1 Right (✓) or wrong (✗)? Correct the wrong sentences.

1 I asked him to give back it a week ago. ✗

I asked him to give it back a week ago.

2 You can find a lot of information on the Internet. ☐

....

3 When he arrives late he always tries to make it up for, but it's not good enough. ☐

....

4 When I was tidying my room I came across some old photos of when I was a baby. ☐

....

5 The doctors were trying to bring round her for an hour. ☐

....

6 She always gets it away with when she cheats in exams. ☐

....

2 Complete the sentences. Use the right form of the phrasal verbs in the box. You may have to add a pronoun.

send off   look up   put up with
find out   ~~take back~~   go up

1 I regretted what I said to her so I tried to *take it back* .

2 It was obvious that he would .... the truth sooner or later.

3 If you're not sure of a word in English you should .... in a dictionary.

4 Our neighbours are so noisy. Nobody should have to .... that.

5 If you don't .... the present tomorrow it won't arrive in time.

6 The price of oil is .... every week.

3 Rewrite the sentences using the word given. Do not change the word. Use between two and five words, including the word given.

1 The children always escape without punishment when they're naughty.

get

They always *get away with* being naughty.

2 I was given a free meal to compensate for the cockroach I found in my food.

make

I was given a free meal .... the cockroach I found in my food.

3 Try to convince your mum to let you go to the party.

bring

Try to .... to the idea of letting you go to the party.

4 His salary increases every year.

goes

His salary .... every year.

5 The detective is investigating the case.

looking

The detective is .... the case.

6 To find somebody's phone number you can use a telephone directory.

look

To find somebody's phone number you can .... in a telephone directory.

4 Read the text. Some of the lines have an extra, unnecessary word. Write the words at the end of the line. If the line is correct, put a tick (✓).

Dear Sir/Madam,

I am writing for to complain about the	1	*for*
terrible service I received from your airline	2	✓
company the last week. The plane was	3	......
delayed for five hours and if the	4	......
passengers were given no information or	5	......
food and drink vouchers to make it up for	6	......
this. When we eventually took it off, the	7	......
plane was dirty and the staff were rude. I	8	......
do not know how you get on away with	9	......
such appalling service.	10	......
I would like for you to give me back the	11	......
money I paid for the flight. Why should we	12	......
put on up with such terrible service?	13	......

Yours faithfully, Joanna Cole.

RESOURCES UNIT 9

Communication activity 10

Grammar practice 10

1 Complete the sentences with question tags.

1 She looks really sad, *doesn't she* ?
2 Your dad's a builder, ... ?
3 They wouldn't agree to help, ... ?
4 I've already apologised, ... ?
5 You're going to Australia this summer, ... ?
6 She could have waited, ... ?

2 What would you say in these situations? Write a statement with a question tag.

1 The sun is shining and the sky is blue. (nice day)
It's a nice day, isn't it?
2 Your friend now has pink hair. (dye hair)
....
3 You leave the cinema with a friend. You think the film was excellent. (great film)
....
4 You think your friend might be late to meet you. You don't want him to be late. (not late)
....
5 You're shopping with a friend. You try on a jumper. You don't think it looks good on you, but you want a second opinion. (not look good)
....
6 You're not hungry and you want to wait before you have a snack. You want to know if your friend is hungry yet. (not hungry yet)
....

3 Read the sentences. Cross out the words in *italics* if they are not needed.

1 *Guernica*, ~~*which was*~~ painted by Picasso, is in a museum in Madrid.
2 Microsoft, *which* Bill Gates created, is one of the biggest companies in the world.
3 Those houses, *which were* built in the 1970s, are about to be knocked down.
4 Robbie Williams, *who* does a lot of charity work, is one of the most popular musicians in Britain.
5 More than 200 people, *who were* taken on by the factory over 30 years ago, are about to lose their jobs.
6 Ferrán Adriá, *who* has just won another prize for his cooking, is one of the best chefs in the world.

4 Rewrite the sentences. Add *which* or *who* + the verb *to be*.

1 Zinedine Zindane, sent off in the 2006 World Cup final, grew up in Marseilles.
Zinedine, Zindane, who was sent off in the 2006 World Cup final, grew up in Marseilles.
2 *Marina d'Or*, famous for its sea-water spa, is one of the biggest holiday complexes in Europe.
....
3 MP3 players, designed to be the modern-day 'Walkman', are really popular.
....
....
4 Television, invented in the 1920s, really changed the way people viewed the world.
....
....
5 Muhammad Ali, once the best boxer in the world, has been a peace ambassador for the UN.
....
....

Communication activity 11

Names →				
1 Could you tell me how you feel about ....?				
2 Can I ask you ....?				
3 Why do you think there is/are ....?				
4 ....?				

Grammar practice 11

1 Rewrite the indirect questions as direct questions.

1 Could you tell me where the bus station is, please?

Where's the bus station?

2 Do you know where the first computer was invented?

....

3 Can you tell me what the time is, please?

....

4 Could you tell me when you're planning to tidy your bedroom?

....

5 Do you have any idea where I left my keys?

....

6 Can I ask you what you think about the election results?

....

2 Rewrite the sentences using the word given. Do not change the word. Use between two and five words, including the word given.

1 What time does the film start?

know

Do you *know what time the film* starts?

2 Do you think UFOs exist or not?

whether

Could you tell .... you think UFOs exist?

3 Where has the teacher gone?

know

Do you .... gone?

4 Why is she behaving so badly?

idea

Have you got any .... so badly?

5 Why didn't George come to school yesterday?

wonder

I .... come to school yesterday?

6 Which is your favourite band at the moment?

is

Can you tell me .... at the moment?

3 Join the two sentences to make one.

1 Why did they allow the golf course to be built there? I wonder.

I wonder why they allowed the golf course to be built there.

2 Where will they build new houses when there's no land left? I don't know.

....

....

3 How should we protect our planet for future generations? It's important to think about it.

....

....

4 What happened to all the money from the charity concert? It's difficult to find out.

....

....

5 How often does it rain in the south of Spain? I'm not sure.

....

....

4 Complete the indirect questions in the dialogue.

A: Hello, it's Paulo. Could I speak to Alba, please?

B: Hello, Paulo. I'm sorry, but Alba's not at home at the moment.

A: Could you tell me [1] *where she is* ?

B: She's gone to the cinema.

A: Do you know [2] .... ?

B: She left at about 6 o'clock.

A: Have you got any idea [3] .... ?

B: I think she went with Chris.

A: Oh! Can you tell me [4] .... ?

B: She'll be back before 10pm, but don't call then because I'll be asleep.

A: Do you know [5] .... ?

B: Yes, Paulo, I think she is going to Teresa's party. Look, why don't you call Alba tomorrow and speak to her yourself?

A: OK, I will. Just one last question. Do you know [6] .... ?

B: Paulo! It's really none of your business whether my daughter is going out with Chris or not. I have to go now. Goodbye!

Communication activity 12

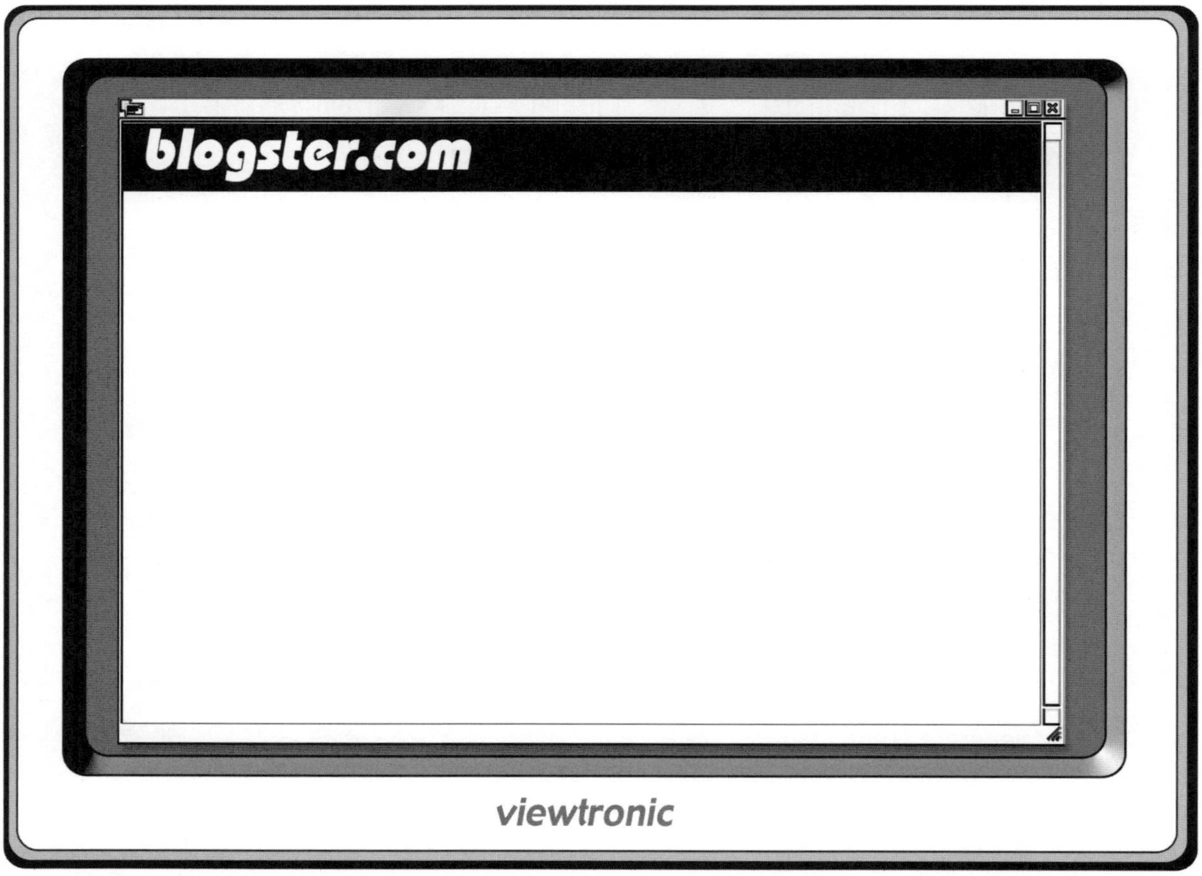

Grammar practice 12

1 Read the sentences. Write *A* (we are certain the action happened) or *B* (we don't know if the action happened).

1 I needn't have arrived on time as everyone else was late. *A*

2 He didn't need to tell her because she already knew. ....

3 Kevin needn't have done the homework as the teacher forgot to collect it. ....

4 She didn't need to bring me a present. ....

5 You needn't have done all the washing up. ....

6 I didn't need to go to school today. ....

2 Rewrite the sentences using *didn't need to* or *needn't have*.

1 I watered the plants in the garden in the afternoon, but then it rained all night.

I needn't have watered the plants.

2 It wasn't necessary to confirm the reservation, so he didn't.

....

3 She phoned her friend to tell him the news about Jim, but he already knew it.

....

4 I took my mobile phone on a skiing holiday, but it didn't work in the mountains.

....

5 The museum was free yesterday, so we didn't pay to go in.

....

6 She spent hours doing her hair in a special style then decided to wear a hat, so doing her hair was a waste of time.

....

3 Join the two sentences to make one.

1 We walked along the beach. We saw a beautiful sunset.

Walking *along the beach, we saw a beautiful sunset* .

2 He hasn't got any money. He's unemployed.

Being ....

3 She had a good breakfast. It made her feel energetic all morning.

Having ....

4 He was running down the street. He fell over.

Running ....

5 I went to bed early. I was exhausted.

Feeling ....

6 She rode her bike to work. She needed a shower.

Having ....

4 Join the two sentences to make one. Use participle clauses.

1 We arrived in Thailand in the morning. We took the train to Chang Mai.

Having arrived in Thailand in the morning, we took the train to Chang Mai.

2 We did a Thai cookery course. We prepared a delicious green curry.

....

3 We rode elephants all afternoon. We had a quiet evening in the hostel.

....

4 We trekked through the jungle. We slept really well that night.

....

5 We learned some Thai. We practised our new phrases at the night market.

....

6 They studied the map carefully. They set off.

....

Communication activity 13

A

You are a special investigator for the government. You have been sent on a mission to Changa, a tiny country in the Indian Ocean, to find out about the environmental and political crisis there.

You have made notes from your mission and now you have to tell the president what you have discovered. Use your notes and remember to speak in a very formal way!

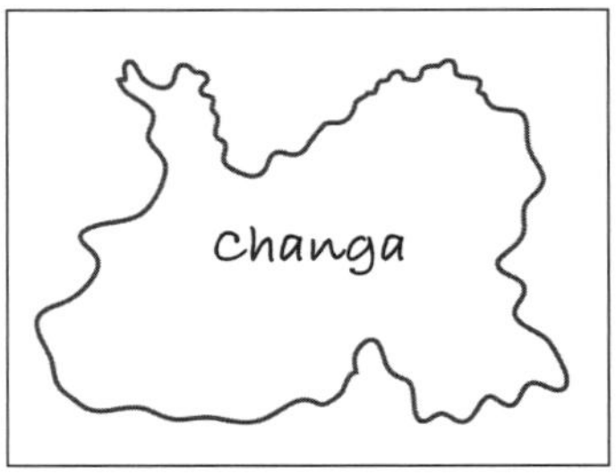

- Experts believe oil supplies will run out completely by the beginning of next year.
- People think that there are now no clean water supplies in rural areas – this affects two-thirds of the population.
- Aid workers say that 90 per cent of the population doesn't have enough to eat. Tell the president about meeting the Tindi family.
- The people of Changa need help immediately.

B

You are the president of your country. Your special investigator has been sent to find out about the problems in Changa, a tiny country in the Indian Ocean. Changa has serious environmental and political problems and you want to make an action plan to help.

You need to know about the following:

Presidential Office

- *Oil supplies?*
- *Clean water?*
- *Enough food?*
- *Drought. How long?*
- *Best way to help?*

Grammar practice 13

1 Rewrite the sentences.

1 Most wine is believed to improve with age.

People believe that most wine improves with age.

2 Interest rates are estimated to go up again next month.

Experts estimate that ....

3 Kiwi fruit is known to have a very high level of vitamin C.

We know that ....

4 Mandarin Chinese is said to be one of the most difficult languages to learn.

They say that ....

5 Too much fast food is known to be bad for us.

We know that ....

6 The Mediterranean diet is considered to be one of the healthiest.

People consider ....

2 Right (✓) or wrong (✗)? Correct the wrong sentences.

1 He is knew to be the richest man in the world. ✗

He is known to be the richest man in the world.

2 She is believed to be one of the rudest actresses in Hollywood. ☐

....

3 The film is said being based on a true story. ☐

....

4 It is considered to be one of the most difficult puzzles in the world. ☐

....

5 There are estimated to be over two million people unemployed in our country. ☐

....

6 This book has said to be her finest novel. ☐

....

3 Rewrite the sentences using the word given. Do not change the word. Use between two and five words, including the word given.

1 They say that Kate earns €1000 per hour for a photo shoot.

said

Kate *is said to earn* €1000 per hour for a photo shoot.

2 They estimate that the contract will be worth €5 million.

estimated

The contract .... worth €5 million.

3 They think that the prince will make an appearance later on in the evening.

thought

The prince .... making an appearance later on in the evening.

4 The journalists presume the couple have married in secret.

presumed

The couple .... married in secret.

5 The reporters say that she is living in Paris.

reported

She .... living in Paris.

4 Rewrite the sentences using passive report structures.

1 Experts think it is the worst flood in recent history.

It is thought to be the worst flood in recent history.

2 People consider it to be the best restaurant in London.

....

3 Reporters say it is the worst road accident this year.

....

4 People believe it is the most challenging race of all time.

....

5 People expect it to be the busiest shopping day before Christmas.

....

RESOURCES UNIT 13

Communication activity 14

Well, in order to ....

So as not to ....

... have you got a bandage on your head?

... is your little brother locked in his bedroom when you were supposed to be looking after him?

... were you playing computer games all afternoon instead of doing your English homework?

... did your teacher call me at work and ask me to come in to school for a meeting tomorrow?

Free square **RELAX!**

Free square **RELAX!**

WHY ON EARTH ... ?

Free square **RELAX!**

... is there no milk, when I specifically asked you to buy some?

... is there a moustache drawn on the photo of your great-aunt?

... is there a big blue stain on the new carpet?

... haven't you tidied your room for six months?

START

... did you eat all the cake that was in the fridge? It was for a dinner party tonight!

... did you arrive home at 11.30pm when you should have got home before 10pm?

So as to ...

In order not to ....

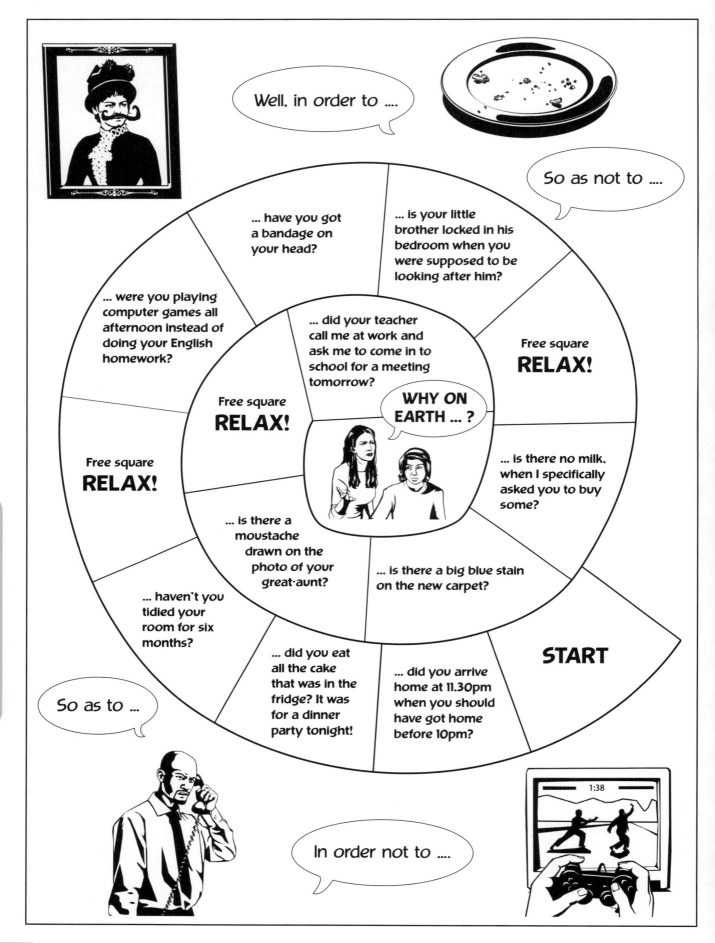

Grammar practice 14

1 **Match the two parts of the sentences. Then join them using *so* or *such (that)*.**

1 The trainers were very expensive
2 He is a kind person
3 The children were really tired
4 The boss made a very big mistake
5 He earned very little money as an actor

a he gets on well with everybody.
b he apologised to all the employees.
c he couldn't pay the rent.
d they fell asleep on the sofa.
e I decided to wait for the sales.

1 *The trainers were so expensive that I decided to wait for the sales.* ....
2 ....
3 ....
4 ....
5 ....

2 **Rewrite the sentences, adding *not* so that they make sense. Then translate them into your language.**

1 He was really quiet so as to wake her up.
He was really quiet so as not to wake her up.
2 She always arrived home on time so as to get in trouble with her parents.
....
3 He put on sun cream so as to get burnt.
....
4 He set his alarm clock in order to oversleep.
....
5 He wrote himself a shopping list so as to forget anything important.
....

3 **Write the answers to the questions.**

1 Why are you studying English?
so as / be able / speak / foreigners
I'm studying English so as to be able to speak to foreigners.
2 Why do people eat in restaurants?
so as / not / have / cook / home
....
3 Why do you use the Internet?
to / find out / information / school projects
....
4 Why has he bought a car?
in order / drive / his new job
....
5 Why do people travel?
so as / learn / different cultures
....

4 **Rewrite the sentences using the word given. Do not change the word. Use between two and five words, including the word given.**

1 He worked in a restaurant all summer because he wanted to go travelling.
order
He worked in a restaurant all summer *in order to go* travelling.
2 He trains every day because he wants to be fit enough to run the marathon.
so
He trains every day .... enough to run the marathon.
3 It was a really good party and they didn't want it to finish.
such
It was .... that they didn't want it to finish.
4 He practised a lot so he would pass his driving test.
in
He practised a lot .... his driving test.
5 She went to the airport because she wanted to meet her friend.
to
She went to the airport .... her friend.

Acknowledgements

The publishers are grateful to the following contributors:

Pat Chappell, Vanessa Manhire and Caroline Mapus-Smith: editorial work

Gill Adams: contributions to the 'Memos from Mario'

Pentacor plc: text design and layouts

The publishers are grateful to the following illustrators:

Anna Lazareva (Lemonade)
Mark Reihill (Lemonade)
Mark Watkinson (Illustration)